Sexual harassment
at the workplace
in the European Union

Employment & social affairs

Equality between women and men

European Commission
Directorate-General for Employment, Industrial Relations
and Social Affairs
Unit V/D.5

Manuscript completed in 1998

The contents of this publication do not necessarily reflect the opinion or position of the European Commission, Directorate-General for Employment, Industrial Relations and Social Affairs.

A great deal of additional information on the European Union is available on the Internet.
It can be accessed through the Europa server (http://europa.eu.int).

Cataloguing data can be found at the end of this publication.

Luxembourg: Office for Official Publications of the European Communities, 1999

ISBN 92-828-6217-8

Printed in Belgium

Table of contents

FOREWORD

"Unwanted conduct of a sexual nature, or other conduct based on sex affecting the dignity of women and men at work, including the conduct of superiors and colleagues, is unacceptable".

This assertion was made in the 1991 Commission Recommendation on the protection of the dignity of women and men at work. It should be regarded as a statement of the obvious. To tolerate such conduct would be tantamount to a failure to respect the dignity and freedom to which every human being is entitled. All those who believe that this right to dignity is a universal fundamental value cannot accept the idea that the Community remains silent and inactive on this issue.

It has to be accepted - and the studies support the fact - that sexual harassment is still endemic, often hidden, affecting all Member States and existing in all kinds of companies. Yet it is still not viewed as a problem which has to be systematically tackled. Despite the absence of an universal definition and despite the various methods used to measure sexual harassment, figures show that between 30% and 50% of female employees still experience some form of sexual harassment.

Since the Council Resolution of 29 May 1990 on the protection of the dignity of women and men at work[1], the Community institutions have been actively working towards raising the level of awareness of the negative consequences of sexual harassment. Special reference must be made in this respect to the actions undertaken by the Parliament, in particular in its Resolution of 11 June 1986 on violence against women[2] and in its Resolution of 11 February 1994 on a new post of "confidential counsellor" at the workplace[3].

The Commission has furthermore consulted the social partners on a possible initiative on this issue.

The publication of these two studies presenting an overview of all relevant research projects conducted over the last ten years represents another step in awareness raising. This is more than ever necessary. Indeed, one of the first things which struck me while reading these reports is the poor level of awareness, at all levels, in most of the Member States. The Commission will continue to reflect on how to improve further awareness about the issues raised by sexual harassment.

Another element stressed by these studies and which caused me some dismay is the fact that it is still usually the harassed employee, rather than the harasser, whose career is negatively affected. This situation definitely deserves more attention and action. This need for further attention is reinforced by the fact that the studies have shown that where they exist actual means to combat sexual harassment do not always prove effective.

---

[1] OJ C 157, 27.6.1990, p. 3
[2] OJ C 176, 14.7.1986, p. 79
[3] OJ C 61, 28.02.94, p. 246

However, further Community action, on its own, whatever the form it takes, will not bring a full remedy to the victims of this problem. A real improvement of the situation requires a change in mentality and the commitment of all of us. However, I would like to believe that further action can be undertaken at Community level to raise the level of awareness and find the means to combat sexual harassment. I would therefore be grateful for your comments and suggestions.

Pádraig Flynn

Member of the Commission

EXECUTIVE SUMMARY

General conclusions on the Dutch and Spanish studies

A. COMMON FEATURES IN NORTHERN COUNTRIES AND SOUTHERN COUNTRIES

1. The definition of sexual harassment

a. The lack of an universal definition

The Commission definition, found in its 1991 Recommendation, is not known throughout Europe, specially in southern Member States. Furthermore, it is not accepted in all Member States and is not necessarily used in studies trying to measure sexual harassment. The debate about what constitutes sexual harassment is still going on among researchers and at least one Member State (France) has concluded that the definition of sexual harassment as sexual discrimination is inadequate.

It should also be pointed out that the same conclusion can be drawn as regards people surveyed. Not surprisingly men tend to confine sexual harassment to its most serious forms (physical assault), but even among women there are varying perceptions of what constitutes sexual harassment.

b. Various types of sexual harassment

Forms of sexual harassment are usually are usually divided into three different types : verbal (remarks about figure/look, sexual jokes, verbal sexual advances), non verbal ("staring and whistling") and physical (from unsolicited physical contact to assault/rape).

2. The ways to measure sexual harassment

The lack of an universal definition of what constitutes sexual harassment makes it more difficult to objectively measure and quantify it.

3. Percentages of female employees sexually harassed

The lack of an universal definition and the various ways used to measure sexual harassment make it more difficult to interpret correctly the results of the surveys and studies.

However, it is indisputable that sexual harassment is not an occasional occurrence, but, on the contrary, appears to occur in virtually all workplaces to a varying degree. Very roughly, the percentage of female employees who have received unwanted sexual proposals (experienced some forms of sexual harassment) can be estimated at between 40% and 50%.

The verbal form of sexual harassment is the most common one. It is experienced by nearly two-third of female employees, but unsolicited physical contacts are also commonly suffered by female employees. At the other extreme of the scale, sexual assaults/rapes are reported by less than 5% of women.

4. Profile of harassed female employees

Although such a profile changes from one country to another, it can be said that women who are between 30 and 40 years of age, single or divorced, with a lower level of education are more likely to experience sexual harassment.

5. Profile of the harassers

Harassers are overwhelmingly men. Perpetrators of sexual harassment are mostly colleagues or superiors. Far behind, are patients or clients and finally subordinates.

6. Costs and consequences of sexual harassment

Almost all people suffering sexual harassment report negative consequences, both private and regarding their job. As regards the former, psychosomatic symptoms, loss of self-esteem, interference with private life are most commonly reported. As regards the latter, it appears that harassed employees experience a negative impact on their career more often than the harassers.

B. DIFFERENCES BETWEEN NORTHERN AND SOUTHERN COUNTRIES

The studies clearly indicate that the problem of sexual harassment is not uniformly perceived and/or addressed in northern and southern countries.

1. The importance given to the problem of sexual harassment

Sexual harassment is common in both southern countries and northern countries. However, it seems that, save in France and Italy, much less importance is attached to the issue of sexual harassment in southern countries and the level of awareness is not very high. This is in particular evidenced by the fact that many fewer studies and surveys have been conducted in southern countries than in northern countries in the last ten years. Indeed, in southern countries it is only very recently that the problem gave rise to such surveys, which often are not entirely reliable.

2. How sexual harassment is perceived by female employees.

Studies seem to indicate that the way female employees in the southern countries and northern countries perceive sexual harassment is different. Women in southern countries tend to consider that sexual harassment is something they have to put up with because it is part and parcel of being a woman. Such a feeling is in particular induced by the attitude of men who do not perceive their behaviour as constituting sexual harassment.

3. Position of companies with regards to sexual harassment

Information policies   (brochures, staff magazines, policy statement) seem to be developed on a large scale only in northern countries. In southern countries researchers have underlined the lack of visibility of the problem in most companies as well as the reluctance to put in place an information policy on the issue.   Furthermore, the appointment of a confidential counsellor is a method used in all northern countries save the UK. This method seems to be virtually non-existent in southern countries, although it should be mentioned that where applied, the method of appointing a confidential counsellor gives frequently rise to problems.

Universitair Centrum
Genderstudies
Sociale Wetenschappen

DUTCH STUDY

SEXUAL HARASSMENT IN EUROPEAN WORKPLACES

A review of research in 11 Member States (1987-1997)

Dr. M.C. Timmerman (Coordinator)
Drs C.W. Bajema (Researcher)

Preface

This is the second expert report on sexual harassment in the workplace commissioned by the European Commission (DG V, Medium-term Community Action Programme on Equal Opportunities for women and men, 1996-2000). The first report on the problem was initiated by the Commission in 1987[4].

According to the Council, the European Parliament and the Commission, sexual harassment constitutes a breach of the principle of equal treatment and is an affront to the dignity of women and men at work. Over the past decade the Community institutions have undertaken a variety of initiatives to prevent and to combat sexual harassment at work:

* the European Parliament Resolution of 1986 on violence against women;
* the 1990 Council resolution on the protection of the dignity of women and men at work;
* the 1991 Commission recommendation on protecting the dignity of women and men at work with its annexed Code of Practice;
* the 1991 Council Declaration on the implementation of the Commission's recommendation and Code of Practice;
* the 1993 Guide to implementing the Commission's Code of Practice;
* The European Parliament Resolution of 1994 on a new post of a confidential counsellor at the workplace;
* the fourth medium-term action programme for equal opportunities for men and women (1996-2000) adopted by the Council on 22 December 1995 which emphasises the need for decisive action to combat sexual harassment;
* a consultation of management and labour on the prevention of sexual harassment at work, July 1996.

To continue these activities and to develop a comprehensive policy, more recent and valid information was needed about the prevalence, the severity and the consequences of sexual harassment in the Member States. This report presents an overview of all relevant research projects conducted in the Member States between 1987 and 1997 (74 surveys and qualitative studies).

Information was collected by an international team of experts on and researchers on sexual harassment. We would like to thank the following colleagues for their invaluable contribution to this review study in the form of a country report:[5] Kathrina Zippel (Austria), Teija Mankkinen (Finland), Kathrina Zippel (Germany), Josephine Browne (Ireland), Anne Werner (Norway), and Ninni Hagman (Sweden).

---

[4] Rubenstein, Michael (1987), The dignity of women at work. A report of the problem of sexual harassment in the Member States of the European Community.

[5] The names of the experts are presented in alphabetical order of the countries for which they gathered information.

We would also like to thank the following people for their participation in our review study: Sybille Opdebeeck, Rien van Meensel, Biche Ehinger (Belgium), Henrik Holt Larsen, Libby Tata Arcel (Denmark), Maddy Mulheims (Luxembourg), Sissel Frøberg (Norway), Jeanne de Bruyn (the Netherlands), Lise Bergh, Gunilla Carstensen (Sweden), Andrea Broughton, Sarah Curteis and Jalna Hamner (United Kingdom).

The additional information resources used to collect the studies include: all University Libraries in the Member States, Women's Studies Databases (e.g. the International Information Centre and Archives of the Women's Movement - IIAV - in Amsterdam), and various Social Sciences Databases in Europe. Further, information about the relevant activities of the European Union was found in Cordis and Europe.

By presenting this comprehensive review of recent research on sexual harassment, we hope to provide assistance in the further development of the Commission's policy to prevent and to combat sexual harassment in the workplace.

Dr. Greetje Timmerman
Drs Cristien Bajema
University of Groningen
University Centre Genderstudies
Grote Rozenstraat 38
9712 TJ Groningen
The Netherlands

Groningen, December 1997

Introduction and summary

A substantial body of research addressing the issue of sexual harassment in the workplace has been developed over the past decade. This report reviews research on sexual harassment in the workplace in the 11 northern Member States (1987-1997). It is the second expert report on sexual harassment and, when compared to the first one (Rubenstein, 1987), the studies reviewed in this report demonstrate an increasing sophistication in definition and methodology. Many quantitative surveys and qualitative studies (74) have been carried out, not only nation-wide surveys but also studies concentrating on specific branches, occupations or firms.

The accumulated evidence from these research activities shows that sexual harassment is prevalent in organisations in all surveyed Member States and functions as a serious barrier to the integration of women in the labour market.

Although percentages differ, partly due to differences in method and definition, the studies estimate that, overall, approximately *30% to 50% of female* employees have experienced some form of sexual harassment or unwanted sexual behaviour. A few surveys studied men's experiences with sexual harassment. The research results suggest that about *10% of male* employees have experienced sexual harassment or unwanted sexual behaviour in the workplace. There are important differences between the sexual harassment experiences of women and men: in general men perceive harassment as less offensive; men experience less negative consequences of harassment; men defined witnessing the sexual harassment of their female colleagues as sexual harassment.

Sexual harassment manifests itself in a variety of behaviour. The most common forms are *verbal* forms such as 'sexual jokes' and 'sexual remarks about body, clothes and sex life'; *physical* forms as 'unsolicited physical contact', and *nonverbal* forms such as 'staring and whistling'. Sexual harassment concerning threats of disadvantage for refusing sexual involvement or other forms of '*quid quo pro*' harassment were experienced by 10% to 26% of the employees. The *severe* forms 'sexual assault or rape' were reported by 1% to 6% of the women.

Most employees *responded* to sexual harassment by ignoring the behaviour or by telling the harasser to stop. The behaviour was ignored because of fear of negative consequences; respondents believed that their complaint would not be taken seriously; or they were too stunned or surprised to do anything. Very few respondents indicated that they contacted a confidential counsellor or a supervisor. Also, very few employees filed a complaint.

There is no typical profile of *harassers* or harassed employees. However, in general *male* workers are the perpetrators of sexual harassment. In most cases the harassers are male *colleagues* (on average 50%) or *supervisors* (on average 30%). *Clients and patients* are mentioned to a lesser degree (on average 15%). However, in 'care' and 'service' professions where employees have contact with patients and clients more frequently, the clients and patients are more often the perpetrators.

Harassed employees are usually women. Young, aged between 20 and 40, single or divorced women are more likely to be harassed than other women. Also, several studies suggest that women with a lower education level and temporary workers are more exposed to sexual harassment. Further, women in *male-dominated* jobs experience more sexual harassment than in other jobs. Harassment-prone occupations include police officer, bus or taxi driver, waitress, nurse, and sales(wo)man.

Not only personal and occupational characteristics relate to the incidence of sexual harassment. There is a growing consensus - as in the United States and Canada - that *organisational characteristics* are critical in determining whether harassment will occur. It is very likely that organisational climate is a primary explanatory variable in the different incidence rates between organisations. For instance, some studies reviewed indicate that organisations characterised by a *sexualised work environment* and a *tolerance* of sexual harassment facilitate the occurrence of sexual harassment.

Although additional research should elaborate on this relationship between *organisational culture* and the occurrence of sexual harassment, some surveys reveal a tendency that employees experienced *less* sexual harassment in organisations which were characterised by a *positive social climate* (employee-oriented instead of job-oriented) and a *sensitivity to the problem for many female workers of balancing work and personal obligations.*

The primary goal of the surveys that have been conducted between 1987 and 1997 was to document the prevalence of sexual harassment in the workplace. This implies that most of the surveys reviewed in this report are of a descriptive nature. Less attention has been paid to the explanation of sexual harassment.

Many researchers assume that *power imbalances* related to *a gendered division of labour* are inherent to sexual harassment. So far, two studies have found empirical support for the theory that (changing) *power balances* between men and women in the workplace influence the incidence of sexual harassment. The lowest rate of sexual harassment was reported by women working in workplaces with relative equality between the sexes. However, the highest rate of sexual harassment was not reported in workplaces where the balance of power was extremely unequal. Most experiences with sexual harassment were reported in workplaces where the balance of power has changed, not to equality but towards a somewhat less uneven balance.

These findings predict that women will express their experiences with sexual harassment more openly with an increase in the number of women entering the labour market. This increase is a temporary effect of the integration of women in the workforce. As this integration continues and women gain more access to the labour market on all levels, it is to be expected that the problem of sexual harassment will decrease.

Sexual harassment has consequences. More than half of the employees reported *negative consequences* for their personal well-being; a third of the harassed employees described negative effects for their work situation such as resignation, reduction in tasks, change of workplace, and poorer working conditions. Also, the harassment had negative consequences for work satisfaction, the working climate and motivation.

When compared to the first research period covered by Rubenstein, more *policy evaluation* studies have been conducted over the last decade. These studies into sexual harassment policies show that countries differ with respect to the implementation of policies and procedures. In a few Member States (United Kingdom, Belgium, Norway, and the Netherlands) organisations have taken the first steps towards setting up a policy structure. These policies usually include information activities such as a policy statement or publication of the policy in staff manuals, the appointment of a confidential counsellor, and the development of a complaints procedure. Generally speaking, organisations have few training possibilities, few grievance commissions, and many firms do not feel responsible for incidences of sexual harassment.

The functioning of the *confidential counsellor* is unsatisfactory. Few of the harassed employees contacted a confidential counsellor. From the studies reviewed it appears that confidential counsellors often lack the necessary facilities to do their work, are too close to management, and are relatively unknown or not trusted. It is also difficult for confidential counsellors to work in organisations that lack an awareness of the problem.

In general, there is a large *discrepancy* between the high numbers of instances of sexual harassment and the low incidence of complaints. Furthermore, several studies show that complaints are usually solved in an informal way, followed by no action taken.

Important *recommendations* for a successful policy are:

*   a change of working culture, with the issue of sexual harassment being taken seriously;
*   providing information about sexual harassment to the entire workforce on a regular basis, and training involved persons;
*   management support;
*   confidential counselling services and grievance committees with the necessary facilities, not directly related to the management;
*   grievance procedures specifically related to sexual harassment;
*   sexual harassment policy should be a part of equal opportunities policy.

Finally, although this review report presents the findings of research activities concerning a wide range of aspects, some topics have received *little attention* and assessment in the research:

*   the sexual harassment of homosexuals and lesbians;
*   the sexual harassment of women and men from ethnic minorities;
*   quantitative and qualitative differences between the sexual harassment of men and women;
*   the consequences for the organisations in terms of financial and economic costs;
*   the influence of organisational culture and structure on the occurrence of sexual harassment;
*   effects of policy measures.

The present report is divided into two parts. The first part is a review of all the surveys and other studies conducted between 1987 and 1997. The second part consists of the country reports on sexual harassment in the workplace.

PART I

SEXUAL HARASSMENT AT WORK IN EUROPE: REVIEW OF RESEARCH

This report presents the results of the review of sexual harassment research in 11 northern European countries, i.e. Austria, Belgium, Denmark, Finland, Germany, Ireland, Luxembourg, the Netherlands, Norway, Sweden, and the United Kingdom. Information has been collected on incidence, types of sexual harassment, responses, profiles of harassers/victims and types of occupations and organisations, costs and consequences of sexual harassment, and policies against sexual harassment.

1 DESCRIPTION OF SEXUAL HARASSMENT IN THE MEMBER STATES

1.0 About the studies

In the period 1987-1997 75 research projects were carried out in the 11 Member States. Some studies are nationwide surveys of several branches of industry (health care, transport, retail trade, government, or commercial services), others were restricted to one branch, occupation or profession, for example the police, secretaries, local government.

Most research determined the incidence and types of sexual harassment by quantitative surveys. Several qualitative studies were also carried out. These studies concentrate on the process of harassment, coping behaviour or policies against sexual harassment. Table 1 presents an overview of the research projects 1987-1997.

	National survey	Branch studies	Total
Austria	1	4	5
Belgium	2	2	4
Denmark	1	4	5
Finland	2	5	7
Germany	1	5	6
Ireland	-	5	5
Luxembourg	1	-	1
Netherlands	1	10	11
Norway	-	8	8
Sweden	1	13	14
United Kingdom	1	8	9
Total	11	64	75

Table 1 Research projects in the period 1987-1997, by country

Response rates

The average response rate was between 45% and 60%. In general the representativeness of the studies is also quite good. The highest response was 100% in an Austrian study on training on the job. The lowest response rate was 10% in a UK branch study amongst employees of an employment agency. In general the questionnaires that were published in journals had very low response rates (about 5% or lower).

Measurement and definition of sexual harassment

Sexual harassment is measured by various instruments. Most studies measured sexual harassment by asking respondents about their experiences with actual behaviour. A complicating factor when measuring sexual harassment is that the perception of which behaviour constitutes sexual harassment differs among respondents. The term sexual harassment usually seems to be applied to instances of sexual assault and other severe forms of inappropriate sexual advances. The studies examined have used different ways of coping with this complicating factor.

* Unwanted sexual behaviour
  The first category of studies asked about unwanted actual behaviour, without mentioning sexual harassment (almost half of the studies). An example of this category is the Swedish FRID-A research in which the following question was asked: "Have you in your working life experienced any of the following unwanted behaviour with a sexual connotation?", followed by an enumeration of behaviour ranging from repeated unwanted remarks about appearance, body, clothes, or private life, to rape or attempted rape.

* Unwanted sexual behaviour & definition of sexual harassment
  The second category of research first inquired about the actual behaviour and then asked the respondents about their perception of sexual harassment; did the behaviour experienced constitute sexual harassment according to the employees? A small group of studies used this kind of measurement, one of them was the German national survey.

* Sexual harassment & types of behaviour
  The third category of studies first asked whether an employee had experienced sexual harassment. In the next question the respondents were asked for details about this behaviour (almost a quarter of the studies). An example of this approach is the Dutch national study in which the respondents were asked about their experiences of sexual harassment in the company they work for. The next question concerned the kinds of behaviour the harassment consisted of, ranging from sexual jokes, unsolicited physical contact, asking for sexual intercourse, to sexual assault/rape.

* Sexual harassment
  The last category of research only asked about experiences with sexual harassment, actual behaviour was not mentioned. About a quarter of the research studied the phenomenon in this way. An example is a question in the Danish national report: "More and more people talk openly about sexual harassment in the workplaces, i.e. that women are exposed to various kinds of sexual approaches, even though they have made it clear that they do not want this. May I ask you whether you have ever been exposed to sexual harassment in the workplace yourself?".

Because of the varying definitions, any comparisons drawn between the results should be made with a degree of caution.

European Commission's definition of sexual harassment

The European Commission's (EC) Code of Practice defines sexual harassment as conduct affecting the dignity of women and men at work: "Sexual harassment means unwanted conduct of a sexual nature, or other conduct based on sex affecting the dignity of women and men at work. This includes unwelcome physical, verbal or nonverbal conduct". In this study it was found that the Code of Practice of the European Commission is well known: almost all recent reports mention the definition of sexual harassment of the Code of Practice.

The EC definition is a comprehensive definition. It includes "unwanted conduct of a sexual nature" as well as gender harassment: "other conduct based on sex affecting the dignity of women and men at work". In this study data were collected on the extent to which gender harassment is included in the various definitions of sexual harassment. It turned out that most research limits sexual harassment to unwanted conduct of a sexual nature. Few studies use the broad definition, for example, in some Austrian research gender harassment is labelled as "hidden sexual harassment" which is gender specific, sexist and experienced daily.

The EC definition distinguishes 3 types of harassment: physical, verbal, and nonverbal sexual harassment. This is a very common subdivision used by many researchers.

Finally, the EC definition includes three conditions:
a. unwanted, improper or offensive behaviour;
b. refusal or acceptance of behaviour influences decisions concerning a job;
c. the behaviour in question creates a working climate that is intimidating, hostile or humiliating for the person.

In this research project it was found that many researchers include one or more of these conditions in their study of sexual harassment. First, almost all researchers used the term "unwanted" in their lists of behaviour. The other terms "improper or offensive" were not referred to. The second condition (b) was included frequently: almost half of the studies inquired about the effects of sexual harassment on the working conditions (dismissal, denied promotion or training, other tasks, preferential treatment). In a couple of studies the third condition (c) was included in the general definition of sexual harassment, for example, the Dutch home care research, which defines harassment as "unwanted sexually tinted behaviour/attention appearing in physical verbal and nonverbal behaviour resulting in a hostile work environment, less pleasure in work, disturbance of productivity, and a worsening of the relationship with the client or organisation". However, in the questionnaires respondents have not been asked directly about the relationship between sexual harassment and a hostile work environment.

Who commissioned the research

In a majority of the countries (7) the national government initiated one or more of the sexual harassment studies. This is certainly the case for Belgium, where all 4 studies in this field were commissioned by the Labour Department. To a lesser extent this applies to Austria, Finland, Germany, Luxembourg, the Netherlands, Sweden, and the United Kingdom: several studies were financed by relevant Ministries or local governments. However, some research was also commissioned by interest groups, labour unions, or Equal Opportunities Commissions.

Further, in Denmark, Ireland, and Norway there has been no assignment for research from the government. Instead the studies were commissioned by labour unions, universities, or by various organisations.

1.1   Incidence and frequency of sexual harassment

> Overall, the studies estimate that approximately one out of every two to three women, and one out of every ten men has experienced some form of sexual harassment or sexually unwanted behaviour.

Most of the studies in this review examine the incidence of sexual harassment. Although the results vary depending on definition and methodology, sexual harassment appears to occur in virtually all workplaces to a varying degree. In general, the studies found that approximately 30% to 50% of women, and 10% of men have experienced some form of sexual harassment.

A few studies present a much higher or lower incidence than the mean results. These varying incidence figures can be linked to:

1) the way of asking about sexual harassment.

The extensiveness of the questions about respondents' experiences with sexual harassment can influence the incidence rate. Generally speaking, only one question about sexual harassment will produce a lower incidence rate than a list of 10 or more questions about actual behaviour. This will be reinforced by the fact that in the perception of many respondents the term sexual harassment constitutes the more severe types of sexual harassment in particular.

Differences in incidence rates can also be attributed to the length of time taken into account. Most researchers do not refer to any period of time ("have you had experiences in this job/company"). In a few studies the respondents were asked to answer the question about their experiences with reference to a specific period of time, for example 3 months, 1 year, or 2 years.

Finally, incidence rates were lower when only personal experiences were involved. However, a couple of studies also inquire about the sexual harassment of others (colleagues) in the respondents' work environments.

2) the representativeness of the research.

Incidence rates can fluctuate as a result of sampling. In general, random sampling produces other (in this case less higher) percentages than nonrandom sampling. For example, in a couple of surveys commissioned by labour unions the sample consisted of all female labour union members. It is to be expected that these respondents are involved in the problem of sexual harassment to a greater or lesser degree. It is probable that more victims than non victims responded to these surveys. This is also the case for self-report samples (e.g. questionnaires in journals).

3) national study or branch study.

Although sexual harassment occurs in almost all workplaces, in some workplaces the problem is more evident than in others. These differences may account for a greater variation in incidence rates in branch studies, as compared to national studies. Table 2 describes the incidence.

	sexual harassment of women	sexual harassment of men
Austria	81% (national study) 73% (local government) 33% (several branches) 17% (training on the job)	
Belgium	29% (secretaries)	
Denmark	11% (national study)	
Finland	34% (11 occupational groups) 27% (national study sexual life) 11% (university staff)*1 17% (Finnish parliament) 9% (SAK, several unions) 17% (union)	26% (11 occupational groups) 30% (national study sexual life) 11% (university staff)*1 3% (SAK, several unions)
Germany	72% (national survey) 80% (local government) 30% (private sector) 50% at least (local government)	
Ireland	25% (civil service) 45% (Electricity Supply Board) 14% (retail sector)	1% (civil service) 5% (retail sector)
Luxembourg	78%-objective criteria (national study) 13%-subjective criteria (national study)	
Netherlands	32% (national study) 58% (several case studies) 54% (local government) 56% at least (police) 25% (secretaries) 13% (industrial office workers) 23% (lesbians, bisexual women)	27% (local government)*2
Norway	90% (women magazine) 8% (several branches) 8% (labour union)	
Sweden	17% (national study) 2% (national study), 22% (health care) 53% (ambulance personnel) 30% (university hospital) 15% (university) 23% (wood industry) 27% (metro) 9% (social insurance office)	1% (national study) 14% (ambulance personnel) 4% (university) 4% (wood industry) 4% (social insurance office)
United Kingdom	54% (national study) 47% (temp agency) 89% (health service) 90% (police '92)	about 9% (national study) 14% (temp agency) 51% (health service)*3

*1 this is an overall rate of both women and men. *2 these are mainly indirect experiences; for example as a witness to the sexual harassment of female colleagues *3 this result is based on a very small sample of 32 responding men

Table 2 Incidence of sexual harassment by country and by sex

1.1.1 Incidence of the sexual harassment of women

As Table 2 shows, the incidence of sexual harassment varies considerably across the countries and the studies.

High incidence rate of 70%-90%
The highest incidence rates were found in the **national** surveys carried out in Austria, Germany, and Luxembourg. The Austrian and Luxembourg surveys reported a rate of 80%, and the German research showed that 72% of employees had been confronted with sexual harassment.

These high incidence rates may partly be attributed to the *comprehensive definitions* of sexual harassment used in the studies. For example, both the Austrian and German national studies included sexist behaviour in the definition of sexual harassment. The Luxembourg study used an extensive enumeration of sexual harassment types. Another possible explanation is the lack of *representativeness* of the research. In the German and Austrian studies the labour unions sent surveys to their (women) members. This group is probably more aware of sexual harassment than a representative sample of all employees. Further, two of the studies had a rather *low response rate*: the German study had a response rate of 20%, and the Austrian research 14%.

A couple of **branch studies** also have a high incidence rate. The Austrian research amongst personnel in public administration, the university, and the private sector reported an incidence rate of 73%, and the German local government study an incidence rate of 80%. In both studies it appeared that respondents were not only asked about their own experiences but also about the harassment they had observed in their work environment. This probably resulted in a higher incidence rate.

The UK police research concluded that 90% of the women had suffered sexual harassment of one kind or another. This could be one of the branches where sexual harassment occurs to a greater extent, opposed to other branches. Other high percentages of sexual harassment were found in a UK study amongst health service workers (89%), and in a Norwegian Women's Magazine study (90%). However, these two studies were self-reporting (non representative) samples: in both cases the questionnaires were published in a journal. The low response rates (less than 1% for the Norwegian study) in both studies suggest that people who have had experiences are more likely to react to journal questionnaires than others.

Medium incidence rate of 25%-60%
In the **national** Dutch, Finnish, and UK studies a somewhat lower incidence figure was reported by female employees: 32%, 27%, and 54%. All three studies were representative samples.

Most **branch** studies belong to this medium category. In various occupations every two to three female employees reported sexual harassment. For example, the Irish report about the Electricity Supply Board found an incidence of 45% of women employees having personally experienced sexual harassment, and a Finnish study amongst 11 occupational groups showed an incidence rate of 34%. Further, 27% of the Swedish Metro employees had been sexually harassed.

Low incidence rate of 2%-25%

A couple of **national** studies present a relatively low incidence rate of between 2% and 17%. The Danish and Luxembourg surveys[6] reported that 11% and 13% of the interviewed employees have experienced sexual harassment. The Swedish national survey showed an incidence rate of 17%. Finally, in the Swedish survey of the Central Statistical Office and the Labour Inspectorate 1 in 50 women (2%) experienced sexual harassment at least twice a month.

Some of the **branch** studies also showed a low incidence rate: the Norwegian research in several branches (8%); a Dutch labour union study amongst industrial office workers (13%); the Irish branch studies in the retail sector (14%), and in the civil service (25%); Finnish branch studies amongst university staff (11%), and in Finnish parliament (17%).

The relatively low incidence rate may be partly attributed to the measurement of sexual harassment. In the national and branch surveys one question about sexual harassment experiences was asked. Another explanation is the length of time. For instance, the Swedish Statistical Office survey covers a short time period of 3 months. All studies were based on representative samples of (female) employees.

1.1.2 Sexual harassment of men

Most studies were limited to women employees. However, 15 (of the 74) surveys studied the incidence of the sexual harassment of men. Although it is overwhelmingly women who experience sexual harassment, men are sexually harassed too. The research results suggest that about 1 in 10 male employees has experienced sexual harassment at the workplace.

Three of the **national** studies asked about the experiences of male employees: the Swedish Statistical Office survey reported an incidence of 1%, the UK study 10%, and the Finnish survey 30%. The Finnish researchers explained this high incidence rate for men by the way the survey question was framed: the question did not refer to unwanted activity, but to activity that the respondents had not sought, probably resulting in a higher incidence rate.

Most **branch studies** report incidence rates of between 1% and 30%. An incidence rate of 1% to 14% was reported by the Irish case studies (civil service 1%, retail trade 5%), and the Swedish studies (university 4%, wood industry 4%, social insurance office 4%, ambulance personnel, 14%). Somewhat higher rates were reported by the Dutch local government employees (27%), and the Finnish several branches respondents (30%). However, from the Dutch study it turned out that the men were mainly reporting indirect experiences: they reported their witnessing of the sexual harassment of their female colleagues. And the Finnish study showed that men have a different attitude towards sexual harassment than women; about 15% of the harassed men found the sexual harassment offensive, whereas half of the sexually harassed women found it offensive.

---

[6] The Luxembourg survey inquired about the incidence rate of sexual harassment in two ways: by asking about experiences with an extensive list of actual behaviour, resulting in a rate of 80%, and by asking the question "have you been sexually harassed at work", resulting in a rate of 13%. These varying incidence rates emphasize the influence of the way of asking about the incidence rate.

An exception was the extent of the sexual harassment of men as measured amongst UK health care workers (51%). However, this rate was measured in a self-report questionnaire published in a union journal. Only 32 men responded, half of them described experiences with sexual harassment.

Experiences of gay men and lesbians
A study in the United Kingdom, "Less equal than others", conducted by the gay lobbying group Stonewall (1993), showed that one in two lesbians and gay men had been harassed in general at work, 48% of them specifically because of their sexuality. Sexual harassment was not mentioned in particular, but the respondents reported these experiences in the category "others": 20 people (2%) indicated experiences of sexual harassment. In most cases this harassment was perpetrated by men. Both lesbians and gay men were harassed by men.

From a Dutch study amongst lesbians and bisexual women (Van Oort, 1993) it appeared that 23% of the respondents had experiences with sexual violence at the workplace. The respondents reported the non-contact types as most common types of sexual abuse (67%), followed by touching in a sexual way (32%). Most harassers were male colleagues.

A Norwegian researcher (Brandsaeter, 1990) investigated the heterosexual arrangement at work. The main result of this study is that heterosexuality is the communication norm at work. Lesbians often find difficulty in expressing their sexual orientation at work. Most of the time they use strategies to prevent colleagues finding out about their lesbianism. Lesbians try to separate private life and work (and sexuality is a private matter) or only talk about their sexual orientation with a small number of women whom they trust. The women interviewed were exposed to unwanted sexual attention at work. Examples concerned the sexual harassment of lesbian women by male colleagues.

Some of the German studies indicated that lesbians and gays are particularly vulnerable to discrimination in the workplace due to their sexual orientation. However, these researchers did not gather information about sexual harassment in particular.

Experiences of migrant women
One study was carried out on foreign women and their experiences with sexual harassment. This is a Dutch study based on interviews with women of Turkish and Hindu descent about their perception of sexual harassment (Tacoma, 1996). In comparison with other women the interviews suggest that migrant women more frequently take preventive measures in advance in their contacts with men in the workplace: they keep a certain distance.

The women responded to sexual harassment with a variety of strategies: direct verbal reaction, indirect verbal reaction such as talking about their own relationships, changing the subject, 'body language', walking away, ignoring the situation. In the long run they said they would talk to the harasser, let other people mediate, or resign. They would undertake action if they thought that the situation was out of their control. They would only lodge a complaint if there was no other possibility. They would never tell their families, because in their view the women are responsible for the occurrence and prevention of sexual harassment at work.

According to the researcher, a policy against sexual harassment should contain a wide/ extensive definition because the term sexual harassment only covers the more severe aspects of sexual harassment. Sanctions should be available within the company because this emphasizes that the management is taking the subject seriously. Talking about sexual harassment is very difficult for women in minority groups because of feelings of guilt and fear of the reaction of their environment. For example, the interviews suggest that Turkish and Hindu women would rather resign than make a complaint.

1.2   Types of sexual harassment; degrees of severity

Overall, the most common forms of sexual harassment are verbal forms such as 'sexual jokes' and 'remarks about body, clothes and sex life'. Furthermore, nonverbal forms such as 'staring, whistling' and physical forms such as 'unsolicited physical contact' are frequently reported.

The studies that asked about quid quo pro harassment (threats of disadvantages if sexual involvement is refused or the promise of advantages as a result of sexual involvement) reported that 10% to 26% of the employees experienced this kind of behaviour. The severe form 'sexual assault or rape' was reported by 1% to 6% of the employees.

On the whole, behaviour which when classified on a continuum is seen as 'lower level' types of harassment is more frequently observed and experienced but is less likely to be identified as sexual harassment.

More than half of the studies distinguish between verbal, physical, and nonverbal types of sexual harassment. The category **verbal** forms includes verbal conduct such as remarks about figure/looks/sexual behaviour, jokes with sexual innuendoes, and verbal sexual advances; examples of **physical** types are touching, forced kisses/hugs, and sexual assault/rape; **nonverbal** forms are staring, whistling, rude gestures, and pornographic pictures or films.

Table 3 presents a summary of the types of sexual harassment that employees reported in the larger, national studies.

	Aus	Dk	Fin	Ger	Lux	Ne	Swe	UK
Verbal								
- sexual jokes		66%	27%	81%	52%		68%	56%
- remarks about figure /sexual behaviour	52%			56%	23%	56%	48%	60%
- asking for sexual intercourse		30%		12%		10%	33%	
- advances (in writing/telephone)		27%		14%		19%	22%	
Nonverbal								
- staring, whistling	48%		13%	84%	58%		68%	60%
- pin-ups, nude calendar	13%	5%		35%	10%			
- suggestive gestures			13%					
Physical								
- (unsolicited) physical contact	55%	90%	7%	70%		59%	71%	20%
- touching body parts (breasts/genitals)	17%			22%	4%			
- (forced) kisses/hugs	31%	37%		15%	5%			
- sexual assault/rape	3%			3%	1%	4%	2%	

Quid quo pro								
- threatening disadvantage if sexual involvement is refused	3%			5%		10%		
- promise of advantages as a result of sexual involvement	7%			7%		16%		

Table 3 Types of harassment reported by the national studies

Overall, the verbal types of harassment are the ones most frequently experienced, followed by the nonverbal types of sexual harassment. On average, the physical forms of harassment are experienced to a somewhat lesser extent.

* *Verbal forms*

Within the verbal forms of harassment, the 'sexual jokes' form is the one most frequently experienced. The 6 national studies in Denmark, Germany, Luxembourg, the Netherlands, Sweden, and the United Kingdom show a similar tendency in the incidence rates of this conduct of around 60% (between 56%-81%). Only the Finnish national study has a lower rate of 27%, but in this study too, 'sexual jokes' is the most frequently experienced type of sexual harassment. The branch and occupation studies present the same tendency. Another frequently reported type of sexual harassment is 'remarks about figure and sexual behaviour'.

* *Nonverbal forms*

Within the nonverbal forms of harassment 'staring and whistling' is the most frequently reported form of harassment. The incidence rate for staring and whistling in the German, Austrian, Luxembourg, Swedish, and UK research is between 50-85%, in contrast with the Finnish studies which have lower incidence rates of 13%. A majority of the branch studies show an incidence rate of between 50-90%.

* *Physical forms*

Within the physical forms of harassment, the most commonly experienced form of sexual harassment is 'unsolicited physical contact, touching', although the incidence rates differ. A majority of the national studies found a high percentage of between 60% and 90%, the UK study and in particular the Finnish study have relatively low percentages of 20%, and 7% respectively. In the branch studies the category touching is also reported quite a lot, but in general with a lower incidence rate (e.g. between 7% and 58%).

The most severe form of physical sexual harassment, 'sexual assault/rape', is reported by 1% to 6% of the female employees.

* *Quid quo pro*

Further, a fourth category 'Quid quo pro harassment' was distinguished. Three national studies inquired about quid quo pro harassment: threats of disadvantage if sexual involvement was refused were experienced by 3% to 10% of the female employees, and promises for advantages as a result of sexual involvement were reported by 7% to 16% of the female respondents. In 3 branch studies quid quo pro harassment was also reported: the rates ranged between 1% and 11%.

1.3 Responses to sexual harassment

Most employees responded to sexual harassment by ignoring the behaviour (fear of negative consequences, the idea that the complaint would not be taken seriously, or respondents were too stunned or surprised to do anything) or by telling the harasser to stop (the assertive response). Further, informal responses such as discussing the incident with partner, friends, and colleagues are regularly reported. However, the formal responses of contacting a supervisor, confidential counsellor, and filing a complaint are rarely indicated.

Although the responses depend on the incident type, the working climate, and the hierarchical position, in general the study results suggest that an assertive strategy appears to be the most effective one, whereas non-interventionist behaviour does not seem to be successful. In some of the studies filing a complaint had a positive and in others a negative effect.

The responses of harassed people may be distinguished into four categories, based on the Belgian study by Bruynooghe (1995), which describes in detail the different strategies harassed employees undertake to stop the violence in the workplace. **Non-intervention responses** are responses where the harassed person ignores the situation/acts as if nothing has happened. With **personal responses** the victims try to solve the problem on their own. A personal response may be 'contacting the harasser to talk about the unwanted sexual behaviour' or 'avoiding the places where harassment is possible'. **Informal responses** are used to get the assistance of friends or family; and **formal responses** to get the aid of professionals, supervisors, confidential counsellors or to make a formal complaint. Most of the harassed employees respond in several ways.

An overview of the responses in the national quantitative surveys is presented in table 4.

	Aus	Ger	Lux	Ne	Swe	UK
Non-interventionist response						
ignored the behaviour	33%	51%		38%	42%	30%
Personal response						
told the harasser to stop/confronted the harasser	18%	38%	22%	45%	55%	42%
physically resisted/pushed the harasser away	16%	27%	21%			
threatened to file a complaint			14%			
walked away				18%		
avoided the harasser	33%	46%		6%		
tried to keep the work relationship good						
dealt with it with humour	18%	40%			38%	28%
Informal strategies						
spoke with colleagues	31%		34%	73%		
spoke with partner/friends	26%		77%			
Formal strategies						
spoke with confidential counsellor				3%		
told supervisor/personnel manager	4%		4%	28%		25%
filed a complaint		9%	7%	4%		5%

Table 4 Responses to harassing behaviour based on the national studies

The table highlights 3 frequently used responses:

1) The non-interventionist response 'ignored the behaviour'.
Around 40% of the harassed women and men used this response. Reasons for not intervening were: fear of negative consequences; the idea that their complaint would not be taken seriously; the hope that by ignoring the behaviour it would stop automatically, and the harassed employees were too stunned, surprised to do anything. In general, in the branch studies a somewhat lower incidence rate was found for this non-interventionist response, i.e. 25%. Of these studies the Dutch government study had the lowest percentage (12%) and the UK temp agency research the highest (39%). The Dutch police survey found that the direct response to unwanted sexual behaviour was usually surprise and being overwhelmed and confused, which resulted in ignoring or avoiding the behaviour.

2) The personal response 'told the harasser to stop, confronted the harasser'.
In the national studies 18% to 55% of the respondents used this assertive response. In the branch studies 27% to 73% of the respondents used the response of telling the harasser to stop. The Norwegian Women's Magazine survey reported that 73% of the respondents confronted the harasser, the Dutch government study mentioned a lower percentage of 27%.

3) The informal response 'spoke with colleagues, partner, friends'.
In those studies which asked about this response, a third to three-quarters of the employees spoke with colleagues about their experience with sexual harassment. Other regularly reported reactions were 'dealt with it with humour', 'avoided the harasser', 'spoke with partner/friends about the incident', and 'physically resisted, pushed the harasser away'.

4) The formal response 'contacting the confidential counsellor, supervisor, filing a complaint'.
The formal responses are not very common: 5% to 9% of the employees filed a complaint. In the Dutch national study 3% of the harassed employees contacted a confidential counsellor. The reasons for not contacting the counsellor included the harassed employees wanting to solve the problem themselves or with help of colleagues, they were unfamiliar with the confidential counsellor, or they did not trust the counsellor. The percentage of employees who told a supervisor or other responsible person (for example the personnel manager) is somewhat higher at 4% to 28%. The results of the branch studies show the same tendency, with one exception being the Belgian secretary study. In this study 18% of the women spoke with a confidential counsellor.

One of the qualitative Finnish studies (Varsa, 1993) reported that the people with experiences of harassment reacted in many different ways. Women almost always let the harasser know that they did not like the situation even though many respondents emphasized the difficulty of taking action. The women who had experienced sexual harassment often blamed themselves. Some of the harassees tried to solve the situation by pretending to be invisible, whereas others took immediate action. There were multiple ways to react against sexual harassment depending on the incident, working climate, and hierarchical position.

Satisfied with way of responding

In some of the studies the respondents were asked whether they were *satisfied* with the way they had responded to the harassment. Half of the respondents in the Dutch police study were not satisfied, they would have liked to have rejected the behaviour more openly. According to the researcher, many policewomen could not react in the way they would have liked because sexual harassment is a part of their normal work culture and thus harassment incidents were ridiculed. In the UK temp agency study the same tendency appeared; the harassed employees stated that if harassed in the future they would be more active than they had been in the past. The Dutch national study asked the harassed employees whether they were satisfied with the result of their response: 3 out of 4 were satisfied with the solution and 1 in 4 was not. Reasons for not being satisfied were: the problem still existed; the organisation did not take the problem seriously; the organisation did not tackle the problem or avoided the problem by dismissing a harasser for another reason.

Effectiveness of responses

The Belgian qualitative study (Bruynooghe, 1995), in addition to describing the different strategies harassed people undertake to stop the violence in the workplace, describes the effectiveness of these strategies. The researchers distinguish 4 types of strategy.

* Non-intervention strategies

The first type is the non-intervention strategy. A section of the harassed employees did not intervene or ignored the harassing behaviour. The most important reasons for this were fear of secondary victimization and fear of escalation of the harassment. According to the researchers the non-intervention strategy is very offender-friendly and will not stop the violence.

* Personal strategies

The second type of response is the personal strategy. Personal strategies range from obliging, to assertive and aggressive strategies. Obliging strategies include avoiding the harasser or places where the possibility of harassment exists. Sometimes sexual harassment can be prevented, but the price for this is high (restriction of own freedom, constant threat of a new incident). With an assertive strategy the harassed respondent makes it clear that she/he does not like the harassing behaviour. An assertive strategy in which the respondent (immediately) makes it clear that the harassing behaviour is unwanted seems to be one of the most effective ways of stopping sexual harassment. An aggressive strategy, physical self-defence, is used primarily against severe sexual harassment. Aggressive strategies are risky: sometimes they work but they may also lead to a further escalation of the harassment.

* Informal strategies

The third type of strategy is the informal strategy. Informal assistance may be called for from colleagues, supervisors, partners, and friends. This strategy may have positive as well as negative effects depending on the reaction of the person the respondent speaks with: if the person reacts with understanding and support then the strategy is successful. If the person reacts with rejection and disapproval then the strategy is not effective. In this case the harassee runs the risk of secondary victimization.

* Formal strategies
The fourth type of strategy is the formal strategy. Harassed employees can contact a confidential counsellor, file a complaint, etc. According to the respondents the help of a confidential counsellor was successful when it was possible to reach a solution within the firm and the offender was approachable about his behaviour. However, counsellors were powerless when the harasser belonged to the top of an organisation. The respondents had no experience with filing a complaint.

Several other studies also asked about the effectiveness of responses. Most studies agree that the *assertive response* is the *most effective* one. In the Swedish national survey the situation improved for half of the women. The German local government study found that more direct ways of dealing with the situation, such as resisting physically and asking the harasser directly to stop his behaviour in front of witnesses or privately, were perceived as more successful. Women felt better afterwards and noticed that the behaviour diminished. In the Dutch national study about half of the women stated that the problem was solved after letting the harasser know that the behaviour was unwanted. In the national UK study the situation of 40% of harassed employees improved after asking the harasser to stop. However, 79% of the respondents experienced an improvement of the situation after filing a complaint. In the UK study filing an complaint was found to be the most effective response.

Some studies also agree that the *non-intervention response has less effect*. In the Swedish research the situation improved only in 20% of the cases. The German research stated that ignoring and other indirect ways of dealing with the situation, such as avoiding the harasser, changing one's clothing or becoming less friendly, did not stop the behaviour, and women tended to feel bad or worse afterwards.

There is no consensus about the *successfulness of filing a complaint*. In the national UK study it appears that the least popular action 'file a complaint' is the most effective response; it improved the situation in almost 80% of the cases. Two of the German studies also concluded that filing a complaint was a successful response: 70% of the women in the German national study said it had improved their situation. As opposed to the UK and German study\ies, the national Austrian study is not positive about the successfulness of filing a complaint. Almost half of the complaints women made did not result in changes in their circumstances. Of the 162 filed complaints, only 24 resulted in the harasser being warned or reprimanded. Women themselves were most likely to experience negative consequences as a result of the complaints: 10 of the women were dismissed, though only 2 of the harassers lost their jobs; 9 women were transferred, though only 3 of the men accused were forced to relocate.

2   PROFILES OF HARASSERS AND HARASSED EMPLOYEES, TYPES OF OCCUPATIONS AND ORGANISATIONS

2.1   Profiles of harassers and harassed employees

> In general men are the perpetrators of sexual harassment. In most cases the harassers are colleagues (on average 50%) or supervisors (on average 30%). Clients and patients are mentioned to a lesser extent (on average 15%). However, in professions were employees have more frequent contact with patient and clients, the clients and patients are more often the perpetrator. The least mentioned category is subordinates.
>
> In general it is women who experience sexual harassment. Young, single or divorced women appear to run a greater risk of harassment. Also, several studies suggest that women with a lower education level and temporary workers are more exposed to sexual harassment.

Harassers of female employees

In general *male employees* are the perpetrators of harassment. The German national study described the typical harasser as a man aged between 30-50, married, who has worked in his job for a long time.

On average the harasser is a *colleague* in almost half of the cases, although the percentages found in the various studies differ from 23% to 75%. *Supervisors* are mentioned to a lesser degree in a third of the cases, ranging from 18% to 66%. For example, the German national study states that harassers were most likely to be male colleagues (50%) or supervisors (29%). In the Dutch national study the harasser was a male colleague in 48% of the cases, in 27% a male colleague from another unit, and in 25% of the cases a supervisor. A couple of studies report a higher rate for supervisors than for employees. One of these studies was the national Danish survey which showed that the perpetrators of sexual harassment are to a great extent superiors: of the harassed women 66% stated that they were harassed by a superior. The Luxembourg study indicated that female employees working in workplaces supervised by women are not sexually harassed as frequently as women supervised by men.

The Swedish national study found that sexual harassment in male-dominated professions was more frequently perpetrated by colleagues, whereas in female-dominated jobs a superior is more often the perpetrator.

Further, some studies (the Belgian secretary study, the national UK study, and the UK temp agency study) suggest that managers at least one level removed from the immediate supervisor are more frequently the harassers than the immediate supervisor.

Patients and clients were the harassers in 15% of the harassment incidences. For example, in the Dutch national study 16% of the harassment is perpetrated by clients or patients. However, in branches where the employees have more frequent contact with patients and clients the incidence rates were higher. For example, in the Swedish national report more than half of the respondents working in the health care sector indicated that the harassment was perpetrated by patients. In the UK police survey the traffic wardens mentioned the public as the main harassers, and in the Austrian study of workers training on the job (mainly hairdressers) 50% of the harassment was perpetrated by clients.

The least reported category of harassers were subordinates. In a majority of studies they were not reported at all, in 4 studies an incidence rate of 2% to 13% was mentioned. For example, in the Belgian secretary study 5% of the harassers were subordinates.

Harassers of male employees

Only two surveys have collected data on the harassers of male employees. According to the German national study, the harassers of man tend to be younger than the harassed person, more frequently of the same sex, and more likely to be on the same hierarchical level in the organisation. The harassers of men were in 63% of the cases male and in 37% of the cases female. The Finnish study of several branches mentioned that the harassers had been of the opposite sex and had acted alone: 9% of the men had been sexually harassed by their supervisor, and 52% of men by a colleague of equal or lower status.

Profiles of harassed employees

It is overwhelmingly women who are harassed. Other personal characteristics which influence the likelihood of harassment are age and marital status: younger women, aged between 20-40, and single or divorced women are more likely to be harassed than other women. Four studies report that women with a lower level of education are more exposed to sexual harassment. For example, the German national study found that women without training were particularly vulnerable. A Finnish study (Högbacka, 1987) showed that women with a low income and a low level of education were more frequently harassed. Two other studies suggest that employees who had worked for a short time at a company or had a student status were more frequently harassed. For example, in the German national study it appeared that temporary workers were more frequently harassed.

2.2   Types of occupations and organisations

Women working in male-dominated jobs have more experience of sexual harassment. A number of the studies suggest that women working in female-dominated jobs also have a higher risk of sexual harassment. Harassment-prone occupations include police officer, bus or taxi driver, waitress, nurse, and sales(wo)men. In addition to occupational characteristics, the organisational context is related to the extent of sexual harassment. A sexualized work environment and a tolerance of sexual harassment facilitates the occurrence of sexual harassment. Less incidence of sexual harassment was found in organisations characterized by a positive social climate and a changing power balance between women and men within the workplace.

Occupational characteristics

The incidence of sexual harassment appears to be related to the sex ratio of the occupation. On the whole, women in male-dominated jobs have more experience of sexual harassment than women in balanced or female-dominated jobs. 7 studies reported the relationship between the sex ratio and the incidence of sexual harassment. In 4 studies it was found that women in male-dominated jobs have more experience of sexual harassment. In 2 other studies it was reported that women in either male-dominated or female-dominated jobs run a greater risk of sexual harassment. Finally, 1 study found that the sex composition did not influence the incidence of sexual harassment.

Many studies did not distinguish between male and female-dominated jobs but rather between occupations (which of course may concern male or female-dominated jobs). In the following occupations employees have more frequently had experience of sexual harassment: police; health carers; retail jobs, women working in shops; waitresses, catering jobs; transport/traffic jobs like chauffeur, conductor, bus or taxi driver (reported in more than 1 study). Further, other occupations or sectors found were: office jobs, printing, private sector, non-profit sector, and cleaning personnel (reported in 1 study).

Organisational characteristics

Although personal characteristics relate to the incidence of sexual harassment, there is a growing consensus that organisational factors are generally critical in determining whether harassment will occur. In Luxembourg and the Netherlands a few studies have concentrated on organisational characteristics that facilitate or inhibit the occurrence of sexual harassment.

* *size of firm*
The Luxembourg study found that the most serious types of sexual harassment were reported by women working in companies employing over 50 people.

* *sex of supervisor*
According to the Luxembourg study it appeared that female employees working in workplaces supervised by women are not sexually harassed as frequently as women supervised by men.

* *organisational culture*
In the Netherlands several studies have focused on organisational features relating to sexual harassment:

(a) sexualization of the work environment

Women reported a higher incidence of sexual harassment in organisations that can be characterized as sexualized work environments. In these organisations explicit sexual forms of behaviour are part of the organisational culture. For instance, the Dutch national study (Amstel and Volkers, 1993) found that the rate of sexual harassment was higher in companies where suggestive remarks about clothes or appearance were daily routine. In general, informal behaviour among employees was male-dominated in these companies, for example, men determined the topics of conversation and the type of humour during the coffee or lunch breaks. The same tendencies were found in the Dutch police study: policewomen working in 'machismo' cultures reported the most incidents of sexual harassment.

(b) tolerance of sexual harassment
In organisations with more permissive norms regarding social-sexual behaviour women experience more sexual harassment than in organisations that are less tolerant. For instance, the Dutch national study found a relationship between the presence of sexual harassment policies and the extent of sexual harassment. Female employees working in

organisations that have implemented an extensive policy reported fewer incidents of sexual harassment than women working in companies without such a policy.

(c) social climate

A Dutch local government study (Zaagsma and Landskroon, 1996) and an empirical research project in a telecommunication company focused on the relationship between sexual harassment and the social climate in the workplace (Bajema and Timmerman, Unpublished Report, 1997). Women and men working in workplaces in which a concern for people (employee-oriented) was important reported fewer sexual harassment experiences than employees working in workplaces in which a concern for getting the job done was the most important goal (job-oriented).

(d) balancing work and personal obligations

The Dutch telecommunication study also found that the sensitivity of the company to the difficulties of balancing work life with family and personal life relates to the extent of sexual harassment. Employees working in organisations that are sensitive to this balancing problem experienced less sexual harassment than employees working in companies that place the priority on corporate rather than personal or family role demands.

*   *unequal power distribution and working culture*

A Dutch study that elaborated on the first national study in the Netherlands investigated the relationship between the power balance in the workplace and the extent of sexual harassment (Timmerman, 1990). The lowest rate of sexual harassment was found in workplaces with little inequality between the sexes. These workplaces were characterized by a relatively equal distribution of women and men throughout the hierarchical structure of the workplace and the sex ratio. On the other hand, women in workplaces with the most uneven balance of power between the sexes did not report the highest number of incidences of sexual harassment; the highest rate of reported harassment was found in those workplaces where the power differentials were still uneven, but to a lesser extent than the most unequal workplaces. In these workplaces women have gradually gained access to a few higher status jobs. The findings suggest that the growing participation of women in working life goes hand in hand with a temporary increase in incidents of sexual harassment.

In general, this study found that (changing) balances of power between the sexes in the workplace were closely connected with changing modes of behaviour. Sexual harassment experiences were hardly ever *expressed* by women in male-dominated workplaces. These workplaces are characterized by segregation of work by sex, a strong cohesion among the male employees, and sex stereotypical attitudes and beliefs. Women did not want to complain about their experiences with unwanted sexual attention because of their fear of stigmatization, isolation or exclusion by their colleagues. Women working in less unequal workplaces were less reluctant to complain about the sexual harassment. In these workplaces the work was less segregated by sex and women and men formed mixed groups. Instead of a male-dominant culture, these workplaces were characterized by a *diversity of opinions and attitudes*. This diversity in the workplace, which goes hand-in-hand with a changing balance of power between the female and male employees, created more opportunities for women to raise the problem of sexual harassment.

3   COSTS AND CONSEQUENCES OF SEXUAL HARASSMENT

Sexual harassment has consequences. It has an impact on the personal well-being of harassed employees as well as on the work situation. In general, more than half of the harassed employees reported negative consequences for their personal well-being as a result of being sexually harassed: emotions such as mistrust, fear, anger, and humiliation; psychosomatic complaints like headaches, stomach aches, and sleeping problems; stress reactions and depression. Further, a third of harassed employees describe negative consequences for the work situation, such as resignation, reduction of tasks, change of workplace, and poorer working conditions. Also, the respondents were more dissatisfied about and indifferent to their work and the working climate, concentration and motivation decreased.

3.1 Consequences for personal well-being

In general, more than half of the harassed employees described negative consequences for their personal well-being as a result of sexual harassment. The Luxembourg national study reported the lowest rate at 46%, in the German national study and the UK health care study more than 80% of the harassed persons experienced negative consequences for their personal well-being.

Sexual harassment may have a wide range of consequences:

* *Emotional and psychological consequences.*
  Many harassed employees reported feelings of mistrust, fear, anger, and humiliation. In the Austrian national study 40% of the harassed women felt mistrust and 35% anger. Feelings of insecurity and helplessness were described by 1 in 10 of the respondents. The national Luxembourg study found that 9% of the employees complained about nervousness and depression and 19% have become distrustful.

* *Psychosomatic symptoms.*
  The results of one of the Norwegian studies suggest that muscular pain, back and neck trouble were the consequence of sexual harassment. The Swedish national study showed that 18% of the harassed women reported headaches and muscle aches, 16% experienced stress reactions such as palpitations and sleeping problems, 12% became depressed and 2% had considered suicide. The Swedish Metro study reported that the harassment had effected the health of the respondents: psychosomatic problems (25%), stress reactions (28%), and thoughts of suicide (4%).

* *Interference with private life.*
  Finally, some studies found that harassment interferes with the private lives of the employees. In the German national study 5% of the employees who had experienced sexual harassment also disliked sexual activities in their private lives. In the UK health care study 59% of the harassed employees reported an adverse effect on relationships with family and friends. The national UK study reported effects on an interpersonal level: tension in relationships (24%), feeling hostility towards others after experiencing sexual harassment (14%), withdrawal from contact with other

people (9%), emotional detachment from those who are normally meaningful in your life (5)%, and becoming repulsed by or afraid of touch (5%).

3.2 Effect on careers, jobs and working climate

In addition to consequences for the personal well-being of harassed workers, sexual harassment also negatively affects careers, the ability to work, the working climate, and motivation.

* *Effect on careers and jobs.*
The 7 studies which asked about the effect of harassment on careers show that a substantial number of harassed respondents experienced a negative impact on their career.

It appears that a considerable proportion of harassed employees leave their jobs, either by giving notice or by taking leave of absence or sick leave. Also frequently reported are a change of workplace or being fired. Table 5 shows some of the most frequently reported results.

	B	D	Lux	Swe	UK
- change of workplace		17%			4%
- fired/quit the job		8%	16%		
- poorer working conditions		2%			6%
- less promotional opportunities			5%		4%
- absenteeism/sick leave					5%
- various negative impacts	30%			33%	

Table 5   Effects of sexual harassment on the careers of harassed employees

The Swedish national survey and the Belgian secretary study reported an overall figure for professional consequences of around 30%. The Swedish survey reported various negative impacts: reduction in duties; less remuneration; higher demands on work performance; unreasonable criticism; and isolation. Some of the respondents were unable to find any other solution to the problem than leaving the job, either by giving notice or by taking leave of absence or sick leave. The Belgian secretary study described the following career effects: dismissal, resignation, decreased motivation, poorer working conditions, and no promotion. According to the Norwegian several branches study (Moland, 1997), sexual harassment had a negative impact on sick leave: harassed persons were ill twice as often as their colleagues. Further, the Swedish University study mentioned the following negative consequences on careers and jobs: loss of tasks, new tasks under the level of competence, no promotion or increase in wages, exhortation to seek another job, and 4% had given notice.

* *Factors affecting the ability to work.*
One of the national studies examined consequences of sexual harassment that affected the employees' ability to work. The UK study found that 24% of harassees experienced difficulty in thinking clearly as a consequence of being harassed, 18% reported an inability to concentrate, 11% indicated a decrease in productivity, and 13% claimed to have experienced interference with their problem-solving abilities and judgement.

* *Consequences for the working climate and motivation of the employees.*
Sexual harassment affects the working climate and motivation of employees. In the Finnish qualitative research (Varsa, 1993) many women reported that harassment called their professional qualifications into question. The Finnish University study stated that staff members felt isolated from their colleagues, thought that they had received unjust criticism from their colleagues for complaining about sexual harassment, and, consequently, their work motivation decreased. The experiences of sexual harassment had a demoralising effect on the general atmosphere at work and on job satisfaction. The Swedish University study reported also negative consequences for the working climate: isolation (17%), spreading of rumours (10%), uneasiness at going to work (17%), unwarranted criticism, and change for the worse in working condition. One Norwegian several branches study (Einarsen, 1993) found that women with sexual harassment experiences were more negative about their working climate. One of the German several branches studies showed that women who had experienced sexual harassment were less satisfied with and felt more indifferent about their work. The Austrian 'training on the job study' reported that 50% of the harassed women had less joy in their occupation.

4 EXPLANATIONS OF SEXUAL HARASSMENT AT WORK

The main purpose of the surveys that have been conducted between 1987 and 1997 has been to document the prevalence of sexual harassment in the workplace. This implies that most of the surveys reviewed in this report are of a descriptive nature. Less attention has been paid to the explanation of sexual harassment. Some researchers have attempted to interpret their empirical findings in the context of existing theoretical perspectives. However, few theories are empirically grounded. This chapter discusses major views of sexual harassment in the workplace that have been considered in the studies reviewed.

4.1 (Individual) power perspectives

Sexual harassment can be explained as an abuse of power that is exercised by those with power, usually male supervisors over low-status employees, usually women. Although this individual power perspective was not empirically examined, it is assumed in several surveys that sexual harassment by senior colleagues is a result of the power differential between harasser and harassee. Most surveys have found some support for this view with (on average) 30% of the incidents involving sexual harassment perpetrated by supervisors or senior colleagues (see paragraph 2.1).

The individual power view also suggests that particular groups of women are more vulnerable to sexual harassment than others, for example women from minority groups, young women and women working in low-paid, low-status jobs. Most studies that examined the relationships between personal characteristics and experiences with sexual harassment found that young women, aged between 20 and 40 years old, single or divorced, with a low education level and temporary jobs, are more likely to be harassed than other women. None of the surveys systematically investigated the influence of minority status on the likelihood of sexual harassment.

4.2 Organisational (power) perspectives

There is a growing consensus in the literature that an individual's formal position within an organisation is a poor indicator of his or her actual power (to sexually harass). Men who want to sexually harass female employees have more opportunities to do so when the organisational context permits or facilitates such behaviour. This explains why in some organisations the estimates of incidents of sexual harassment are considerably higher than in other organisations.

From this view structural and cultural characteristics in the organisation are considered to be the main explaining factors of sexual harassment. Differences in the incidence of sexual harassment are explained by differences in organisational climate and organisational structure.

From an organisational perspective it is hypothesised that the following aspects of organisational context are critical antecedents to sexual harassment:

organisational culture:
* a sexualized work environment;
* organisational tolerance of sexual harassment;
* a positive social climate;
* acceptance of balancing work and personal obligations.
*

organisational structure:
* a gender-based hierarchical structure;
* sex segregation of jobs, departments, workplaces;
* sex ratio within the job.
*

Several studies have examined one or more of these contextual factors. Although further studies should more systematically elaborate structural and cultural factors to explain sexual harassment in the workplace, probably all of these factors are of relevance in explaining the incidence of sexual harassment (see paragraph 2.2).

The Established and the Outsiders
One of the theories empirically applied to the problem of sexual harassment in different workplaces is the theory of Established-Outsider relationships (Elias, 1965). Established-Outsider relations are unequal power relationships between social groups. When the balance of power between these groups is extremely unequal, both groups usually believe that the unequal power balance is just and natural. The Established think of themselves as people with superior qualities. Stigmatization and marginalization are a very common element in situations with such highly unequal power balances.

When the power balances become less uneven, inequalities previously taken for granted are challenged. Members of the Outsider group who have gained access to higher status positions express their claims for equal treatment and equal opportunities more openly. At the beginning of this process of changing power balances, the Established refuse to consider these claims and are unwilling to negotiate. However, as the struggle proceeds the balance of power gradually tilts. At the beginning of this process, conflicts and tensions between both groups increase. However, when the power balance shifts to a more even power ratio, tensions and conflicts decrease.

One Dutch study (Timmerman, 1990) found empirical support for this theory. Most sexual harassment experiences were reported in workplaces in which the power balance between male and female employees has changed, not to equality but towards a somewhat less uneven balance. Where the balance of power between men and women was extremely unequal (very few -token- women in high status positions) female employees reported fewer incidents of sexual harassment. The lowest rate of sexual harassment was reported by women working in workplaces with relative equality between the sexes.

In general, the Established-Outsider theory predicts that women will express their experiences with sexual harassment more openly as the number of women entering the labour market increases. This increase is a temporary effect of the integration of women in the workforce. As this integration continues and women gain more access to the labour market - both numerically and hierarchically - the balance of power between men and women will change to a less uneven relationship and as a result the incidence of sexual harassment will decrease. The Belgian evaluation study (Garcia, 1994) and the Dutch police study support this hypothesis. The Belgian study concludes that the proportion of women in the company influences the number of sexual harassment cases: in companies that employ over 75% of women no cases of sexual harassment were reported. The majority of cases (81%) occurred in companies where the number of men and women was practically equal. Furthermore, the Dutch police study indicates that units consisting of 50% women reported less sexual harassment than units consisting of only 20% women.

4.3   Misperception theory

This theory addresses the possibility that sexual harassment may result from men's misperceptions of women's behaviour and intentions. It is hypothesised that men who tend to misperceive women's friendly, outgoing behaviour as a sign of sexual interest or availability are more likely to endorse and engage in the sexual harassment of women. Some surveys in this review have discussed this perspective as a plausible explanation (e.g. Brandsaeter and Widerberg, 1992), however, none of them have examined it empirically.

4.4   Token theory

The theory of tokenism refers to the discrimination and marginalization of the members of a group in a minority position (Kanter, 1977). This theory proposes that members of any social group will be discriminated against if their group makes up less than 15% of an organisation. As yet the token theory is not supported by research. The theory of token discrimination was developed using evidence from women's experience of harassment and marginality in male occupations. No support is found for negative tokenism effects when men are in the minority. Men entering female-dominated jobs are generally welcomed, or, at the very least, there is little evidence that they are marginalized by their female colleagues.

Although the sex ratio of occupations was an important contextual variable in many surveys, the effects of tokenism were not examined in the studies. However, one survey, the Finnish national study, reported the finding that women and men are more likely to experience sexual harassment if they are the only representatives of their own sex in their job. Most surveys studied the occurrence of sexual harassment in sex-typed occupations. These studies showed that women in male-dominated occupations were more likely to experience sexual harassment than women in other occupations (see paragraph 2.2).

5   POLICIES

A third of the countries carried out evaluation studies into sexual harassment policies. The overall picture presented is that organisations have made a start with policy against sexual harassment. The first steps are setting up a policy structure usually including information activities like a policy statement or publication of the policy in staff manuals, a confidential counsellor, and a complaints procedure. In general, the rest of the policy is not that well developed (no regular information activities, few facilities for involved persons, few grievance commissions, organisations do not feel responsible for incidences of sexual harassment).

One of the main problems is the high number of instances of harassment and the low incidence of reporting. Some critical comments are made with regard to the functioning of the confidential counsellor: few harassed employees consult the counsellor; a lack of facilities for the counsellor; the position of the counsellor - too close to management, relatively unknown or not trusted; and a lack of awareness of the problem in the organisation. Further, several studies show that complaints are usually solved in an informal way, followed by no action taken. Important recommendations for a successful policy are: 1) a change of working culture, with the issue of sexual harassment being taken seriously; 2) providing information about sexual harassment to the entire workforce on a regular basis, and training involved persons; 3) management support; 4) confidential counselling services and grievance committees with the necessary facilities, not directly related to the management; 5) grievance procedures specifically related to sexual harassment; 6) sexual harassment policy should be a part of an equal opportunities policy.

Research projects into the effectiveness of sexual harassment policies have been carried out in the United Kingdom, Belgium, Norway, and the Netherlands. Although relatively few research projects have been conducted to evaluate the effectiveness of sexual harassment policies, it appears that most policies usually consist of the same components: information activities such as publicising a policy statement, a confidential counsellor, and a grievance procedure.

5.1   Information and training activities

Providing information about the policy for the whole workforce and educating involved persons are helpful tools to raise awareness of the issue and the company's procedures for tackling the problem. A substantial number of the organisations have taken steps to communicate their sexual harassment policies in one way or another.

Information activities

According to the Dutch national study, 2/3 of the surveyed companies who already had policies have developed information activities (Amstel and Volkers, 1993). Most of these firms provided information about sexual harassment in brochures, in the staff magazine or at work meetings. In the Dutch local government research information was provided at work meetings, in the personnel magazine, and by a lecture or video. The respondents were satisfied with this information dissemination. The Dutch home care study concluded that information and education is the basis of a good policy, however, the respondents were not satisfied with the information policy; they would like to see more structural and qualitatively improved information about sexual harassment.

The 1996 UK study concluded that over 90% of the organisations surveyed had taken steps to publicise their sexual harassment policy by issuing copies of the policy to all employees, by publication in staff manuals, by the distribution of leaflets, and by the display of posters and notices.

A policy statement is one of the ways to communicate about harassment. According to the 2 national Belgian studies, a large majority of the firms have a statement of principles or have changed their labour regulations. This was one of the measures suggested by the Royal Decree. In almost all cases the statement of principles took the form of a prohibition. However, the Flemish researchers suggest that the policy statement is to all intents and purposes only a paper measure because organisations reported that they did not feel responsible for the incidence of sexual harassment and they did not take other preventive measures.

In the UK 1996 research it appeared that 72% of the surveyed organisations had a policy statement on sexual harassment as part of the equal opportunities policy. These are often general policies covering all forms of harassment.

Training activities

The UK 1996 study found that just over half of the employers with policies provided training for staff involved in the sexual harassment policy. These training programmes vary according to whether an employee acts as a first-line recipient of complaints or whether they are responsible for investigating and determining the validity of the complaints. Approximately 40% of companies with a policy also provide training concerning sexual harassment for other groups of staff, for example, awareness training for all employees.

5.2   Confidential counsellor

Although a variety of policies and procedures to prevent and combat sexual harassment are implemented in the Member States, the great majority of organisations in this review study have appointed a confidential counsellor. However, in the United Kingdom the confidential counsellor is appointed much less frequently than in the other countries.

In Belgium many companies have appointed a confidential counsellor (the Royal Decree of 1992 requires employers to designate a confidential counsellor). The two Belgian studies suggest that as yet about 4 out of 5 companies have indeed appointed a confidential counsellor. The Dutch national study selected companies that have developed a policy against sexual harassment. The researchers conclude that in this sample 2 out of 3 of the organisations have designated a confidential counsellor. The national UK study reports a lower incidence of 20% for those organisations that provide confidential counselling services, and the 1996 UK policy evaluation reported that equal opportunity officers, harassment officers or counsellors were potential contacts in some organisations, but that in 80% of the organisations the line manager was the first person a harassed employee should approach.

The confidential counsellors are selected from different locations. The counsellors are usually personnel managers or health professionals. Sometimes one of the general managers or one of the employees is appointed. The tasks of a confidential counsellor differ between countries. In the Netherlands the counsellor's tasks are relieving, advising, and the aftercare of employees who have been harassed. According to the Royal Decree in Belgium, the counsellor, just as in the Netherlands, is supposed to play the role of a social worker, however, the dominant role of the counsellor in Belgium could be described as 'examining magistrate/judge'. The counsellor has a role in the formal settlement of grievances: hearing complaints; judging the justness of a complaint, and proposing sanctions. Another difference is that a (small) majority of the Belgian counsellors are male, as opposed to the Dutch situation in which almost all counsellors are female.

Evaluation of confidential counsellor

1. FACILITIES

Many of the counsellors did not have protection as a counsellor, did not have a description of their tasks, nor did they get extra time for their counsellor tasks. Another problem was a lack of training and special competence concerning the subject of harassment. The Norwegian several branches study concludes that the confidential counsellor was not the right person to solve conflicts about sexual harassment at work because the counsellors lacked training and special competence concerning the subject of harassment. This situation made the personal characteristics of the counsellor very important for the way the counsellors handled a complaint. The Belgian (Flemish) evaluation study also reported that almost no one of the confidential counsellors was educated on the field of sexual harassment. Only in the Netherlands, according to the national study, a majority of the confidential counsellors were trained.

2. INDEPENDENCY

In Belgium, a number of the counsellors were employers or belonged to the management group, which may have a deterrent effect on contacting a counsellor. According to the Belgian evaluation study, the 'management counsellors' regarded sexual harassment as less of a real problem than the other counsellors. The other counsellors received the largest number of complaints. These differences, according to the researchers, could probably be explained by the different tasks of the groups. The management staff is responsible for the company and its image in the outside world. Sexual harassment may influence the company's reputation; a counsellor from the management staff would be reserved in cases of sexual harassment.

Moreover, the counsellor/supervisor may be the perpetrator of the harassment. In these cases it is highly unlikely that the victim will contact the counsellor to file a complaint.

In the United Kingdom this is also an important issue, because in UK organisations a majority of harassed employees should contact their line manager (or the personnel manager or another manager), with the same problem of (in)dependency. The UK 1996 evaluation study reports the following problems:
- the immediate supervisor is frequently the accused harasser, and in these cases it is highly unlikely that the victim will pursue a complaint;
- the embarrassment of women involved in raising a complaint with their line manager may dissuade them from pursuing a complaint.

3. SEX OF THE COUNSELLOR

In Belgium about half of the counsellors are male. The Belgian secretary study suggests that this is a problem. Because it is women who are to a great extent harassed it is probably more convenient to talk about the experience with another women. The same problem is stated in the UK 1996: because the line manager is most likely to be a man, harassed women are less motivated to contact their line managers about sexual harassment incidents.

4. COUNSELLOR IS UNKNOWN OR NOT TRUSTED

In the Dutch national survey one of the reasons for not contacting the counsellor is that the confidential counsellor is relatively unknown or is not trusted. The Belgian secretary study stated that respondents were not satisfied with the counsellor because they did not know him/her.

A basis of trust appears to be an important issue. In the Belgian qualitative study, this was also expressed by the employees who reported a trusting relationship between the victim and the confidential counsellor as one of the factors for being satisfied with the help of the counsellor. In the Dutch home care study the employees were satisfied when they could openly tell their story, were believed and supported.

5.3   Dealing with complaints

Grievance procedure

Another measure regularly employed by organisations is establishing a grievance procedure. The UK organisations surveyed (1996) had implemented a complaints procedure relating specifically to sexual harassment in 70% of the cases. In the other cases a formal complaints procedure was available. Research carried out earlier, such as the national UK study (Industrial Society, 1993), showed a lower incidence of 40% of the employers in Britain providing swift and thorough investigation of complaints. This difference can be explained by a doubling of UK employers with sexual harassment policies since 1992, as found by the 1996 policy study.

In Belgium two-thirds of the companies had grievance procedures. In the Netherlands a third of the organisations had a grievance procedure specifically for sexual harassment and one in five had a grievance procedure for all kinds of complaints.

Grievance commission

In Belgium and the United Kingdom hardly any companies had grievance commissions. According to the Dutch study, a higher incidence of 29% of the firms had a grievance commission specifically for sexual harassment. Further, 1 in 7 of the firms had a general grievance commission which also handled sexual harassment complaints. The task of a grievance commission in the Netherlands is to handle a complaint, another task is give advice about sanctions, and 1 in 4 of the commissions could also enforce these sanctions. The personnel manager was almost always a member of the grievance commission.

Incidence of complaints

Several studies inquired about the number of sexual harassment complaints in an organisation. In approximately 20% to 50% of the organisations sexual harassment cases were reported.

According to the Belgian evaluation research there had been complaints in less than 20% of the Flemish companies and in 29% of the Walloon and Brussels companies, to a great extent in large firms. The most frequently reported complaints concerned unwanted physical behaviour followed by verbal forms. The victims were usually married women aged between 35-40, secretaries, saleswomen or office workers/clerical staff. The perpetrators were usually married men aged between 35-40, in almost half of the cases in higher hierarchical positions. The proportion of women in the company is related to the number of sexual harassment cases. In companies that employ over 75% of women no cases of sexual harassment were reported. The majority of cases (81%) occurred in companies where the number of men and women was practically equal.

In the 1996 UK policy report it appeared that in more than half of the companies surveyed (54%) employees reported cases of sexual harassment during the past year. Cases were reported in all sizes of organisation and in firms where women represented the majority or the minority of the total workforce. The reporting of harassment complaints appears to be linked to the existence of sexual harassment policies: organisations with a policy have a higher number of complaints, suggesting that harassed persons are more willing to come forward in organisations that adopt specific procedures for resolving sexual harassment complaints.

The Dutch national study found that complaints about sexual harassment were filed in almost two third of the organisations during the past 2 years. To a great extent the complaints concerned verbal types of sexual harassment and they were most frequently filed by employees in lower administrative occupations. This study also found that organisations with a comprehensive policy have a higher number of complaints than firms with a minor policy.

Sanctions

The overall picture is that in the most cases harassers receive a (formal or informal) warning, followed by no action taken.

According to the UK management study (Davidson, 1991), the most common punishment for someone found guilty of harassment was either an official or unofficial warning. The next most likely outcome was no action whatsoever. Furthermore, the victim of sexual harassment had a greater likelihood of being relocated as compared to the harasser.

In the UK office study (Alfred Marks Bureau, 1993), both the temp agency workers and the clients' agency were asked about the results of filing a complaint. In general, the employees were less positive about the results than the client/employer. According to the employees the most common response to reporting an incident to the senior staff was no action (43%), followed by resignation of the victim, and, less likely, dismissal of the offender (4%). The employers, however, said that the most common response was that the offender was disciplined (43%) or that the incident was reported but the company took no action (32%). The employers believe that their organisation takes more notice of the problem than their employees believe they do.

The 1996 evaluation study found that the vast majority of complaints of sexual harassment (70%) were upheld following an internal investigation. The most common actions taken were formal warnings or disciplinary action against the harasser, reported by 50% of the employers. The next most common measures were informal warnings to the harasser (34%), and the transfer of the harasser (32%). A small number of the complaints of sexual harassment were not upheld resulting in no further action; the employee making the accusations received an informal warning; or the employee who made the accusations was dismissed.

The Belgian national study concluded that most of the complaints were solved in an informal way, even the more severe physical forms; the perpetrator received a final warning and not an official sanction.

The Dutch home care study showed that the measures taken most often were that the harasser received a warning letter, or that a different carer -who was not always informed of the sexual harassment incident- was sent to the harassing client. The final sanction of stopping the assistance to the perpetrator was rarely made.

Effectiveness of the complaints procedure

Some studies inquired about any problems the organisations may have experienced when handling sexual harassment complaints. The problems reported were:

1. LACK OF AWARENESS IN THE ORGANISATION

In two UK studies, about 50% of the employees reported that the employers were not effective in dealing with sexual harassment. The most common reason given was that it was not taken seriously by management or generally in the workplace, frequently because the management, the union or the workplace was male-dominated.

2. PRACTICABILITY OF THE SANCTIONS

The Belgian qualitative study reported that filing a complaint with the counsellor was successful when it was possible to reach a solution within the firm, when the offender was approachable, and when the victim and offender could be split up. Counsellors, however, were powerless in the case of an offender at the top of an organisation.

In the Dutch national study one of the pressure points the counsellors described was that dismissal or relocation of a harasser was not always practicable, for instance because of the high position of the harasser within the organisation.

5.4   Effects of policies on the incidence of sexual harassment

According to the Dutch national study sexual harassment is experienced less by employees in organisations with a detailed policy. In companies with a minor policy 37% of the employees reported sexual harassment, as opposed to 21% in organisations with a detailed policy.

In the UK study about discrimination and sexual harassment amongst lesbians and gay men it appeared that respondents whose employers had implemented an equal opportunities policy including sexual orientation were less likely to conceal their sexuality at work. This suggests that a good policy makes it easier for lesbians and gay men to come out at work. Alternatively, it could be that in a more accepting environment it is easier to lobby for inclusion in the equal opportunities policy.

REFERENCES

Alfred Marks Bureau (1991), *Sexual harassment in the Office. Report 1: A quantitative report on client attitudes and experiences. Report 2: A quantitative report on employee attitudes and experiences*, Richmond-upon-Thames: Adsearch.

Amstel R. van and H.J. Volkers (1993), *Seksuele intimidatie: voorkomen en beleid voeren, Ervaringen bij 50 arbeidsorganisaties*, Onderzoek uitgevoerd in opdracht van het Directoraat-Generaal van de Arbeid door het Nederlands Instituut voor Arbeidsomstandigheden, Den Haag.

Bajema, C.W., M.C. Timmerman (1997), *Sexual harassment in a telecommunication firm*, University Centre Genderstudies, Groningen (unpublished manuscript).

Brantsæter, M.C., K. Widerberg (red.) (1992), *Sex i arbeid(et)*, Tiden, Oslo.

Bruynooghe, R., S. Opdebeeck, C. Monten, L. Verhaegen (1995), *Geweld, ongewenste intimiteiten en pesterijen op het werk: een beschrijving van klachten en strategieen om er mee om te gaan*, Diepenbeek.

Davidson, M.J., S. Earnshaw (1991), Policies, Practices and attitudes towards sexual harassment in UK organisations, *Women in Management Review and Abstracts* 6: 15-21

Einarsen, S., B.I. Raknes, S. Berge Matthiesen (1993), *Seksuell trakassering:* Bøllen og blondinen på norske arbeidsplasser, Bergen.

Elias, N. (1965), *The established and the outsiders: a sociological enquiry into community problems*, Londen.

Garcia, A., G. Colard-Dutry, C. Tholl (1994), *Etude portant sur la mise en place des directives decoulant de l'A.R. de 18 septembre 1992 visant la protection des travailleurs contre le harcelement sexual sur les lieux de travail*, Louvain-La-Neuve.

Högbacka, R., I. Kandolin, E. Haavio-Mannila, K. Kauppinen-Toropainen (1987), *Sukupuolinen ahdistelu ja häirintä työpaikoilla: Suomea koskevia tuloksia.*

Industrial Society (1993), *No offence? Sexual harassment, how it happens and how to beat it*, London.

Kanter, R.M. (1977), *Men and women of the Corporation,* New York.

Moland, L.E. (1997), *Ingen grenser? Arbeidsmiljøog tjenesteorganisering i kommunene*, Oslo, *Faforapport 221.*

Rubenstein, M. (1987), *The dignity of women at work, A report on the sexual harassment in the Member States of the European Communities*, Commission of the European Communities.

Stonewall (1993), *Less equal than others, a survey of lesbians & gay men at work*, by Anya Palmer.

Tacoma, L. (1996), *Grenzen in de omgang, Turkse en Hindoestaanse vrouwen over hoe zij omgaan met grensoverschrijdend gedrag op het werk*, Onderzoek in opdracht van Pres Emanciaptiebureau Utrecht in het kader van het project seksuele intimidatie en zwarte/migranten/vluchtelingenvrouwen, Utrecht.

Timmerman, G. (1990), *Werkrelaties tussen vrouwen en mannen, een onderzoek naar ongewenste intimiteiten in arbeidssituaties*, Amsterdam.

Varsa, H. (1993), *Sexual Harassment in Working Life: the Finnish Experience*. Ministry of Social Affairs and Health, Tasa-arvojulkaisujasarja A, Tutkimuksia, Helsinki.

Zaagsma, A.W., A.M. Landskroon (1996), *Onderzoek Seksuele intimidatie*, Groningen.

PART II

45

COUNTRY REPORTS

This part describes the studies that have been carried out in each of the 11 Northern European countries in more detail. The countries are presented in alphabetical order. The structure is as follows: after a short summary of the studies, the national studies are presented -if available-, next followed by studies concerning several branches, and by surveys concerning one branch or occupation. Each country report ends with the references used.

I   AUSTRIA

Kathrina Zippel

One large-scale quantitative study has been conducted in Austria, financed by the Austrian Women's Office of the Ministry for Labour and Social Affairs. Further, three studies have dealt with sexual harassment in branches such as public administration, health care, university, and the private sector. The initiators included the government, both ministries and local government, and universities.

1   National study

1.1   Definition and method

The first and, to date, only major large-scale quantitative study on sexual harassment in the workplace in Austria was commissioned and financed by the Austrian Women's Office of the Ministry for Labour and Social Affairs (Hopfgartner and Zeichen, 1988).

In the large-scale study, the methods used included both qualitative in-depth interviews of 14 women employees and a large quantitative survey. The 10,000 questionnaires were sent to labour unions which were asked to distribute them to female employees via female employee representatives in companies and industries. No men were interviewed. The representativeness of the study, however, is limited. The response rate was low (14%); the authors explain the low response rate by noting the sensitivity of the issue, as well as the distribution of the survey in the summer months of July and August. These limitations do not mitigate the fact that the sample was not selected using a specific quota system or random sampling.

In this study, sexual harassment was defined as "one-sided, unwanted, sexual advances which have a negative impact on the working and living conditions of the person who is confronted". The authors state explicitly that they do not mean to study or question consensual, voluntary social or sexual relationships in the workplace. They define sexual harassment with language that is close to the EEOC guidelines: "sexual harassment is repeated and unwanted behaviour, which emphasizes the sexuality of the person in the workplace," and they state that "sexual harassment includes sexual expressions which can be verbal or physical, ranging from personal remarks, deliberate touching and fondling to coercion".

The study distinguishes between two forms of sexual harassment, differentiated by the intent and the goals of the perpetrator. First, "secret" sexual harassment occurs when the sexually harassing behaviour has the goal of creating an actual sexual contact. Because of hierarchical power differentials in organisations, these expressions of sexual interest can take on a coercive nature. Second, "public" sexual harassment functions to make women insecure by turning them into sex objects. Thus, by demonstrating women's subordinate status in the work place, women's employment is fundamentally challenged. This type of harassment functions as a reprimand to women for not fulfilling their "true gender role". Both forms of sexual harassment constitute a serious burden for women and discrimination for women in the workplace.

1.2   *Results*

The main finding of this survey is that for a high percentage of women employees sexual harassment is part of their everyday working lives; and thus "Austria is no isle of the blest concerning this matter". About 80% of the women employees who participated in the study were confronted with sexually harassing behaviours throughout their working lives. Those forms considered least serious were reported by the women most often: almost 3/4 of the women had been patted, called pet names, whistled at, kissed on the cheek, and/or embraced against their will. 70% of the women reported serious forms of sexual harassment, including unwanted sexual remarks about their bodies or appearance and being stared at. Women were continually being invited for dates in which they were not interested, and many had been patted on the bottom. Even the most serious physical forms of harassment, which are the least controversial types of sexual harassment, had been experienced by almost 1/3 of the women. Such women received invitations with the explicit intention of sexual intercourse, and they had been pinched and touched against their will and without their permission. Moreover, 3% of the women reported they had been coerced to sexual contact under the threat of disadvantage for refusal; and 7% of the women had been promised professional advantage if they became sexually involved. Furthermore, 3% of women had heard about a rape occurring at the workplace.

The study found that almost all women agreed that sexual harassment is neither amusing nor complimentary. Respondents were asked to interpret three scenarios that tested levels of agreement on this issue. The respondents had very similar interpretations of the following three scenarios. 16% of the women had heard about an incident in which a woman was offered a job if she would "go to bed" with the new boss. Almost all of the respondents (95%) interpreted this behaviour as harassment, 3/4 of the women thought it was threatening and 89% of the women said it was humiliating for the woman. The women had similar perceptions about the second scenario, in which a supervisor "accidentally" touches the female employee's breasts. The most frequently recognised scenario was a male colleague making sexual remarks about a woman's bottom and breasts in public. The judgment of how severe the harassment was for the woman who was confronted with the behaviour in the scenarios is interestingly related to how familiar the respondents were with these incidents. Thus, while only 40% of the women thought sexual remarks about the body in public were humiliating for this woman, 70% of all women thought that touching a woman's breasts was degrading, and 89% of the women thought that the offer of the job on the condition of having sex with a supervisor was humiliating.

Women with university degrees regard physical incidents and sexually harassing remarks as more severe than women with less education. The differences in women's interpretations when correlated to their education might derive from the different status women gain in organisations. Those women in higher positions might have higher self-awareness and self-confidence and thus be less likely to accept these forms of behaviour from colleagues and supervisors. Most often, women had repeatedly experienced these forms of behaviours. For 3% of the women, these incidents were part of their everyday working lives, 34% of the women said these incidents happened every couple of days, and 41% were confronted with this kind of behaviour on a monthly basis.

In the qualitative interviews, women said that the colleagues or supervisors who had demonstrated sexually harassing behaviour had also expressed hostility towards women at work in general. Sexual harassment thus constitutes a special burden at work with which specifically women are confronted, through which women are hindered in their access to paid employment, and by which means women are discriminated against.

Because women anticipated negative consequences and feared for their jobs as a result of registering a sexual harassment complaint, 1/3 of the women did not take any action and ignored the behaviour. Another 1/3 of the women tried to avoid the man. The study found that "passive" reactions by women should not be taken as evidence that women did not object to such behaviour, they were bothered by them and felt harassed but a more active reaction was necessary to make the behaviour stop. Women did encounter resistance when they disapproved of sexual jokes and remarks.

Women tended to speak about incidents of sexual harassment only to those with whom they had trusting relationships. Such people included colleagues (31%), partners or spouses (14%), or friends and relatives (12%). But the least likely reaction (less than 4%) was to talk about the incident with the employees' representatives, supervisors or the personnel managers. Included among the active strategies women adopted were ridiculing the behaviour (18%), confronting the harasser (18%), and complaining to responsible persons (14%). Physical defences included pushing the harasser away (13%) and slapping the perpetrator's face (3%).

The fear of negative consequences as a result of complaints is real. The study found that almost half of the complaints women made did not result in changes in their circumstances. Of 162 complaints filed, only 24 resulted in the harasser being warned or reprimanded. The women themselves were more likely to experience negative consequences as a result of the complaints. Ten of the women were dismissed, though only two of the harassers lost their jobs; nine women were transferred, though only three of the men accused of harassment were forced to relocate.

Most often, harassers in the Austrian study were male colleagues (48%). Less often, women reported having been harassed by supervisors (18%). Only in 7% of the cases were the harassers clients or patients, and in 2% of the cases subordinates had harassed the women. The consequences of the harassment for the women were more severe when the harasser was a supervisor. Of those women who had left their jobs because of the harassment, 16 out of 18 had been harassed by the supervisor. Furthermore, 90% of the women in the study said the men who harassed them had harassed other women, too. Thus, sexual harassment is not the expression of a personal relationship but instead the pattern for some men who demonstrate harassing behaviour towards many women on a regular basis. The study did not ask about the women's experiences of harassment from other women. Because the study asked about women's experiences during their working lives, no conclusions could be drawn from the data about the women's ages.

Nevertheless, a common reaction is to blame the women for the harassment. Other women are seen as having sought advantage for themselves, and they are held responsible for the incidents instead of the harassers. Almost 10% of the women respondents, when asked to interpret the scenario, thought the women had provoked or incited the men, or attracted this behaviour. The researchers found that older women in particular (over 50 years of age) blamed the harassed women themselves for the incidents. Women often think that the harassing behaviour was incited, solicited or wanted by the harassed women when they observe other women being harassed; this is less often the case if they are being harassed themselves. A third of the women agreed that "women who are harassed by men asked for it". But even though less than 20% of the women said that they themselves would find it flattering if a colleague or a supervisor found them sexually attractive, the majority still thought other women would be flattered. When women experience harassing behaviour themselves they are more likely to blame themselves than the harasser. If they see fault with the perpetrator, they use psychological explanations to rationalise or even to excuse the behaviour, or see it as the uncontrollable "natural" behaviour of men. In the interpretation of the scenarios, 1/3 to 1/2 of the women thought the harasser had done it to prove himself and about 1/4 thought the men suffered from psychological disorders. And in explaining why the man made sexual remarks about a woman's body more than 1/4 of the women believed it was in the "nature of the man".

The authors see the women's responses to sexual harassment and the allocation of blame as closely connected. They argue that women blaming themselves or other women, and finding "explanations" for the harassers' behaviour, diminishes their feelings of responsibility for incidents in which they are harassed; women justify their "inadequate" reactions to the behaviour even if they are aware that they are being treated in a demeaning way.

The emotional and psychological consequences even of "less" severe forms of harassment can be similar to those of sexual assault and rape. If the harasser was a supervisor the negative impact on a woman can be even greater. Of the respondents to the survey, 39% stated that the harassment "did not affect them at all". The other employees reported feelings of anger (35%), insecurity (12%), humiliation (10%), helplessness (8%), and fear (4%). Another 4% of the women said they were flattered. 4% of the women felt guilty, and felt they were responsible for the incident. In the qualitative interviews, it often took women a longer time to remember the effects the harassment had on them because of the nature of sexual harassment. Sexual harassment can be experienced as an intrusion of privacy, and because it is still a taboo topic women might not associate negative effects on their well-being with incidents of sexual harassment.

2   Several branches

2.1   *Public administration, university, private sector*

2.1.1   DEFINITION AND METHOD

The women's section of the city of Graz commissioned a study on the work-related satisfaction of women and discrimination against women in public administration, in the university, and in the private sector (Kapeller, 1994).

The study asked about three different forms of harassment including, first, "hidden sexual harassment" which is gender specific, and harassment experienced daily which is sexist but not defined as sexual harassment. Second, more direct approaches than the first type, and third, sexual harassment including promises for professional advantage for engaging in sexual contacts, physical threats and rape.

2.1.2   RESULTS

The Graz survey found that 73% of the 362 women respondents had themselves been confronted with harassment by men or had witnessed men harassing another woman. Remarks about bodies against the women's will were the most often reported forms of harassment (64%). While staring and being observed in a critical, examining way was experienced by 57% of the women, 46% of the respondents had noticed being whistled at. Almost 50% of the women remembered observing women being put down verbally by men, and 43% remembered men using pet names for women. About 46% of the women noticed men not keeping the appropriate distance from women. Physical harassment, including touching, was reported by 37% of the women. Types of harassment categorised in the third category, more obvious or severe forms of sexual harassment, were reported less frequently. 11% of the women had been offered a sexual relationship by a man with the promise of professional advantage. 10% of the women had been directly asked to have sexual contact. 5% of the women knew about women being physically threatened by men. And rapes in the workplace were reported by 6 women.

The study found a connection between satisfaction in the workplace and the observation or experience of harassing behaviour. Those women who reported more harassment showed more work-related dissatisfaction, while the women who were more satisfied tended to report less harassment. The longer women had been employed in the organisation, the more often they observed harassment. Moreover, women in the production sector were more likely to perceive harassing behaviour than those in the public sector. The experience of harassment did not depend on the sex composition in the workplace.

2.2   Nurses, saleswomen, secretaries

2.2.1   DEFINITION AND METHODOLOGY

Roethleitner (1995) studied the relationship between work-related dissatisfaction among women and sexual harassment in the workplace. The convenience sample was composed of 1/3 nurses, 1/3 saleswomen, and 1/3 secretaries. The overall response rate was 55%.

2.2.2   RESULTS

The main finding was that women working in shops were more often harassed and more likely to be harassed physically, while secretaries and nurses experienced more verbal harassment and interpreted more situations as harassing than saleswomen. Furthermore, single women and women between 20 and 30 years of age were more likely to be harassed. Also, those women who had worked for less than five years for the same employer experienced more harassment.

Both the level of education and the length of time working for this employer correlated with job-related satisfaction. Women working as nurses showed the highest satisfaction with both their lives in general and their work (more than 3/4), whereas less than half of the secretaries were satisfied, and the saleswomen were the most dissatisfied; only

26% were satisfied with their jobs and only 36% were satisfied with their lives in general.

Women who had not reported sexual harassment were more satisfied with their work and felt less indifferent towards their work than those who had experienced sexual harassment. 2/3 of those women who had not experienced sexually harassing behaviour said they were satisfied with their work, but only 40% of those who had been harassed did. Although the percentage of women who were dissatisfied with their work was surprisingly higher among those who had not been harassed (21%) as compared to those who had been harassed (15%), overall the result is that most importantly, the women who had been harassed were more indifferent towards their work than those women who had not reported harassment. The small number of cases, unfortunately, did not allow the researchers to control for other factors, such as the correlation of tenure in the job, sexual harassment, and job satisfaction. Thus the author argues that it is too simplistic to say that those women who feel harassed in the job are more dissatisfied with their professional environment. However, this study could not answer the question of whether the sexually harassed women experienced a change in their satisfaction with the job.

3   Branch studies

3.1   Public administration

3.1.1   DEFINITION AND METHOD

The state of Salzburg carried out a survey of 700 women employed in public administration concerning issues of gender equality, in which sexual harassment was one of the subjects (Raos and Eder, 1991). Because sexual harassment was only a small part of this survey of employees, sexually harassing behaviour was defined narrowly and did not include some of the more frequently experienced types of harassment such as staring, leering, being whistled at, and receiving "accidental" touches.

3.1.2   RESULTS

In the Salzburg study the incidence rate was that almost 1 in 3 women employees had experienced sexual harassment. They reported the following forms of harassment: 1/4 of the women had been confronted with personal remarks or "dirty" jokes; physical harassment such as patting and grabbing was reported by 1/9 of the women; and 1% of the women had been promised professional advantage if they engaged in a sexual relationship. Women with higher education and in higher positions tended to report less physical forms of harassment, but reported the same amount of verbal harassment as women with less education.

3.2   Army

In 1995, political discussions about the possible recruitment of women to the Austrian military brought sexual harassment and misogyny to the attention of the public. The Ministry for women's affairs commissioned a study about the integration of women as soldiers in the military. This international comparative study found that sexism and hostility towards women, especially in the military, was of great concern to women soldiers and a barrier towards the integration of women. It emphasized that one could not expect the mere integration of women soldiers to eliminate the masculine-martialist nature of military culture, which was seen as one cause of sexual harassment. Instead, the presence of women may even enhance and stabilise the masculine tendencies and the exclusion of the female minority. Since February 1997, women have had access to careers and jobs in the Austrian military, but do not have to undergo military service.

3.3   Training on the job/vocational school

3.3.1   DEFINITION AND METHOD

The study is based on a survey of 189 women conducted in a vocational school. Although this study is not based on a representative sample of women apprentices, the response rate of 100% does support the validity of the results.

3.3.2   RESULTS

Sexual harassment is a problem for women even in their first years of training on the job. Karrer (1996) found that 1 in every 6 young women between 15 and 20 years of age had already experienced sexually harassing behaviour in their brief working lives.

Because 90% of the students worked in female-dominated occupations such as hairdressing (10% of the students were graphic artists), most of the students (90%) had only women as colleagues or worked mostly with women, and the majority had women supervisors (61%). This specific working environment helps to explain that, in almost half of the incidents reported, the harasser was a client, and that in 23% of the cases the women had been harassed by a colleague. However, it is alarming that in 1/3 of the cases the harasser had been a supervisor.

Furthermore, the fact that most of these young women had only worked for about three years and that some had already experienced severe forms of sexual harassment, indicates the high vulnerability of this group to harassment. Of the 30 women who reported having been harassed, 3 women had been sexually assaulted, 1/3 had been confronted with physical approaches, and 70% reported having frequently been "accidentally" touched. Two of the women had been offered advantages or threatened with disadvantage if they did or did not engage in sexual acts.

Most frequently experienced and most often reported types of harassment were staring and whistling; 90% of the respondents reported being the object of this type of behaviour. Two-thirds of the young women had been confronted with sexually harassing jokes, and 60% had frequently encountered overly personal remarks. Finally, 1 in every 3 women had been called pet names. For most of the harassed women, the incidents did not have consequences, but 50% of the women experienced less joy in their occupation, 1/3 of them felt helpless, and 40% felt mistrust.

The study found that the perception of which behaviour constitutes sexual harassment differed with the "degree" of its severity. While about 1/3 of the respondents found the "light" forms of harassment, including whistling, staring, sexual jokes, remarks, and being called by pet names sexually harassing, the majority, about 70%, did not. But more than 94% of the respondents agreed that the "medium" and "severe" forms constituted sexual harassment. The "medium" forms included offensive posters, sexual invitations and telephone calls; and the "severe" forms included promises of advantage for sexual "favours", the threat of disadvantage for sexual resistance, sexual coercion, and asking for sexual intercourse. A fourth category were "ambivalent" types of behaviour, for example, invitations with unclear intentions, physical approaches, and accidental touches. Nevertheless, 70% of the women found this kind of behaviour harassing.

According to this study, almost 3/4 of the respondents understood sexual harassment as an expression of power by men (72%), and did not agree with blaming women for harassment (81%), nor did they agree with excusing men for their harassing behaviour.

References

Hopfgartner, A., M.M. Zeichen (1988), *Sexuelle Belästigung am Arbeitsplatz,* Frauenreferat, Schriftenreihe No. 20., Wien.

Kapeller, M. D., E. Scambor (1994), *Die Zufriedenheit von Frauen am Arbeitsplatz im Raum,* Frauenreferat der Stadt Graz, Graz.

Karrer, H. (1996), *Tatort - Arbeitsplatz: Sexuelle Belästigung von Frauen, die in Ausbildung stehen,* Diplom Arbeit, Institut für Erziehungswissenschaft, Universität Graz.

Raos, J., F. Eder (1991), *Mitarbeiterbefragung in der Landesverwaltung, Detail-ergebnisse,* Amt der Salzburger Landesregierung, Landesamtsdirektion Referat Statistik.

Roethleitner, C. (1995), *Untersuchung zur sexuellen Belästigung von Frauen am Arbeits-platz und ihre Auswirkungen, unter Berücksichtigung der Arbeitszufriedenheit,* Diplom Arbeit, Salzburg Universität.

Zirngast, W. (1995), *Frauen im Heer im internationalen Vergleich,* Studie im Auftrag des Bundesministerum für Frauenangelegenheiten in Wien, Bericht an das Österreichische Bundeskanzleramt.

II   BELGIUM

Cristien Bajema

In the mid-1980s, sexual harassment became a research issue in Belgium. In the period 1987-1997 4 studies were carried out: one mentioned the incidence of harassment in secretarial jobs, one concentrated on the coping strategies of harassed employees including policy measures taken by organisations, and the other two studies dealt with the evaluation of measures against sexual harassment. Compared with other countries, Belgium has carried out more research into policy evaluation. The reason for this could be the Royal Decree of 1992, in which employers were obliged to develop a policy against sexual harassment. It is remarkable that all the studies have been commissioned by the Labour Department of the Government.

1   National studies

1.1   Definition and method

Two 'national' studies focus on the evaluation of policy, especially on the evaluation of the Royal Decree of 1992. According to the Decree each firm should have a statement of principle, a confidential counsellor, a grievance procedure, and sanctions. This policy should be described in the labour regulation of the companies.

The first evaluation study about the Royal Decree concerns companies in the Walloon provinces and Brussels (Garcia, Colard-Dutry, et al., 1994). Of the 159 firms contacted, 76 (48%) participated in the research. The most frequently mentioned reasons for not participating were either because they felt that they were not concerned with such a problem or because they had not appointed a confidential counsellor. In general the information was gathered by interviewing the confidential counsellor.

The second study concentrated on Flemish organisations (Van Meensel, Van Gyes, et al., 1995). Of the 127 firms approached, 68 (response rate 53%) participated in the research project. Reasons for non response included not being interested in the subject or no time. The firms varied in geographical location, branches of industry and company size. In most cases the confidential counsellor was interviewed.

1.2   Results

Of the companies participating in the Walloon provinces and Brussels, almost all had changed their labour regulations and 4 out of 5 had appointed a confidential counsellor. The counsellor could be a member of the management staff (31%), one of the employees (22%) or a medical/psychosocial/ health professional (41%). The age of the counsellors was rather high, since 47% were between 40 and 50 years of age. Half of the counsellors were female and half were male.

Just under two-thirds estimate that they do not profit from a certain protection as counsellor, but then this only seems to be problematic for a minority, mainly for those from the group of 'employees'.

Twenty-two companies, mainly large firms, had received complaints of sexual harassment. Six complaints concerned verbal types of harassment, three complaints mentioned anonymous phone calls and messages. According to the researchers 11 cases concerned 'serious' sexual harassment such as improper gestures, compromising propositions, asking for sexual favours, and physical violence. Almost all the victims were women with an average age of 33 years who occupied less important positions within the company. The harassers were practically always men, with an average age of 40 years. More then 40% were employees and 31% were managers. The confidential counsellor reacted in different ways when an employee reported a complaint. The most common scenario was that the confidential counsellor first had a meeting with the person who had experienced sexual harassment, followed by a meeting between the counsellor and the harasser to discuss the harassment case. Other possibilities were that the confidential counsellor made an appointment for a meeting with both the victim and the harasser, or that the counsellor did not contact the harasser but rather concentrated on supporting the victim. The counsellors estimated that of the 22 complaints 8 had not been resolved, usually because the victims were afraid of the possible consequences of having filed a complaint.

Half of the confidential counsellors felt that the Royal Decree's aim of preventing sexual harassment had been achieved. On the other hand, the other half felt that drawing attention to sexual harassment by way of a legal measure could induce acts of sexual harassment or incite the personnel to bring up problems of sexual harassment wrongly. 20 out of 70 respondents proposed improving the protection of workers against sexual harassment. The main propositions were the following: the personnel should be better informed; the aim should be respect of professional ethics at all levels; the confidential counsellor should be independent of the company; there should be a policy of equality between men and women.

The counsellors from the management group were more sceptical about sexual harassment than the health professionals; the latter group regard it as a real source of problems amongst personnel. Relatively speaking, the health professionals received the largest number of complaints. According to the researchers, these differences could probably be explained by the different tasks of the groups. The management staff is responsible for the company and its image in the outside world. Sexual harassment can influence this reputation, so a counsellor from the management staff would be reserved in cases of sexual harassment. The health professionals, however, are much less concerned with the image of the company. Their role is to make sure the personnel is in good health and has proper working conditions. Therefore they will take a complaint of sexual harassment more seriously.

The proportion of women in the company influences the number of sexual harassment cases. In companies where over 75% of the employees are women, no cases of sexual harassment were reported. The majority of cases (81%) occurred in companies where the number of men and women employed was virtually equal.

The researchers point out that, ideally, two confidential counsellors should be appointed, of different sexes and of different status. One of the counsellors should be close to the personnel and the other should have a certain authority within the firm.

According to the Decree, companies are free to define the role of the counsellor themselves. This leads to a lot of ambiguities and difficulties, for in general their role is rather undefined by the companies. It seems that the largest number of inaccuracies occurs at the level of formal treatment of the complaint. In certain labour regulations, the complaint must be filed with the counsellor. In others, it must be filed with the personnel officer or the management officer.

A great majority of the Flemish organisations had a statement of principle: in almost all cases this was in the form of a prohibition. The companies reported that they did not feel responsible for the incidence of sexual harassment and that they did not take preventive measures.

The companies did appoint confidential counsellors, but the counsellors did not have a description of their tasks, and were not trained on the field of sexual harassment. The dominant role of a confidential counsellor was the role of 'examining magistrate/judge'. The counsellor had a role in the formal settlement of the grievances: hearing complaints; judging the justness of a complaint, and proposing sanctions. The interpretation of the tasks of the confidential counsellor was in contrast with the Royal Decree, in which the counsellor is supposed to play the role of a social worker. Remarkable was that more than half of the counsellors are management members and not one of the counsellors is from a labour union. Further, more men than women were counsellors, in small firms in particular the counsellor tends to be a man. Two-thirds of the companies had grievance procedures, only one of the firms had a grievance commission. In many of the companies informal solutions were possible; the counsellor could mediate between victim and perpetrator.

There had been complaints in less than 20% of the companies. The most reported forms were unwanted physical behaviour followed by verbal forms. The victims were usually married women between the ages of 20-40 in functions such as secretary, saleswoman or office worker/clerical staff. The perpetrators were usually married men between the ages of 35-40, in half of the cases with a higher hierarchical position. Most of the complaints were solved in an informal way, even the more severe physical forms; the perpetrator received a final warning and not an official sanction.

2 Strategies of harassed employees

2.1 Definition and method

A qualitative study about strategies of harassed people to stop violence in the workplace was carried out in 1995 (Bruynooghe, Opdebeeck, et al.). The researchers searched for respondents with experience of sexual harassment on the job. With the help of social workers, confidential counsellors and by appeals in labour union magazines and professional journals they reached their target group. Most participants were interviewed. In addition, one day a week respondents could phone the researchers to tell them of their experiences with sexual harassment. The interviewers did not define sexual harassment; the definitions of the respondents themselves was the starting point.

The researchers distinguished between non-intervention strategies (ignoring the situation/acting as if nothing has happened); personal strategies (active and passive self-defence, avoiding conflict situations, and threats); informal calls for assistance strategies (aid of family, friends); and formal calls for assistance strategies (aid from professionals). The harassed people usually used several strategies. Furthermore, the study examined which strategies were the most successful at stopping the harassment.

2.2 Results

A section of the respondents did not intervene/ignored the behaviour. The most important reasons for this was fear of secondary victimization and fear of escalation of the harassment. A couple of respondents said that they ignored the behaviour because they wanted to spare the harasser or the work climate. The non-intervention strategy is very offender-friendly and will not stop the violence.

Personal strategies range from obliging to aggressive strategies. Obliging strategies are avoiding the harasser or places where the possibility of harassment exists. Other strategies are trying to break the contact and leaving the work situation. In general the obliging strategies were not the most effective strategies for stopping sexual harassment. Sometimes sexual harassment could be prevented, but the price for this was high (restriction of own freedom, constant threat of a new incident). With an assertive strategy the harassed respondent (immediately) makes it clear that the harassing behaviour is unwanted. This strategy seemed to be one of the most effective ways of stopping sexual harassment. The last personal strategy (physical self-defence) is an aggressive strategy. Physical self-defence was used primarily against severe sexual harassment. Aggressive strategies were risky: sometimes they worked but they might also lead to a further escalation of the harassment.

Informal assistance may be called for from colleagues, supervisors, partners, and friends. There was a wide range of reactions from understanding and support to rejection and disapproval. Informal assistance strategies always carries the risk of secondary victimization: the environment did not support the victim but thought she had provoked the harasser. But according to the researchers there was an even greater risk in not telling anyone about the harassment, namely the risk of becoming a misunderstood victim; there were physical or emotional consequences of sexual harassment but no one knew that these were caused by the harassment.

The study also evaluates two measures against sexual harassment begun in 1992/1993: the confidential counsellor, and a help line for sexual harassment. The employees were satisfied with the confidential counsellor when they could openly tell their story and if they could keep control over the interventions. The confidential counsellors in Belgium were not only supportive but they often also mediated between victim and offender. The respondents evaluated this task positively. The help of a confidential counsellor was successful when it was possible to reach a solution within the firm: the offender was approachable concerning his behaviour, and/or the victim and offender could be split up (profession, workplace). Counsellors, however, were powerless in the case of an offender at the top of an organisation.

The help line for sexual harassment was not evaluated as positively as the counsellors: some people were very pleased with it, others were not pleased at all. It depended on the reason for phoning: people who phoned for initial relief after experiences of sexual harassment evaluated it positively, but people who had questions about concrete strategies were more negative about the help line.

3   Branch studies

3.1   Secretaries

3.1.1   DEFINITION AND METHOD

The most recent survey is the study about incidence and types of harassment in one occupation, namely secretaries. The 1997 research was carried out by the secretary journal 'Secretaresse'. Of the 3600 subscribers to the journal, 182 (5%) filled in the questionnaire. In the questionnaire an enumeration of types of harassment was given.

3.2   Results

The study shows that 29% of the respondents reported unwanted sexual behaviour on the job. The types of harassment most reported by secretaries was the verbal form of sexual innuendoes (24%) and, to a lesser extent, sexual/incriminating proposals (10%). 16% of the secretaries reported the nonverbal form of staring/whistling and the physical form unsolicited physical contact. Of the respondents, 2% mentioned the severe form of physical sexual harassment: sexual assault/rape. Furthermore, 5% of the secretaries said they were threatened with disadvantage if they refused sexual involvement.

The perpetrators of harassment were in 33% of the cases colleagues, 33% were the manager (higher supervisor), 21% were the immediate supervisor, 8% were friends of the management or customers, and 5% were subordinates. About 70% of those harassed spoke about their experience with others; usually with a colleague (41%) or partner (30%). The confidential counsellor was consulted in 18% of the cases.

Experiencing sexual harassment can be of influence to people's careers. For 30% of the sexually harassed secretaries it had indeed had an influence: dismissal, resignation, decreased motivation, poorer working conditions, or no promotion. Also, psychological effects such as stress, less concentration and fear were reported by the respondents.

Further, some questions were asked about the policy of the firms the secretaries worked for. It appeared that about 40% of the firms had a procedure for handling sexual harassment and 20% of the firms had appointed a confidential counsellor. Three-quarters of the secretaries who had experience of sexual harassment could contact a confidential counsellor, however, more than half of the respondents were not satisfied with this counsellor: the confidential counsellor was the perpetrator, the counsellor was relatively unknown, the counsellor was (too) close to management, or the counsellor was a man.

References

Bruynooghe, R., S. Opdebeeck, C. Monten, L. Verhaegen (1995), *Geweld, ongewenste intimiteiten en pesterijen op het werk: een beschrijving van klachten en strategieen om er mee om te gaan*, Diepenbeek.

Garcia, A., G. Colard-Dutry, C. Tholl (1994), *Etude portant sur la mise en place des directives decoulant de l'A.R. de 18 septembre 1992 visant la protection des travailleurs contre le harcelement sexual sur les lieux de travail*, Louvain-La-Neuve.

Meensel, R. van, G. van Gyes, J. Bundervoet (1995), *De implementatie van het KB ter bescherming van werknemers tegen ongewenst seksueel gedrag op het werk. Een verkennende rondvraag bij 68 Nederlandstalige bedrijven*, Leuven.

Secretaresse Vakblad, (1997), Ongewenst seksueel gedrag op het werk, enquete 1997, In: *Secretaresse, vakblad voor het dynamisch secretariaat*, april 1997, p. 23-25.

III   DENMARK

Cristien Bajema

Five surveys have been carried out in Denmark. One of them is a national study about the incidence, types, and consequences of sexual harassment. Three are more or less inventory qualitative studies. The fifth study is the so-called Cranfield survey, a survey about organisational policies and practices in human resource management, which includes two questions about sexual harassment at work.

1   National survey

1.1   Definition and method

The only national study was carried out by the Danish Gallup Institute (Schultz, 1991). A representative sample of 1300 adult women, aged between 15-70, participated in the project. They were interviewed about their experiences with sexual harassment at work. It should be noted that the institute only used female interviewers, just as interviews were only conducted with respondents who were alone during the interview. The following question was asked: "More and more people talk openly about sexual harassment in the workplace, i.e. that women are exposed to various kinds of sexual approaches, even though they have made it clear that they do not want them. May I ask you, have you ever been exposed to sexual harassment in the workplace yourself?".

1.2   Results

Of the Danish women, 11% reported that they had been sexually harassed at work. The physical form touching and the verbal form dirty remarks were the most common types of sexual harassment; 9 out of 10 women reported touching and 66% mentioned dirty remarks. Other regularly reported types were kisses (37%), requests for sexual intercourse (30%), and requests for sexual activities other than intercourse (27%). The nonverbal form pornographic pictures was mentioned by 5% of the respondents.

Many women had been exposed to more than one kind of harassment. The assumption by the researchers that it was usually male superiors who offend against their female employees was confirmed: to the question "Was the sexual harassment perpetrated by your superior?" 66% of the harassed women answered "yes".

For a majority of the women (65%) the sexual harassment had no consequences for their work situation. However, 8% stated that they were fired and 17% reported that they changed their place of work. Poorer working conditions were experienced by 2% of the respondents.

More than three-quarters of the women who experienced sexual harassment were very open about it and spoke to colleagues, family and acquaintances about it. They didn't treat their experiences 'as a guilty secret'.

With regard to the question "Do you think there is too much fuss about sexual harassment, or do you think the subject ought to be taken very seriously", 53% of the women said that it should be taken seriously and 34% said that there is too much fuss about it.

2 Small scale qualitative reports

2.1 Larsen's research

2.1.1 DEFINITION AND METHOD

In 1988 Larsen interviewed a small group of employees to obtain a first-hand impression of experiences with sexual harassment. The respondents were asked about their personal opinions about and experiences with sexual harassment.

2.1.2 RESULTS

Larsen's main results were:

* Most respondents were surprised to be asked about this subject, and they were unsure about which behaviour constituted sexual harassment.

* Initially the respondents, men in particular, trivialised the problem.

* Almost all the respondents had experienced some form of sexual harassment in the past, but not everyone was immediately conscious of this: after discussing the subject, they remembered these experiences.

* Many men and a few women thought that women were jointly responsible for the harassment: women could fight harassment by clearly stating that the behaviour was unwanted.

* After a general discussion, when respondents started to talk about their own experiences they stated that sexual harassment was more common and more serious then they had thought at the beginning of the interview.

* Unwanted physical contact was the most commonly experienced harassment, followed by verbal intimidation. In particular, the unwanted physical contact had negative consequences: many women who reported this type of harassment had resigned from their jobs.

2.2 Petersen's service industries study

2.2.1 DEFINITION AND METHODOLOGY

Petersen interviewed 36 women working in service industries (health care unit, creche, social affairs office, and administration office) about their experiences with and responses to sexual harassment.

2.2.2   RESULTS

A third of them reported sexual harassment. Verbal forms were the most common, followed by unwanted touching. In general, women reacted individually to the harassment. Only in one case there was a collective reaction from a group of nurses with regard to a harassing doctor. The respondents stated that the incidence of sexual harassment was not that high because the women had no difficulty in rejecting the harasser, and because they were not dependent on the harasser for their job or salary.

2.3   *Process of sexual harassment study by Tata Arcel*

2.3.1   DEFINITION AND METHOD

In 1992 another qualitative study concerning sexual harassment was carried out (Tata Arcel). This research is based on four interviews with harassed women, two interviews with women who are working in a working environment in which sexual harassment occurs, and with reports of court sessions. The researcher's starting points were: sexual harassment is related to the psychological working environment and is a threat to the psychological health of individuals; therefore sexual harassment should be prevented, just like other damaging factors in the working environment.

According to Tata Arcel sexual harassment consists of the following elements: a sexual incident or advance; a certain amount of pressure used by the harasser; the harassee refuses permission in one way or another; and there are then consequences for the working environment.

2.3.2 RESULTS

Tata Arcel describes in detail the process of harassment, the different strategies of harassed women, and psychological consequences of harassment. The process of sexual harassment starts with a nice and sweet harasser: the women receive attention, interesting work tasks and they feel valued. But after a time the tune changes, although the women do not immediately notice this. One of the women related that when her supervisor arrived in the morning he started with "shall we give each other a morning hug?". She always said, 'No I don't like that', and pushed him away. Then it becomes increasingly clear that the approaches could be defined as sexual harassment. The men start to try more open sexual advances. For example, after 2 weeks one of the harassers started to touch a respondent's legs, and tried to kiss her on her neck and mouth. The respondent found it very unpleasant, but she was afraid to tell him directly that he had to stop because she thought she would be dismissed. Thus she turned and walked away when he did or said something unpleasant.

Tata Arcel describes the starting of terror as the next step in the harassment process. When the harasser figures out that the woman will not give in, he begins terrorisation by exercising his power. For example, one of the women related that she was the only one in the office who had to work overtime, and when she once said "no", he reacted with "aren't you happy with your job then?". This is the moment when the interviewed women realise what kind of a person their boss is, and they start talking about the things that have happened with friends, colleagues, and family. At this stage the women display physical and psychological stress symptoms. In general, the colleagues do not know what to do about it. Some are afraid for their own positions and others do not believe the things told about the harasser. Overall, the friends and colleagues do not help very much. In the last stage the women realise that in this situation they cannot keep their jobs; something has to be done. The interviewed women report ill or try to change workplace.

The study shows that the harassment had severe consequences for the victim: psychosomatic symptoms like headaches, sleeping problems, palpitations, and stomach aches; concentration problems; depression and thoughts of suicide; dislike of sexual activity in the private life; and mistrust of friends.

2.4   Management

2.4.1   DEFINITION AND METHOD

In the Cranfield survey (Brewster and Hegewisch, 1994), 2 questions were asked about sexual harassment: managers were asked about their experiences with and opinions about sexual harassment. 730 companies, with more than hundred employees, took part in the research.

2.4.2   RESULTS

In each firm the human resource responsible (usually the manager) was asked whether there had been concrete cases of sexual harassment within the organisation. A great majority of the managers answered negatively (81%), 5% positively and a group of 15% did not know. The second question was whether the respondents thought that sexual harassment is an area to which the manager should direct more effort in the future. About 60% of the managers thought they should not, 11% that they should and 30% had no opinion.

References

Brewster, C., A. Hegewisch (1994), *Policy and Practice in European Human Resource Management*, the Price Waterhouse Cranfield Survey.

Holt Larsen, H. (1988), *Ej Blot til lyst- seksuel chikane i arbejdslivet,* København.

Petersen, H. (1988), *Retsbeskyttelse af kvinders vaerdighed. Seksuel chikane i komparativ og retsteoretisk belysning,* Tidsskrift for Rettsvitenskap, 3/88, 253-308.

Schultz, A. (1991), *Sexual harassment on Danish workplaces,* Danish Gallup Institute.

Tata Arcel, L. (1992), *Seksuel chikane. Unfrivillig sex pa arbejdspladsen, hvad kan man gøre ved det?* København.

IV   FINLAND

Teija Mankkinen

Sexual harassment has established itself as a legitimate topic in both the general debate and work research in Finland. In general the phenomenon is regarded as a social problem that also needs to be dealt with means provided by society. The first survey was published by a committee of the Council for Equality between Men and Women (Ministry of Social Affairs and Health) among 11 Finnish occupational groups in 1987. Further, one national study and several case studies have been carried out. Only 3 studies concentrated on sexual harassment, the others focused on working conditions, equal opportunities or sexuality.

1   National study

1.1   Sexuality and sexual harassment

1.1.1   DEFINITION AND METHOD

Haavio-Mannila and Kontula (1993) carried out a representative nationwide survey with a sample concerning sexuality and sexual harassment. The objective of the study was to explore changes in Finnish sexual life over the past 20 years. One of the topics researched was sexual harassment. Sexual harassment at work was screened by the following question: "During the past 24 months, have you experienced the following kinds of sexually related activities or initiatives that you have not sought: sexually biased letters or phone calls, pornographic material – obscene language, dirty jokes, suggestive remarks or questions –, sexually insinuating looks or gestures – groping or pinching –, pressure to have intercourse or an equivalent sexual activity?"

The research material consisted of 3000 questionnaires sent to randomly chosen people, and several qualitative materials (newspaper articles, biographies, etc.). The questionnaire approached sexual harassment from a number of different angles. Comparison with other studies on the same topic is problematic because the definitions and concepts used differ from the terminology in earlier studies.

1.1.2   RESULTS

Of the respondents, 30% of males and 27% of females had been subject to some kind of sexual advances or harassment during the past two years. The percentage of sexually harassed men is exceptionally large. The researchers explained this by the way the question was framed: the question did not mention unwanted activity, only activity that the respondent had not sought. Age played a significant role in the workplace: 38% of men and 34% of women under 35 had been sexually harassed, whereas the corresponding percentages for men and women over 55 were 15% and 9%. The study showed that men had a different attitude towards sexual harassment than women: about

68

15% of the harassed men found the sexual harassment offensive, whereas half of the sexually harassed women found it offensive. The most common form of sexual harassment was obscene language, ambiguous jokes, remarks and questions (every fourth man and woman). A little over a tenth of the respondents had observed sexually suggestive looks and gestures and 4% of the men and 9% of the women had been groped or pinched.

2   Several branches

2.1   11 occupations survey

2.1.1   DEFINITION AND METHOD

The study by Högbacka et al. (1987) within 11 occupations was the first published research on sexual harassment at work in Finland. In the presentation of the issue and setting of the questions the study followed to a great extent the prevailing research approach in the United States. The study also adopted the American practice of including as many different forms of sexual harassment as possible under the definition of sexual harassment. Sexual harassment was defined to include the following: rape or attempted rape or sexual abuse, pressure to have intercourse or equivalent sexual activity, groping or pinching, sexually insinuating looks or gestures, sexually biased letters or phone calls, pornographic material, obscene language, dirty jokes, suggestive remarks or questions.

The study made use of both quantitative and qualitative material. The primary quantitative material consisted of 120 questions about working conditions and the quality of work, interaction at work, social support, family and work, free time, lifestyle, and self-image. There was a total of five questions on sexual harassment. Occupational groups in the survey that were female dominated included dentists, nurses for the mentally handicapped, and waitresses. The male-dominated occupations included architects, police officers, technicians, metalworkers, and construction workers. Occupations that were not gender specific included reporters, psychiatric nurses and workers in the rubber and plastic processing industries. The questionnaire was sent to 150-200 men and 150-200 women in each occupation in Southern Finland, randomly chosen from the membership records of trade unions in the relevant fields. A total of 887 men and 957 women returned the questionnaire. The percentage of returned questionnaires varied according to gender and occupation.

The qualitative research material consisted of interviews conducted as part of the same survey into 'quality of work and social relationships', and including the occupations of engineers, kindergarten teachers, industrial workers, secretaries, and childminders working at home. A total of 163 women and 102 men were interviewed; the interviews consisted of over 200 questions and lasted between 1.5 hours and 3.5 hours.

2.1.2 RESULTS

The study revealed that 34% of the women and 26% of the men had been subject to some form of sexual harassment during the past two years. The most common forms of sexual harassment were obscene language and jokes, and sexually suggestive remarks and questions (27%). Next came sexually insinuating looks and gestures (13%), and the third most common form of sexual harassment was groping and pinching (7%). Women had been subject to groping and pinching twice as often as men. Other forms of sexual harassment were very rare. The most harassment-prone occupations were waiter/waitresses and psychiatric nurses: about half of the respondents in both occupations had been sexual harassed in one way or another. Also, 70% of female police officers and 60% of female construction workers had experienced sexual harassment. In addition to waiters and male psychiatric nurses, male nurses for the handicapped had been subject to sexual harassment (36%).

One of the most significant findings of the study was that both women and men are more likely to encounter sexual harassment if they are the only representative of their own sex in the working place. For women, age and marital status had an effect on the likelihood of being exposed to sexual harassment: young and single women were harassed more frequently. The level of income and education was also decisive: women with high incomes were less frequently sexually harassed than women with low incomes. Discrimination at work was often felt to be closely related to sexual harassment: women who had been sexually harassed by their colleagues - subordinates or superiors - often felt that the sexual harassment had hindered their career advancement.

Usually the harasser was of the opposite sex and had acted alone. 16% of the women and 9% of the men had been sexually harassed by their superior; 58% of the women and 52% of the men had been sexually harassed by a colleague of equal or lower status. For less than half of those who had experienced sexual harassment, the harasser had been a customer or a patient.

2.2 *Finnish Institute of Occupational Health*

2.2.1 DEFINITION AND METHOD

The Finnish Institute of occupational Health carried out a study on equality during the summer of 1996. The main purpose of this study was to inquire attitudes and readiness to promote equality between women and men at the company level. The final sample of this study was 425 enterprises (over 30 employees) from the register of enterprises.

2.2.2 RESULTS

Of the surveyed employers, 11% evaluated that there has been sexual harassment cases in their company during the previous 5 years.

2.3   Trade union members

2.3.1   DEFINITION AND METHOD

A survey of the attitudes of the members of the Confederation of Finnish Trade Unions (SAK) was conducted in January/February 1995 via a postal questionnaire. The participants in the study were selected by means of random sampling. The final sample consisted of 7,929 people, of which just over 4, 000 responded, yielding a response percentage of 53. This questionnaire contained questions about sexual harassment.

Another trade union study is the one among members of the Central Union of Special Branches within Akava, AEK (1994). The survey covered many different things, including one question about sexual harassment. The sample was 1940, of whom 1486 (77 %) members responded.

2.3.2   RESULTS

The central result of the study among members of the Confederation of Finnish Trade Unions, was that 5 % of all members had experienced sexual harassment. On a gender basis, this was maintained by 9% of female respondents and 3% of male respondents. Women aged between 26-35 and women working in the private service sector were most likely to have experienced harassment.

According the Central Union of Special Branches study, 17% of women had experiences of sexual harassment in their present workplace. In top positions the incidence rate was even higher: 22 % of women. Sexual harassment was more common in private than in public sector's workplaces.

2.4   Process nature of sexual harassment

2.4.1   DEFINITION AND METHOD

In 1989 the Equality Ombudsman started a study into sexual harassment in Finland, commissioned by the Ministry of Social Affairs and Health (Varsa, 1993). The approach was qualitative because of the hidden nature of workplace harassment and focused on the process nature of harassment. Varsa's project also included a study by Mankkinen on sexual harassment encountered by psychiatric nurses (Mankkinen, 1994, see paragraph 3.1). To a great extent, Varsa's definition of sexual harassment was based on the definition in the European Community report "The dignity of women at work". In her study she used the following definition of sexual harassment: - it is physical, verbal or written sexual attention - it is unwelcome and one-sided - it often involves either direct or indirect pressure or it creates an uncomfortable working atmosphere - it entails negative consequences or the threat of them for the person who has experienced sexual harassment.

Varsa's research material consisted of letters (18), personal interviews with harassed people (39), and group interviews (5). The material contained descriptions of the sexual harassment process and workplaces, consequences of sexual harassment and survival strategies.

2.4.2.   RESULTS

The main focus of Varsa's study was on understanding the process nature of sexual harassment. Varsa considers sexual harassment to be a long process which severely affects the harassed person's integrity and circumstances in the workplace, even though it may have started with a single, seemingly harmless incident. Sexual harassment in working life was related to power and the misuse of power. Many women reported that harassment made their professional qualifications questionable.

The forms and interpretations of sexual harassment varied greatly according to employment sector and workplace. Also, the proportion of men and women seemed to affect the definitions and experiences of sexual harassment. For example, in some female-dominated fields mild forms of sexual harassment were thought to belong to the job because other women in the workplace were treated in the same way. Women in male-dominated fields were more readily conscious of sexual harassment because men were not harassed in the workplace.

The status of the respondents in the workplace hierarchy also affected the interpretations. For example, one interviewed women in a top position did not experience client or fellow workers' sexual proposal or innuendoes as sexual harassment, because they did not have actual power on her. On the other hand, women experienced all, also light, forms of such conduct as sexual harassment if a harasser worked at a higher level of hierarchy.

Different types of sexual harassment were found at construction sites and in offices. In construction sites verbal types of harassment, such as suggestive remarks, innuendoes, offensive comments about appearance, are more frequent experienced than in offices. In general, workers in construction sites do not define them as sexual harassment; it is part of the working culture. In offices sexual harassment is usually more hidden.

People who had experienced sexual harassment and took part in the research reacted in many different ways. Women almost always let the harasser know that they did not like the situation even though many respondents emphasized the difficulty of taking action. This was partly due to the progressive nature of sexual harassment. The women who had experienced sexual harassment often blamed themselves. Some of the sexually harassed people tried to solve the situation by pretending to be invisible and by moving about as little as possible in the workplace, whereas others took immediate action. There were multiple ways to react against sexual harassment, depending on the incident, the persons involved, their hierarchical position, and the atmosphere within the working community.

3 Branch studies

3.1 Psychiatry

3.1.1 DEFINITION AND METHOD

This study contains a theoretical reconstruction of sexual harassment in the light of previous research, and a description of the phenomenon from the point of view of psychiatric nurses. An important point is defining the phenomenon in a certain workplace context - how a general definition can be applied to a local context. The data consists of one-week period of observation and 17 theme interviews. Eight of the informants were women and nine men, and their mean age was 34.

3.1.2 RESULTS

The research on sexual harassment is divided into three orientations that differ by their geographical location, socio-political contexts and the concepts of power - which is the most important aspect of the phenomenon. The first research orientation is located in the United States. It is called human rights-orientation, because the background discussion of the research is related to the general discussion on human rights in the USA. The main point is to clarify the frequency and the societal meaning of sexual harassment. The phenomenon is interfered with legislation and because of this the definitions are quite stable. In this orientation power is seen as institutional and stable.

The second research orientation, women studies orientation, is located in Europe. The view point is now shifted from the organisational level to individuals, especially women. Sexual harassment is described as a phenomenon that changes according to the context, situations and people involved. Power is seen as interaction, techniques that are used in different ways in different situations and by different people.

The third, equality-orientation, is located in the Nordic Countries. In this orientation it is focused on the new conceptualisation of sexual harassment, taking into account the local and general levels of the phenomenon, methodological questions and the role of the researcher. In this orientation power is seen both interactional and institutional. The orientations are not chronological, research is still done according to all the orientations. This study is located in the latter orientation.

Sexual harassment was part of every day life of nurses. The following description of sexual harassment is derived from the data: The experience of sexual harassment is unwanted and one-sided, it causes uncertainty and feelings of uneasiness and it breaks the borders of what is professional and what is private. The experience of sexual harassment depends also of the grade of the patient's illness and whether the harassment is directed to other people also. The idea of ordering modes of sexual harassment into a scale according to the seriousness of the harassment as done in previous research turned out to be impossible. Physical harassment was not always experienced as the most severe, like it had been thought in previous research. In many cases rude talk of the patients was experienced as more serious.

Types of sexual harassment varied very much and most nurses said that it was much easier to handle "concrete" harassment such as touching, grabbing etc. It was part of a everyday life and one had tools for that (orders, sanctions, rewards etc.). According to many nurses the worst thing was a situation where "nothing really happens, but you know that there is something going on". Further, if sexual harassment continues day after day it became more serious. Also, if a nurse was in a situation alone, was more stressing.

In the study it is stressed that the definitions of sexual harassment depend on the culture of the workplace. A general definition must be brought into the local context. In this case, psychiatric hospital, the mental illness of the patients was an important part of the working environment and determinant of the atmosphere, and it also affected the ways power was manifested. The power of the nurses was mainly institutional, while the patients used interactional power, for example making comments on the nurse's looks.

The harassment was experienced in different ways by men and women. Men took the harassment more personally than women, who said that they were so used to it, that they did not care anymore so much. This can be interpreted through the general positions and roles of men and women in the society: women in their lives in general were used to being objects of sexual harassment (while men were not) and this is why they did not take it so affectionately. Also the positions of men and women had some influence on the phenomenon: women were more objects of continuing oral sexual harassment, while men experienced harassment in certain working situations, when a patient had to be isolated.

3.2 University

3.2.1 DEFINITION AND METHOD

In the spring of 1995 the Equality Committee of the University of Helsinki launched a study on sexual harassment at the University. This study was the first study on sexual harassment in the Finnish academic world that was conducted with a representative sample. The study adopted the same definition of sexual harassment as was used by Varsa's study. The study included a questionnaire that was sent to 1002 academic and non-academic staff members, all chosen at random. In each group women constituted 50% of the group. 74% of the staff members returned the completed questionnaire, which contained a number of open questions. This study combined a qualitative and a quantitative research approach. Sexual harassment experiences were surveyed from three points of view: 1) how many had been subject to sexual harassment during their careers, 2) how many had encountered sexual harassment during the past two years, and

3) how serious had the sexual harassment been. The material was analysed by qualitative contents analysis and statistical methods.

3.2.2 RESULTS

The study revealed that 11% of the academic and non-academic staff members had been subject to sexual harassment at some point during their time at the University. During the past two years, 7% of the staff members had been sexually harassed. Of those staff members who had experienced sexual harassment during the past two years, 78% were women. This study attested to the conception that sexual harassment is a gender-specific phenomenon.

The most common feelings aroused by sexual harassment among women were embarrassment and bewilderment, as well as anger and feelings of being offended. For men, too, the most common reactions were embarrassment and bewilderment, but also humour. The fact that of the 62 female staff members who had been sexually harassed during the past two years 15 had become deeply distressed, but that none of the men had felt distressed, clearly demonstrates the difference in the nature of sexual harassment and gender-specific reactions. The most common ways of coping with sexual harassment were ignoring and/or avoiding the harasser. More women than men had told their harasser to stop.

Sexually harassed staff members felt isolated from their colleagues, thought that they had received unjust criticism from their colleagues for complaining about sexual harassment and, consequently, their motivation for work had decreased. Thus, sexual harassment has a demoralising effect on the general atmosphere of the working community and on job satisfaction.

The sexual harassment experiences described by the respondents in the open questions were divided into four categories according to the hierarchical status of the harasser, the serious consequences, the duration of the sexual harassment, and the frequency of the sexual harassment. Serious consequences included resigning from the job or changing to another working unit, sick leave or leave of absence due to the sexual harassment, and health problems. The described sexual harassment incidents, which totalled 83 for the faculty and staff members, were classified in the following manner: 24 respondents reported 'sexual favours as a precondition for career advancement', 6 people mentioned 'systematic sexual harassment of long duration'. Sex role spill-over was mentioned by 10 staff members, ambivalent sexual harassment by 25 respondents, and 7 staff members were sexual harassed by a student.

3.3 Parliament

3.3.1 DEFINITION AND METHOD

In November 1995 the Chancellery Commission of the Finnish Parliament set up a working group to investigate how equal opportunities were implemented in the personnel policy of the Parliament and its offices, and to draw up guidelines for equal opportunities (Eduskunta, 1996).

The questionnaire was returned by 167 staff members (not MPs), that is, 107 women and 60 men. The percentage of returned questionnaires for women was 46% and 40% for men. Sexual harassment was screened with the question "Have you ever been subject to sexual harassment at your workplace?"

3.3.2 RESULTS

17% of the female respondents (n=18) said that they had experienced sexual harassment at their workplace. One male respondent answered the question affirmatively. As the question did not include any specification as to the date of the sexual harassment the answers give no indication as to when the sexual harassment took place. Also, the answers do not reveal who the harasser was nor under what circumstances the sexual harassment took place.

References

Eduskunta (1996), *Selvitys tasa-arvon toteutumisesta eduskunnan ja sen virastojen ja laitosten henkilöstöpolitiikassa*, Helsinki.

Erkkilä M., (1996), *Tietoa, toimintaa ja rutvallisuutta, SAK: n liittojen jäsentutkimus 1995*, Jyväskylä.

Haavio-Mannila, E., O. Kontula (1993), *Suomalainen seksi. Tietoa suomalaisten sukupuolielämän muutoksesta*, WSOY Porvoo-Helsinki-Juva.

Högbacka, R., I. Kandolin, E. Haavio-Mannila, K. Kauppinen-Toropainen (1987), *Sukupuolinen ahdistelu ja häirintä työpaikoilla: Suomea koskevia tuloksia.*

Jaakkola, T. (1995), *AEK: n työmarkkinatutkimus 1994*, Akavan Erityisalojen Keskusliito, Helsinki.

Mankkinen, T. (1994), *Sukupuolisen häirinnän ja ahdistelun teoreettinen rekonstruktio mielisairaalaa koskevan tapausanalyysin valossa*, Helsinki.

Mankkinen, T. (1995), *Survey on Sexual Harassment at the University of Helsinki. Helsingin yliopiston tasa-arvotoimikunta*, Helsinki.

Varsa, H. (1993), *Sukupuolinen häirintä ja ahdistelu suomalaisessa työelämässä-näkymättämälle nimi*, Tasa-arvojulkaisujasarja A: Tutkimuksia, Helsinki.

V   GERMANY

Kathrina Zippel

Several studies have been carried out into the incidence, types, and perceptions of sexual harassment in Germany. One national study, commissioned by the Ministry of Women, Family, Youth, and Health, surveyed the incidence, responses to, and consequences of sexual harassment. Further, other studies have reported on harassment in both the public and private sectors. No research has been conducted into the effectiveness of policy measures against sexual harassment.

1   National study

1.1   Definition and method

The first nationwide study in Germany was commissioned and financed by the Ministry of Women, Family, Youth, and Health and was conducted by the Sozialforschungsstelle Dortmund (Holzbecher et al., 1991). The methods used included both qualitative interviews and large-scale quantitative surveys. The total number of women surveyed was 3951, and the number of men was 265. The nationwide survey involved 1981 women employees. A complex sampling method was used to achieve a nationally representative sample: unions representing ten industrial sectors sent surveys to their women members selected by means of probability sampling. The average response rate was approximately 20%. Other parts of the study included case studies of public sector firms and a case study of secretaries. In addition, qualitative interviews with individuals and groups who had experienced harassment (26 interviews) and/or were in management positions (50 interviews) were conducted.

1.2   Results

The results of the surveys showed that 93% of the women employees have personally experienced some form of the incidents listed in the questionnaire, independent of whether they perceived it as sexually harassing or not. When including only those forms of behaviour that at least 73% of the respondents interpret as sexual harassment, 72% of the women had experienced sexually harassing behaviour in their workplace. On average, women had been confronted with four to five different forms of behaviour. 40% of the women gave detailed descriptions of events they particularly remembered. Sexual harassment happens without warning for those targeted, most often in the everyday work environment and not just at company parties, and more often than not is repeated and frequent behaviour.

In the study, the respondents first identified whether certain behaviour constitutes sexual harassment, and then whether they had ever experienced these types of behaviour themselves. The most frequently experienced categories of behaviour were the following: staring, whistling (84%), jokes with sexual innuendoes (81%), and "accidental" touches (70%). On the one hand, the majority of women did not think of these three types of behaviour as constituting sexual harassment. On the other hand, approximately 30% of the women respondents did interpret them as sexually harassing. The researchers found a surprisingly similar judgment from men and women; however, the quality of the survey results from the men may have been compromised because the questionnaires tended to be filled out in incomplete and often contradictory ways. The authors argue that the results from the men can only be interpreted as trends.

Further, 56% of the female employees reported remarks about figure or sexual behaviour in private life and 35% pornographic pictures, unwanted invitations with definite sexual intentions, and pinching or patting on the behind.

There were differences in the experiences of sexual harassment between women in different types of occupation: women in blue-collar occupations reported more physical behaviour such as pinching and touching of the breasts, whereas women employees in white-collar occupations reported more jokes and remarks with a sexual content. The authors point out an inverse correlation between the interpretation and experience of the behaviour. For example, although women in police and construction work were those who most often experienced sexually harassing behaviour, they were less likely to judge this behaviour as harassment.

On the one hand, although women of all educational and training backgrounds were harassed, a particularly vulnerable group of women was women without training. Women in this group were the most likely to experience physical harassment incidents, and, among this group, temporary helpers were especially vulnerable. On the other hand, women with university training were the least likely to be harassed. Furthermore, women with some supervisory duties and in middle management positions reported a higher frequency of incidents than those who were working for someone else or working autonomously, or whose work was more oriented towards co-operation. The sex composition of the workplace also had an effect on the likelihood of women being confronted with sexual harassment. Women whose colleagues are mainly or exclusively men are more likely to experience sexual harassment. This was the case for approximately a quarter of the women.

Indirect strategies were the main response of women to sexual harassment: 51% of women in the national study ignored the offending behaviour, 46% tried to avoid the harasser, and 40% attempted to deal with it with humour. Further, a considerable number of women responded actively: 38% confronted the harasser and told him to stop, 27% of the women resisted physically, 14% threatened to file a complaint, 9% filed a complaint, 6% threatened to tell others, and 1% sued the harasser.

The women interpreted the success of these responses. The highest interpretation of success was for "filing a complaint" (70%), confrontation of the harasser (63%), and physical resistance (63%). In addition, the majority of women who had responded by threatening to make the behaviour of the harasser known to others, either by telling others themselves or by filing a complaint, perceived this strategy as successful. The authors, however, warn against interpreting these high frequencies of resistance as the overall success of women in resisting sexual harassment. For example, a third of the men whom the women confronted did not take the women's complaint seriously.

The isolation of those who experience sexual harassment is high. Approximately a sixth of the women in the nationwide study and a third of the secretaries in the case study responded that they had not talked to anyone. When women talked to someone, they chose carefully who to talk to. The majority of women in the survey, but only 30% of the secretaries, had spoken to colleagues about the incidents. Others had talked to female or male friends or partners. Only approximately 10% of the women had talked to a supervisor, and fewer still to personnel managers or employees' representatives.

Harassers were most likely to be male colleagues (50%), or supervisors (29%). 13% of the harassers were male clients or patients, and 3% were training supervisors. According to the study the typical harasser is between 30-50 years old, married, and has been in his job for a long time, often more than 10 years. The typical woman who experienced sexual harassment was between 20 and 30 years old, unmarried and without children, and had worked for this employer for a short time. 22% of the women said they had been harassed during their training and had short-term contracts.

The 19% of men who had experienced some form of harassment were in 37% of the cases harassed by a woman and in 63% of the cases by a man, in 18% male colleagues, and in 18% clients or patients. In contrast to the people who harass women, the harassers of men tend to be younger, more often of the same sex, and more likely to be on the same hierarchical level in the organisation. The study did not ask for the nationality or ethnicity of the women who had experienced harassment or of the harassing person. However, based on the qualitative interviews it seems to be a tendency that women were more likely to file complaints against harassers when they were non-nationals.

Sexual harassment effects women's health and well-being in serious ways: 80% of the women who had experienced sexual harassment reported in the survey that they noticed physical or psychological changes as a consequence of the harassment. The women most often reported feelings of fear, insecurity, and mistrust (27%). 23% reported being more sensitive. 4%-5% had psychosomatic symptoms including headaches, stomach aches, sweating, sleep deprivation. And 2% indicated that they had suffered from depression. 12% of the women said they became more aggressive. 5% of the women reported that they felt a disinclination for sexual activity with their partners in their private lives as a consequence of the harassment. In the in-depth interviews women described that they felt a broad range of consequences which can be categorised into those during and immediately after the harassment, and those that have more long-term effects. The immediate effects included women feeling helpless, humiliated, hurt, and degraded, in a situation where they could see no way out. As a more long-term consequence of the harassment, some women experienced a deep break in trust with their colleagues in a previously good working climate.

As a consequence of the harassment, for one in five women the experience of sexual harassment lead to less work-related satisfaction. They reported that they enjoyed work less. Women who filed complaints or made the harassment public often experienced secondary victimization through the reactions of colleagues and those they had reported the incidents to. Almost half of the women had job-related disadvantages because of the harassment, 6% of the women left their jobs and 3% asked to be transferred. Ten women in the study (1%) reported that they had sued the harasser. However, of these ten cases only four were successful for the women. In only three cases was the harasser convicted, and in half of the cases the women had to pay the legal costs.

The researchers conclude that sexual harassment cannot be explained by sexuality or eroticism, but instead that sexual harassment is a question of unequal gender relations and may be explicitly linked to sex discrimination: "Sexual harassment is an expression of the pervasive social and political secondary position of women, that is reflected in, among other things, sex discrimination in the workplace." They concluded that the responses of organisations to sexual harassment need to be improved.

2 Several branches

2.1 Public sector

2.1.1 DEFINITION AND METHOD

In 1989, the first study about sexual harassment in the German public sector was commissioned and financed by the Equal Opportunity Office for Women in Hamburg, and conducted by Andrea Schneble, Michel Domsch and the F.G.H. Forschungsgruppe. The study was based on a survey of 682 employees (464 women and 135 men) of the city and federal state in Hamburg, which has a total of approximately 110,000 employees. The response rate was 32%. The employees worked in sectors including administration, education (including schools and universities), justice (including prisons, courts and the police), building management, and medical and pharmaceutical services. The study also included focus groups of interested and concerned women, and interviews with persons responsible for personnel management or who serve as representatives of employees.

The researchers defined sexual harassment as "unwanted male behaviour that degrades and objectifies women and does not treat women as equal colleagues. Harassing behaviour is part of the everyday professional life and results in extreme psychological consequences and strains for women."

2.1.2   RESULTS

The study found that sexual harassment happens more often than previously assumed and not only in isolated cases. It occurs in all branches and on all hierarchical levels in the public sector.

In the survey women were first asked whether they had themselves experienced or observed specific types of incidents and behaviour, and second, whether they perceived these types of behaviour as sexual harassment. Over 80% of the women respondents in the public sector had experienced or observed sexually harassing behaviour. The most frequent behaviour, which almost 2/3 of the women experienced themselves, was being stared or whistled at, hearing jokes and remarks with sexual innuendoes, and hearing jokes which put down or debase women. More than half of the women had been touched "accidentally", and about 30% had been involuntarily kissed or hugged. More than 40% of the women had experienced or witnessed "slogans, comics, posters, or calendars with sexual content" in their everyday working lives and have had to listen to unwanted remarks about their figures or private lives. Almost 1/5 of the women had received unwanted invitations with definite sexual intentions or sexual advances by phone or in writing, which more than 84% of all women consider strongly sexually harassing. And even the most explicit forms of harassment, the promise of professional advantages through sexual involvement, had been experienced by 8% of the women.

Both men and women showed broad agreement in their judgments about what constitutes explicit and severe forms of sexual harassment. In general, these included direct behaviour targeted at a specific woman's personality or work situation, and include obvious unwanted physical advances. Thus insistent advances, remarks about a woman's figure or private life, invitations with definite sexual intentions, and implicit threats or promises about consequences for a woman's job constitute definite and strong harassing behaviour, according to more than 3/4 of the respondents.

In contrast, "indirect" behaviour is harder to define, it is a "borderline case". It may be classified on a continuum of types of harassment as "lower level" because these incidents and behaviour are less likely to be interpreted as sexual harassment. However, these indirect forms of harassment are more often experienced or observed than the direct forms. Everyday "normal" behaviour including jokes with sexual innuendoes, slogans, comics and posters are less often considered sexually harassing by the respondents. However, more than 40% of women still do find these "everyday" forms of behaviour clearly sexually harassing. In addition, in the course of the qualitative group interviews the respondents pointed out that the frequency and repetition of these "indirect" or "lower level types of harassment" also have damaging consequences for women.

The study showed that there are significant differences between the perceptions of men and women about what sexual harassment is: women are more likely to interpret certain behaviour as sexual harassment. Women respondents find certain behaviour more harassing than men do. Women also usually observe more sexual harassment than men with the exception of slogans, cartoons, and posters with sexual content.

The most common reaction of the women who had been harassed was to ignore the behaviour and do nothing about it. However, ignoring and other indirect ways of dealing with the situation, such as avoiding the harasser, changing one's clothing, or becoming less friendly, did not stop the behaviour, and women tended to feel as bad or worse afterwards. In contrast, more direct ways of dealing with the situation, such as resisting the harasser physically, directly asking the harasser to stop his behaviour, either in front of witnesses or in private, or filing an official complaint were perceived as more successful. Women felt better afterwards and felt that the behaviour diminished.

The typical harasser in a third of the cases was a male colleague. Almost one in four women (24%), however, had been harassed by a male supervisor. 16% of the women were harassed by male clients, citizens, and patients. Least frequently, 8% of the time, the respondents had experienced harassment from a man they supervised. Younger women were more often the targets of sexual harassment. In the age group 16-20, 20% reported having been harassed. Women between the ages of 21 and 30 most often experienced sexual harassment (38%). Nevertheless, one in four women were in the 31-40 age range.

As a consequence of harassment, women and men reported either having experienced themselves or having observed in others the following emotional responses: insecurity, flattery, anger and irritation, guilt, intimidation, confusion, insult, and fears or discomfort about going to work. Interestingly, both women and men more often thought that a woman they had observed felt flattered (about 12%), than women who had themselves experienced sexual harassment (only 5%). Also, fewer people thought that the person they had observed as the target of the behaviour was angry (17% of women and 14% of men), than was reported as felt by the individuals who had been harassed (24%).

The researchers concluded that "sexual harassment consists of behaviour by men that women experience as degrading, humiliating, or hampering and that men should have known was unwanted." Sexual harassment damages the personal integrity of the woman and results in personal and health encumbrances which make the working environment very uncomfortable and have negative impacts on work productivity. The researchers argue that sexist behaviour in the workplace and indirect and subtle forms of sexual harassment are related. They recommend more awareness of the problems of sexual harassment and that discriminating unequal and disrespectful working relationships for women be challenged. Further, measures should be developed to assist women who have experienced sexual harassment, for example, trained personnel should be available for consultation and legal information. On an institutional level, awareness programmes, especially for personnel managers, should be conducted, and better institutional means to solve conflicts should be developed.

2.2 Private sector

2.2.1 DEFINITION AND METHOD

The first German study about sexual harassment in the private sector was commissioned by the women's unit of a large union and was conducted in 1994 by Heike Maenz. The company chosen for the study had only 8% of women among its workers. Two-thirds of these women worked as employees (white-collar), and a third as (blue-collar) workers. The number of women who responded to the survey was 622, a response rate of 42%. Out of concern for anonymity, however, the respondents were not asked their age or the length of time or kind of position they held in the organisation. Therefore it is not possible to determine whether the study was representative of all female employees. The respondents were asked what sexual harassment meant to them and how they interpreted specific behaviour. They were given a list of types of behaviour and the answer categories always, often, and rarely. Because of the ambiguity of the question, about 20% of the respondents did not give coherent answers to this part of the survey.

2.2.2 RESULTS

The researchers found that the women's judgments as to whether certain behaviour was sexual harassment or not depended on the degree of sensibility and experience of the respondents. Those women who had felt sexually harassed before and those who thought that sexual harassment could or did occur in their working environment were more likely to interpret "accidental touching" as sexual harassment. The women who had experienced sexual harassment more often felt harassed by remarks about their figures, by nude photographs on walls and by lewd jokes than those who said they had never been harassed. But the majority of women, independent of their own experiences, found the most threatening and clearly intrusive types of behaviour as sexually harassing. These included threats of professional disadvantage or promises of professional advantage in connection with sexual demands or sexual physical contact.

30% of the women reported sexual harassment experiences. The most frequently reported types of harassment were physical intrusions: 52% of the women experienced unwanted touching. Other frequently described behaviour included suggestive, lewd jokes (38%), remarks about their figures (35%), pinching or patting the behind (33%), and nude photographs on walls (32%). 15% of the women had felt harassed when being whistled at and 12% who had been touched on their breasts or thighs. 4% of the women had felt harassed by the demand to have sex. Of the most severe physical offences, attempted rape had been experienced by 2% of the women, and 1% of the women had been raped at their workplace.

Most often the harassers were male colleagues (66%). Further, 19% of the harassers were male supervisors, and in 11% of the cases the harasser was an instructor, a situation in which women are even more dependent and vulnerable. 7% of the harassers were workers' representatives and in 4% of the cases the harasser was from outside the company.

The study showed that sexual harassment is still a taboo topic; 95% of the women in the study thought that women would not dare to talk about sexual harassment. Only 1 in 4 women who had experienced sexual harassment talked about the incident to colleagues, and only 1 in 10 to a supervisor. Only 4% of the women spoke to workers' representatives about the sexual harassment incidents.

The researcher recommends institutional measures in the form of internal agreements within businesses and factories to prevent sexual harassment, and measures to increase the competence of those in responsible positions to take action in cases of sexual harassment. And equally important, these measures should be designed to increase the trust women have in the institutional mechanisms for dealing with sexual harassment.

3   Branch studies

3.1   Local government

3.1.1   DEFINITION, METHOD AND RESULTS

Bitsch (1993) reports on a study conducted by the city of Frankfurt/Main in co-operation with the Union for the Public Sector (OETV) in which 301 women were interviewed. The women reported the following harassment incidents: one woman had been raped and 11 women were sexually coerced. A third of the women had been touched sexually, 8 women experienced exhibitionism in the workplace, and about half of the women had heard offensive remarks. Yet only 1% of these women had filed a report with the police, and only 1% filed an official report in their workplace.

3.2   Responses to sexual harassment

3.2.1   DEFINITION AND METHOD

In 1992 a study was carried out into the subjective experience of sexual harassment, based on 6 interviews of about 2 hours each, with women in different occupations. The authors, Ursula Brandstedt, Gabriele Elke and Heike Schambortski (1992), defined sexual harassment as a "condition or action that is unwanted and disturbing and is solely oriented toward the sexuality or sex role of a person in such a way as to interfere with the condition (or health) of the person and/or to limit the scope of his or her actions."

3.2.2 RESULTS

The researchers highlighted the fact that although there is a variety of strategies women use to deal with sexual harassment, strategies of adaptation are the most common ones. Women experience sexual harassment not only on an individual level as feelings of unease, but also on an interaction level, which has important implications for their relationships at work. The impact it had on the interactional level were feelings of insecurity, dependency, helplessness, isolation, and fear of disapproval after being sexually harassed. Moreover, sexually harassed women experience a break of trust with the person who harassed them and the loss of trusting collegial relationships.

Women find it difficult to resist the harassers through direct confrontations or through "joking" with quick-witted remarks, although some would like to. The fear of not being understood, the fear of the reactions of colleagues, feelings of helplessness, or feelings of dependency keep women from reacting on the spot and from confronting harassers. In addition, to be dependent on supervisors who are harassing them is an even greater problem if women have the impression that sexual harassment is tolerated within the organisation.

There are a variety of adaptive responses that women use. Women interpret the behaviour as "normal" and instead of reacting they blame themselves. They interpret their own feelings of shame, embarrassment or unease with the situation as deviations from the normal. Avoidance of the harasser or harassing situation is a widespread form of adaptation. The pressure on women, especially in male-dominated working environments, not to show feelings that would be perceived as weakness leads women to hide their feelings of offence and hurt. In addition, women identify with the aggressors and try to think and feel "like men," and thus not be vulnerable to behaviours and remarks that devalue women.

Because sexual harassment is an impediment to the professional development of women, the researchers argue for institutional measures. In addition, they recommend specific measures for trainees and women early on in their careers, and assertiveness and self-defence training programmes for all women. Moreover, they call for public statements from companies which should emphasise that sexual harassment is unwanted and has a negative impact on the working climate. Most importantly, they recommend that sexual harassment be made a public issue, to "bring it out of the corner of ridicule and embarrassment" so that women feel that it is their right to take action against sexual harassment.

3.3   Gay men and lesbians

Studies on sexual harassment did not ask about the sexual orientation of the respondents and assumed sexual harassment in general to be "heterosexual" harassment. In addition, studies about the work experiences of sexual minorities often did not specifically ask what kind of discriminating incidents gays, lesbians, bisexual, or transsexual employees experienced. A study commissioned by the Social Ministry of the State of Niedersachsen in 1994 pointed out that lesbians and gays are especially vulnerable to discrimination in the workplace due to their sexual orientation. "Project Lesbians and Gays in the Working World" at the University of Munich (Knoll et al., 1995) conducted a nationwide survey in which 81% of the respondents (gay men and lesbians) reported having experienced discrimination. Lesbians were more likely to suffer physical repercussions from the discrimination than gay men. 23% of the lesbians experienced health-related consequences while 17% of the gay men did. Heiliger (1992) argues that there is ample evidence to show that if women are publicly known as lesbians in their workplace they are often the target of harassment and discrimination. Lesbians experience job loss either because they find themselves in working environments that are unbearable, or because they are fired. Even if women are not "out," they are likely to be isolated from other colleagues and avoid situations in which they are confronted with personal questions.

Just as women, independent of their sexual orientation, find sexist jokes degrading, jokes and remarks with homophobic contents can have negative effects on lesbians and gay men. Often homophobic jokes and remarks use sexual connotations and explicit sexual references. Thus lesbians and gay men can be targets of harassment just as much as heterosexuals. Because those lesbians who prefer not to be "out" in their workplace are perceived as being single, they are as likely to be confronted with sexual harassment as single heterosexual women are. In addition, sexual harassment can use homophobic messages. For example, a man who repeatedly unsuccessfully approaches a female colleague might spread the word that this woman must be a lesbian since she has declined his sexual offers. Considering sexual harassment as an intrusion and a threat to women's sexual self-determination demonstrates the necessity to study the connection between sexual harassment and harassment based on sexual orientation further.

3.4   Theoretical interpretation

Kuhlmann (1996), in her review and theoretical interpretation of these German empirical studies of sexual harassment, emphasizes that further studies on sexual harassment should elaborate more systematically structural and cultural factors to explain sexual harassment in the workplace. The author argues that historically, sexual harassment has been closely linked to the discrimination of women in the labour market and to the gender-based hierarchical structure of work organisations. Sexual harassment is a social problem because it is a barrier against equal professional opportunities for women and men. Because sexual harassment is pervasive, it is structural discrimination and not just a matter of isolated incidents that affect individual women. When women and girls choose or avoid certain jobs not only based on experiences of sexual harassment, but also based on the anticipation of sexual harassment, for example, in male-dominated occupations, then sexual harassment constitutes a barrier to equal opportunities for women in the workforce. The evidence that women early on in their careers are affected by sexual harassment reveals that sexual harassment is an impediment to the professional development of women.

Kuhlmann argues that sexual harassment is "a dynamic process which develops within the context of specific labour market structures and cultural patterns. It is a process that is influenced by legal rules and frameworks, political decisions, personal characteristics and experiences." Thus she recommends short-term and mid-range preventive strategies that eliminate sex segregation in the labour market, and strategies to develop concrete legal guidelines to pursue incidents of sexual harassment. These measures can function both as deterrents for potential perpetrators and to allow individual women to pursue their rights to sexual self-determination and equal chances in the labour market.

References

Bitsch, C. (1993), Wenn wir darauf reagieren würden, kaemen wir ueberhaupt nicht mehr zum Arbeiten. Was macht die Beschwerde ueber sexuelle Belaestigung so schwer?, In: *Grenzverletzungen. Sexuelle Belaestigung Am Arbeitsplatz,* edited by Renate Sadrozinski, Frankfurt am Main, Germany, p. 71-80.

Brandtstedt, U., G. Elke, H. Schambortski (1992), *Sexuelle Belaestigung Am Arbeitsplatz: Wahrnehmung und Bewaeltigungsstrategien Berufstaetiger Frauen; eine Studie.* Frauenforschung 10(1/2), p. 84-104.

Heiliger, A. (1992), Sexismus gegen Lesben am Arbeitsplatz, In: *Tatort Arbeitsplatz: Sexuelle Belaestigung von Frauen,* edited by U. Gerhart, A. Heiliger, A. Stehr (eds.), p. 79-86, Muenchen.

Holzbecher, M., A. Braszeit, U. Müller und S. Plogstedt (1991), *Sexuelle Belästigung am Arbeitsplatz* No. 260 in the series of the Bundesministeriums für Jugend, Frauen und Gesundheit, Stuttgart.

Knoll, C., M. Bittner, M. Edinger, Dr. G. Reisbeck, R. Schmitt, Prof. Dr. H. Keupp (1995), *Studie 'Lesben und Schwule in der Arbeitswelt, Ergebnisse zur Diskriminierung von Lesben und Schwulen in der Arbeitssituation,* Projekt Lesben und Schwule in der Arbeitswelt, Institut fuer Psychologie -Sozialpsychologie der Ludwig-Maximilians-Universitaet Muenchen.

Kuhlmann, E. (1996), *Sexuelle Belaestigung von Frauen am Arbeitsplatz,* Pfaffenweiler.

Maenz, H. (1994), *... und Kaum eine Traut Sich, Darueber zu Sprechen" : Sexuelle Belaestigung Am Arbeitsplatz; eine Umfrage bei Thyssen-Stahl Hamborn/Beeckerwerth,* Edited by Beratungsgesellschaft fuer ISA-Consult GmbH, Innovation. ISA-Schriftenreihe, vol. 19, Bochum.

Meschkutat, B., M. Holzbecher, G. Richter (1993), *Strategien Gegen Sexuelle Belaestigung Am Arbeitsplatz* : Konzeption -Materialien - Handlungshilfen, Koeln.

Schneble, A., M. Domsch (1989), *Sexuelle Belaestigung von Frauen Am Arbeitsplatz: Eine Bestandsaufnahme Zur Problematik; Bezogen auf Den Hamburger Oeffentlichen Dienst.* Hamburg: Leitstelle Gleichstellung der Frau, Hansestadt Hamburg.

VI   IRELAND

Josephine Browne

In Ireland the subject of sexual harassment at work has not been well researched, nor is there a basis of funding for research projects. No comprehensive national quantitative or qualitative study is available on sexual harassment in Irish workplaces. Two larger studies have been carried out. One surveyed managers about the incidence of sexual harassment complaints, their policy and their perceptions of sexual harassment. The other study was a questionnaire in the Sunday Press into the incidence of sexual harassment. Further, a few studies have been carried out within one company or branch.

1   Several branches

1.1   Management

1.1.1   DEFINITION AND METHOD

In 1993, the first attempt to provide a national overview of the incidence of sexual harassment complaints in Irish workplaces was the survey by the Rape Crisis Centre with the assistance of the Institute of Personnel Management in Ireland. They surveyed 1,090 firms, and asked employers about the incidence of sexual harassment complaints, whether they had a policy against sexual harassment, and what they considered to be sexually harassing behaviour.

1.1.2   RESULTS

According to the study, two out of every five companies had received reports of sexual harassment in their workplace but less than half of them had any policy to deal with sex pests annoying their staff. This survey found that sexual harassment is a national workplace problem.

The survey also aimed at determining how seriously Irish employers viewed sexual harassment. The report found that the following acts constituted sexual harassment in the Irish workplace for almost all employers: demands for sexual favours (98%), physical assault (94%), unwanted contact (89%), and compromising behaviour (88%). There was less consensus about suggestive remarks (62%), offensive pin-ups or calendars (52%), leering or eyeing up a person's body (51%), and sexist or patronising behaviour (47%).

1.2 Sunday Press research

1.2.1 DEFINITION AND METHOD

In 1993 a Lansdowne Market research survey, commissioned by and reported in the Sunday Press, was carried out on the issue of sexual harassment. The survey was conducted among a representative sample of 504 adults between the ages of 23 and 33.

1.2.2 RESULTS

According to the study, a considerable number of Irish women had been sexually harassed. The following types of harassment were reported: touched/brushed against (14%), sexual jokes/remarks (12%), stared/leered at by men (11%). Furthermore, 7% stated unwanted demands for sex or dates, being grabbed, and being exposed to pin-ups. The survey clearly revealed that women were ill-informed as to what sexual harassment is, given that 46% did not regard being grabbed by men as constituting harassment.

2 Branch studies

2.1 Electricity Supply Board

2.1.1 DEFINITION AND METHOD

One of the major Irish employers, the Electricity Supply Board (E.S.B.), which employs approximately 8,500 people (87% male and 13% female), carried out a survey into sexual harassment in 1990.

2.1.2 RESULTS

The study found sexual harassment to be a workplace reality for the E.S.B. The report found that just under half of the women surveyed stated that they had personal experience of sexual harassment at work. Fifteen percent of all women reported this as occurring at least sometimes. The report concluded that for an important minority of women in the E.S.B. this is an unwelcome and very real part of their experience of employment. However, there is no definitive survey available of sexual harassment in this company.

2.2 Higher civil servants

2.2.1 DEFINITION AND METHOD

In 1993 the Association of Higher Civil Servants in Ireland (a trade union for senior civil servants) reported on the extent of sexual harassment within middle and senior grades in the Irish civil service. The survey sampled approximately 1,550 male and female middle and senior Irish civil servants. There was a response rate of 46%; with 84% of the respondents being male and 16% female. It should also be noted that female participation in the senior grades of the Irish civil service is low. This report considers the sample as reasonably representative of the higher civil service grades in Ireland. The respondents were asked if they had ever experienced sexual harassment in their jobs, but they were not asked when the harassment occurred, and the report points out that it is most likely that the vast majority of instances predate the publication of the civil service guidelines on dealing with sexual harassment, which were published in 1991.

2.2.2 RESULTS

The Civil Service Report found that 5% reported that they has suffered sexual harassment at some stage in their civil service careers. Of those who suffered sexual harassment 85% were female and 15% male. The report also analysed the age of the respondents reporting sexual harassment by sex. In particular, female employees aged between 30 and 40 (22 of the 29 women with experiences) were harassed, the male employees aged between 35 and 45 (4 of the 5 men with experiences) were more often harassed.

Further, the research found that the harasser was in the majority of cases in a superior position to the victim. The verbal types of harassment were the most frequently reported, followed by physical forms of sexual harassment.

The report concludes that it is clear that sexual harassment has presented a problem for a number of officers during their careers in the civil service. However, the report urged that care must be taken in drawing further conclusions due to the small numbers.

2.3 Retail sector

2.3.1 DEFINITION AND METHOD

The retail sector in Ireland employs a very large percentage of women. A recent study from 1996 funded by the European Social Fund and carried out by the Employment Equality Agency, Superquinn (employer), and Mandate (trade union) reported on equality policies in Superquinn, where approximately 56% of all staff are female.

2.3.2 RESULTS

The survey found that whereas the vast majority of men and women had not experienced sexual harassment, 14% of the female respondents stated they had experienced it, and 5% of male respondents stated they had experienced it. The study also reported that 26% of women and 23% of men had observed sexual harassment happening to others in the workplace.

2.4 Policy against sexual harassment

To date, there is no research available in Ireland concerning the effectiveness or impact of sexual harassment policies. However, most large Irish companies have well-developed policies. Most of these policies are based on the Irish Code of Practice, 'Measures to Protect the Dignity of Women and Men at Work', which was issued in accordance with the European Commission Recommendation and Code of Practice 1991. Most policies in existence contain a definition of sexual harassment, the company policy on sexual harassment and a complaints procedure.

References

Association of Higher Civil Servants (1993), *Equality in the Workplace Report,* AHCS Survey, Dublin.

Electricity Supply Board (1990), *The Reality*, Dublin.

Employment Equality Agency (1994), *Code of Practice: Measures to Protect the Dignity of Women and Men at Work,* Dublin.

Institute of Personnel Management in Ireland (1993), *Statement on Harassment at Work,* IPM.

Rape Crisis Centre Survey (1993), *Sexual Harassment in the Workplace*, Dublin.

Sunday Press, (1993), *A Lansdowne Market research survey about the incidence of sexual harassment*, commissioned by and reported in the Sunday Press.

Superquinn/Mandate and EEA Research Report (1996), *Quality for Equality,* Dublin.

VII LUXEMBOURG

Cristien Bajema

In Luxembourg one study has been carried out into sexual harassment in the workplace. In 1993 a group of non governmental organisations commissioned ILReS S.A. Luxembourg to canvass opinion amongst women at work on the extent of the phenomenon. The study was partially financed by the Ministry of Employment and the Commission of the European Community

1. National study

1.1 Definition and methodology

The authors used two different definitions of sexual harassment: an evaluation based on objective criteria, an enumeration of 15 different verbal, nonverbal and physical types of harassment, and the personal subjective opinion of the participating women.

The study is based on a representative sample of 502 working women between 16 and 50 years of age, living in Luxembourg. The inhabitants of the border regions could not be included because of methodological and budgetary constraints. The data were gathered by telephone interviews. The women questioned worked in companies with at least 3 employees.

1.2 Results

Almost 80% of the women had experienced sexual harassment of some kind at least once according to the objective definition. Most frequently reported were verbal and nonverbal types of harassment: looks (58%), dirty jokes (52%), making eyes (44%), whistling (31%), remarks about looks and clothes (23%), and pornographic pictures/naked women (10%). The following physical forms were reported: touching buttocks (8%), kissing (5%), touching legs (5%), touching breasts (4%), and rape (1%). Of the women, 15% experienced one of these situations, 30% two or three, 21% four to five, and 12% six or more of these situations.

The seriousness and the extent of the harassment increased in accordance with the number of people a company employs. The more serious types of harassment are observed in particular in companies employing over 50 people. The branches that are affected most as far as extent and seriousness are concerned are the hotel and catering industries.

In contrast to this evaluation based on objective criteria, the researchers asked the women to give their personal, and therefore subjective opinions on whether or not they had been the victims of sexual harassment. 13% of the women affirmed that they had been the victims of sexual harassment themselves. Even though the difference is important, the smallest figure (13%) still proves that sexual harassment is a risk that is very real for women at work.

Even if a priori nobody is really safe from the risk of being sexually harassed, the risk is not the same for all women. Young women were the ones that were most exposed, and particularly those in the age group of 25 to 29, who suffer more than those in the age group of 16 to 24. When looking at the level of education it appeared that the women who were the most exposed were those who had had secondary education as opposed to those who either had a lower level of education or a higher one. This might be because the first group are confronted less often with men at work, and because the second group is better equipped to defend themselves. Different jobs also mean unequal exposure to the risk, which is illustrated by the observation that clerks run a greater risk than labourers.

Women working under the direction of women (as the person responsible hierarchically) are not sexually harassed as often as those working under the supervision of a man. Women that are separated, divorced or who live together without being married are more vulnerable than colleagues who are single, married or widowed.

The 13% of the women (66 cases) who said that they had experienced sexual harassment in their own definition were asked about their immediate reaction. Of the women, 39% resisted, 22% defended themselves/made a verbal retort, 21% slapped the person in the face or had another violent reaction, 12% made the facts known/talked about it, 10% resigned, and between 2 and 5% of the women threatened to talk about it, walked off, offered no resistance, hid and were afraid. 15% of the victims did not talk to anyone about what had happened to them; the others discussed it with their partner (42%), a friend at work (34%), a friend outside work (24%), parents or family (8%), and male friends (3%). Only 4% contacted an advisory institution or a doctor.

81% of the victims did not take any action, 7% filed a complaint with the management, 4% contacted the personnel representative, and 1% filed a complaint with the police.
54% of the victims feel that these situations did not have any consequences for their personal and professional life; 19% have become distrustful and 9% complain of psychological problems (nervousness, depression etc.); 16% handed in their resignations, and 5% had problems getting promotion opportunities.

References

Margue, C. (1995), *Sexual harassment, A day-to-day reality at the workplace in Luxembourg,* ILReS S.A., Luxembourg.

VIII THE NETHERLANDS

Cristien Bajema

Eleven research projects have been carried out in the Netherlands. One is a national study for the Ministry of Social Affairs and Employment. Other large surveys report on work and stress, including one question about sexual harassment and on (sexual) violence amongst lesbians and bisexual women. The other research projects deal with one or two branches of industry or occupations: the police, home care, local government, telecommunication, secretaries, industrial firms, and office workers. One of the recent reports discusses how foreign women perceive sexual harassment. In the Netherlands, the government, followed by the labour unions, has played an important role in initiating research. Both the incidence of, responses to and policy measures concerning sexual harassment were studied.

1 National study

1.1 National survey on policy against and incidence of sexual harassment

1.1.1 DEFINITION AND METHOD

In the national study, fifty organisations with a certain degree of policy were interviewed by telephone concerning the content of their policies against sexual harassment (Van Amstel & Volkers, 1993). The persons interviewed were the personnel manager, the confidential counsellor, or a member of the grievance commission. The organisations belonged to branches of industry, health care, transport, retail trade, government, and the commercial services industry.

In 14 of these organisations, employees (602 women, a response rate of 58%) filled in a postal survey about the incidence of, types, and responses to sexual harassment in the workplace. The survey first asks about the experiences of colleagues with sexual harassment or annoying behaviour, followed in the next question by an enumeration of types of harassment. Secondly, the respondent is asked about her own experiences with harassment or annoying behaviour, again followed by an enumeration of types of sexual harassment.

1.1.2 RESULTS

Policy measures
The reasons most frequently mentioned for starting a policy against sexual harassment were collective labour agreements, social developments, and research publications – the Working Conditions Law of 1994, which obliges companies to have a policy against sexual harassment, was not yet effective at the time of the interview.
The following policy measures were taken by the organisations:

1.   *Information activities.* In 2/3 of the organisations the confidential counsellor or the management distributed information about the sexual harassment policy. The information was provided at work meetings, in brochures, or in the staff magazine. About half of the respondents evaluated the information activity as successful, the other half did not. Reasons for this were that they suspected that a lot of the information was not red by the employees, that the information was too limited, or was given only once. The survey among the female employees confirmed this last result: in none of the organisations was the policy known to all the respondents. According to the respondents a successful information policy depended on regular information and should be concentrated on specific groups or small groups.

2.   *Confidential counsellor.* 2/3 of the companies had a confidential counsellor. This was usually a woman whose tasks included relieving and advising harassed employees. Other often reported tasks included mediating and the aftercare of employees. A quarter of the organisations chose to appoint more than one confidential counsellor. In general, the counsellor was a personnel officer or a company welfare worker who did not receive extra time to carry out these additional tasks. Two third of the confidential counsellors were educated on the issue of sexual harassment. More than a third of the counsellors spent almost no time on the function of counsellor, about a quarter spent more than 5 days a year on the counselling tasks.

3.   *Grievance procedure.* 1/3 of the organisations had a grievance procedure especially for sexual harassment and 1/5 had a grievance procedure for all kinds of complaints. Some of the companies without a grievance procedure stated that they did not need one because there were no complaints in their organisation.

In general, the procedures state that all employees may use the procedure, and there is no limitation to the period in which a harassment complaint should be filed. A majority of the company procedures report the possibility of the informal treatment of a complaint, this should lower the barriers to contacting a counsellor. In some of the organisations an employee may file a complaint anonymously or a complaint can be filed collectively. Other subjects described in the grievance procedure include: who handles the complaint, the time period within which a complaint should be handled, possible sanctions, the possibility of appeal, and aftercare. In general, the companies with a procedure especially for sexual harassment have a more complete procedure and *more frequently an extensive policy against sexual harassment.*

4.   *Grievance commission.* A grievance commission for sexual harassment was available in more than 1/4 of the firms, in particular in the companies with an extensive sexual harassment policy. Furthermore, 1/7 of the firms had a general grievance commission which also handled sexual harassment complaints. A majority of the organisations stated the tasks of the commission. In addition to handling a complaint, other tasks included advising about the sanctions and reporting annually about the

incidence of complaints. The personnel manager was in all cases a member of the commission, in 2/3 of the commissions at least one women and one employee were represented (usually a member of the works council).

The researchers described a great variety in policy content and expertise ranging from organisations who educated the counsellors and grievance commissions and provided time for carrying out the tasks, to organisations who did neither.

Over the last two years, two-thirds of the 50 organisations had received one or more complaints of sexual harassment. The organisations without complaints of sexual harassment are the 'smaller' companies with less than 500 employees and companies with a limited policy. The percentage of female employees did not influence the incidence of complaints. Over the last two years at least 118 complaints were made, usually female employees who reported to the counsellor. There were proportionately a lot of complaints from employees in low administrative jobs. Half of the organisations with a limited policy thought that all the harassment cases should be filed, as opposed to 10% of the companies with an extensive policy. Of this last group of respondents a majority notes that the complaints filed are just a small part of all experienced cases of sexual harassment.

A third of the companies reported pressure points in the implementation of the policy. Most frequently stated problems were: the onus of proof, lack of a clear grievance procedure and prejudice on the part of the supervisors who should handle the complaints. About 1 in 7 of the respondents report problems with taking measures. For instance, the preferred measure of relocation or dismissal of the perpetrator is not possible because of the important position of the harasser within the company.

Preconditions for a successful policy include educated confidential counsellors, management support, regular information for specific groups, and a grievance procedure especially for sexual harassment cases. What is important is that a combination of measures is needed. Pursuing a successful policy may take a couple of years, as well as a change in working culture towards dignity for both women and men at work.

Incidence and reactions
The survey among the employees themselves indicated that 32% of the respondents themselves, had experienced sexual harassment or annoying behaviour. In total, 193 women reported sexual harassment, as opposed to 47 complaints filed in this organisation. The conducts most complained about were unsolicited physical contact (59%) and suggestive remarks, sexual comments about the body, clothes, and sex life (56%). Less frequent experiences were unwanted pressure for dates (16%) and pressure for sexual favours (10%). The harassers were usually men. It was usually colleagues who perpetrated the sexual harassment (75%), followed by supervisors (25%), patients (12%), and clients (7%).

100

Nearly half of the respondents told the harasser that they didn't like the behaviour, remarks. Almost 40% ignored it, hoping that it would stop automatically, 31% of the women told the harasser to stop, and 18% got up and walked away. Further, 4% of the women asked for relocation and 3% resigned.

The interviewed women spoke with a colleague about the situation (75%), or with a superior (25%), but they rarely made an official complaint or went to the confidential counsellor. Reasons for this included 'the harassed employees wanted to solve the problem themselves or with help of colleagues', 'they were unfamiliar with the confidential counsellor', or 'did not trust the counsellor'.

Were the actions of the women successful? About half of the women stated that the problem was solved after letting the culprit know that the behaviour was unwanted. A quarter of the women reported that the situation was solved because she had left the unit (resignation, transfer) or the harasser had left the unit. In 10% of the cases the problem still existed. More than three-quarters of the respondents were satisfied with the solution, and a quarter was not. Reasons for not being satisfied were: the problem still existed, it was not taken seriously, the company did not take enough action, or the organisation avoided the problem by relocating or dismissing the harasser for another reason.

Sexual harassment was more common in a working culture where employees were used to making suggestive remarks about clothes and looks. Employees working in the Health Services experience more sexual harassment because of certain aspects of the job: working outside ordinary business hours and working in enclosed spaces.

1.2   National survey of work and stress

1.2.1   DEFINITION AND METHOD

In 1994 a survey was carried out about work and stress, including one question about sexual harassment (Diekstra et al.). This statement was: "In my job I have experienced sexual harassment", with answer possibilities ranging from (totally) agree to (totally) disagree. The questionnaire was published in 14 local/regional newspapers, with a response rate ranging from 3% to 13%. In total, 15,000 people filled in the survey.

1.2.2   RESULTS

Of all respondents, 4% had experienced sexual harassment: 7% of the women and 2% of the men. The following groups had a higher risk of sexual harassment: young women; less well-educated; working full time; working in the non-profit sector; and working as conductor, chauffeur, waitress, or cleaning personnel.

2. Several branches

2.1 *Local government and industrial firms* [7]

2.1.1 DEFINITION AND METHOD

In this 1990 study there were interviews at twelve different workplaces; 7 in a local government and 5 in an industrial firm (Timmerman, 1991). Central to this study was the relationship between sexual harassment and the power balance between the sexes in the workplace. The workplaces were categorised into three groups according to the distribution of women and men throughout the hierarchical structure in the workplace.

2.1.2 RESULTS

The lowest rate of sexual harassment was found in workplaces with relatively little inequality between the sexes. The workplaces with a very uneven balance of power held a middle position, and the highest rate of sexual harassment was found in those workplaces where power differences between the sexes were uneven but to a lesser extent than the very uneven workplaces.

Besides the material balance in power, the social and cultural climate in the workplace is strongly connected with the possibilities for women to raise the issue of sexual harassment. In the workplaces with very uneven power differences men had a superior status and they defined the beliefs and values. The segregation of work by sex was strong, social and functional contacts between men and women were very restricted. Sexual harassment could not be expressed openly as a problem. Most men and women were of the opinion that the women should adapt to a male-dominated workplace and that the women who were harassed had asked for it by the way they dressed and behaved at work. The verbal forms of sexual harassment were viewed as an inherent aspect of these workplaces: if you did not like it, you lacked a sense of humour. As a result, those women who reported unwanted sexual advances had ignored this behaviour and had not raised the issue/made complaints. These reactions were related to the social climate: otherwise they ran the risk of isolation and exclusion by their colleagues.

In workplaces with a less uneven power difference there was a lack of consensus, a plurality of opinions and attitudes, which went hand-in-hand with the changing balance of power between the sexes. This situation created more opportunities for women to raise the problem of sexual harassment. The issue of sexual harassment was brought into the open by a substantial number of women. Men responded in a defensive or ridiculing way. Women talked to each other about how to take up the issue and this increased solidarity among them.

---

[7] This study is a thesis elaborating on the research of the Project Group Women's Studies, 1986. The 1986 research is described in Rubenstein's report 'The Dignity of Women at Work'.

The last category of workplace are those with a relatively even power balance. The reported frequency of sexual harassment was rather low. The distribution of women and men throughout the hierarchical structure of the workplace was less unequal, jobs were less segregated by sex, and the informal contacts were mixed. According to the workers, this situation created a climate in which serious sexual harassment was not very likely to occur. More men took the issue of sexual harassment seriously and would support the person being harassed.

These results have consequences for policy: policies and procedures should vary from company to company. In workplaces with a very uneven power balance measures should be focused towards creating an atmosphere in which women feel safe enough to come forward and complain about sexual harassment. The improvement of the position of women in these workplaces, however, remains a necessary condition. In organisations with a less uneven balance between the sexes and a more open climate, grievance procedures could be very supportive to women who want to challenge the issue of sexual harassment.

3. Branch studies

3.1 Police

3.1.1 DEFINITION AND METHOD

In the police survey, commissioned by the Home Department, 1450 policewomen from all over the country were asked to participate in research about (unwanted) behaviour in the workplace (Eikenaar, 1993). The response rate was 42%. In the questionnaire the term sexual harassment was not mentioned; the questions dealt with unwanted verbal, physical and nonverbal behaviour. First, the researchers asked if a certain behaviour was common at the workplace, followed by a question asking whether this behaviour was unwanted or wanted.

3.1.2 RESULTS

Verbal behaviour was the one most commonly experienced: sexual jokes (90%), remarks about women/looks (90%) and remarks about sex (83%). The executive policewomen experienced this more often than women in administrative/technical or cleaning jobs. Physical behaviour - such as touching (88%), playful behaviour (84%) - and other behaviour such as pin-ups (79%), rude gestures (55%), and sex films (38%) were experienced by the executive policewomen in particular. The verbal and physical behaviour may be regarded as a part of the working culture of the executive policewomen. They judge the above-described behaviour less negatively than women in administrative/technical or cleaning jobs; the police has a strong culture in which conformation and loyalty are important.

The next question concerned which of the behaviours experienced were *unwanted*. Of the verbal types of harassment 'remarks about women' were unwanted for 56% of the respondents, and 'remarks about sex' were unwanted for 46% of the policewomen. Unwanted physical behaviour such as touching and hugs/kisses were experienced by 17%, respectively 16% of the policewomen. Finally, of the unwanted other behaviour, rude gestures were reported by 45%, undressing with the eyes by 42%, and pin-ups/sex films by 31% of the policewomen.

In general, the executive policewomen experience more sexual harassment than women in administrative/technical or cleaning jobs. A possible explanation for this could be the higher percentage of women in the administrative/technical and cleaning jobs (48%, opposed to 22% in the executive police jobs), resulting in a less male-dominated working culture. Furthermore, women in the age group 30-40, with higher seniority, and with a middle or higher management job had more experiences of sexual harassment. Women with a partner suffered less personal sexism.

The employees were asked to describe an incident of sexual harassment, a third of the policewomen did this. According to this information a great number of the perpetrators were supervisors/ management members (35%), followed by colleagues (28%). In general the perpetrator was older than the harassed women. In cases where the women were harassed when they were alone, it was always physical types of harassment.

The response to unwanted sexual behaviour/sexual harassment was usually surprise and being overwhelmed/confused, which resulted in ignoring or avoiding the harassing behaviour. About half of the respondents were not satisfied with their own reaction; they would have liked to have rejected the behaviour more openly. The other people present at the time of the harassment reacted by laughing, by joining in, or by ignoring it. Many policewomen could not react in the way they would have liked, because sexual harassment was a part of their normal work culture and thus harassment cases were ridiculed.

As a consequence of harassment about 40% of the harassed respondents changed their behaviour: reacted more assertively, took no notice of the harasser, or avoided certain situations or people. Other effects of the harassment were: less self confidence, psychological problems, less concentration, becoming ill, feeling more isolated or less accepted by colleagues. A couple of women asked for relocation or resigned because of the bad working atmosphere. Three-quarters of the women reported that there were no consequences for the perpetrators and a quarter said there were. The consequences mentioned were sanctions such as a talk with a supervisor, relocation, an official warning, and in one instance the harasser was suspended.

The organisational structure influences the incidence of sexual harassment: units that were 50% women reported less sexual harassment than units that were only 20%

women. Other influences were aspects of the organisational culture: the more machismo, the higher the incidence of sexual harassment.

The researcher made a couple of recommendations for policy. She concluded that unwanted sexual behaviour was structural and therefore an organisational problem. The primary responsibility should be taken by the management. Their first priority should be to make sexual harassment debatable/discussible. If there is no safe working environment to discuss sexual harassment then no one will use a confidential counsellor, a grievance procedure, or a grievance commission. Training and information are very important.

3.2 Home care

3.2.1 DEFINITION AND METHODOLOGY

In 1992 an evaluation study was carried out among 6 home care organisations which already had sexual harassment policies. The research was commissioned by the Foundation against the Sexual Harassment of Carers (Dijkstra, 1992). In total, 42 people were interviewed (carers, supervisors, and management members) about the functioning of the policy and pressure points. Sexual harassment was defined as: "unwanted sexually tinted behaviour/attention appearing in physical, verbal or nonverbal behaviour resulting in a hostile work environment, less pleasure in work, disturbance of productivity, and a worsening of the relationship with the client or organisation". In the interview the respondents themselves defined sexual harassment.

3.2.2 RESULTS

The Foundation against the Sexual Harassment of Carers (STOIG) had developed a model policy plan. This plan consisted of five aspects: (1) information, (2) relief and counselling in cases of complaints, (3) improving the expertise of supervisors, (4) appointing confidential counsellors, and (5) developing a code of behaviour and procedures.

None of the organisations had implemented all five of the aspects of this policy plan. The most frequently implemented measure was the providing of information and appointing a confidential counsellor. 3 of the 6 organisations provided information for carers or appointed a confidential counsellor. However, information for the clients was rarely provided. Education for the supervisors was provided by two home care organisations. The final aspect of the policy plan for the code of behaviour had hardly been developed. Furthermore, all six organisations had a policy plan which mentioned the following subjects: the provision of information at the introduction course for new employees, at work meetings, and in a leaflet for clients; an active attitude on the part of supervisors, and a careful settlement of sexual harassment complaints.

More than half of the carers had experiences of harassment: 11 of the 19 interviewed carers reported sexual harassment. For instance, a client played a sex film while the carer was at work, or questions about the carer's sex life were asked, or remarks about looks were made. After reporting the harassment experience to a supervisor or the confidential counsellor, the harasser usually received a warning letter, or a different carer was sent to the harassing client. The final sanction of stopping the assistance to the perpetrator was rarely made. In general, the carers were satisfied with the reaction of the supervisor; she believed the carers' stories and supported them.

Several pressure points were indicated by the respondents: The carers reported that the providing of information could be improved. They wanted more structural advice and not only written material but also oral information. According to the confidential counsellors, some of the supervisors had not enough skill for a discussion with the client, so the supervisor avoided the problem by sending a different carer – who was not always informed about the sexual harassment incident. From the interviews, it turned out that not every supervisor regarded sexual harassment as a serious problem: some of the supervisors thought sexual harassment occurred rarely, and they found the interests of clients more important than the interests of the carers. The supervisors, counsellors, and carers had expected a more active, stimulating role from the management, as yet the policy has been implemented because of the efforts of a couple of active supervisors and confidential counsellors.

The researcher concluded that it is very important for the home care organisations to have a consistent policy, in which the safety/dignity of the carer should be the starting point, with sanctions for the client after repeated incidents, and with regular information and education.

3.3   Telecommunication firm

3.3.1   DEFINITION AND METHOD

In 1997 a survey was carried out into sexual harassment in a telecommunication firm (Bajema & Timmerman, unpublished manuscript). A written questionnaire was sent to all 458 employees, 181 employees (40%) returned a completed questionnaire. The survey asked about experiences with an enumeration of verbal, nonverbal and physical forms of sexual harassment or unwanted sexual behaviour. Furthermore, the study inquired whether the organisational culture, the dominating norms and values within the organisation, influenced the extent of sexual harassment.

3.3.2   RESULTS

About half of the respondents (54%) had experienced one or more instances of sexual harassment within the department and 64% of the respondents had had personal experience of sexual harassment. With regard to the personal experiences most frequently mentioned are sexual jokes/ambiguous remarks (54%). Other verbal forms are remarks about someone's sex life (22%), and sexually slanted remarks about their appearance (20%).

Of the physical behaviour, unsolicited touching, such as putting an arm around you, hugging, kissing, is mentioned by one in four employees. Among the nonverbal forms, one in five employees still indicate that they have experienced undressing with the eyes/staring/ogling, sexually slanted texts/pictures on the computer, and showing/hanging up pornographic nude calendars.

In general, women experience slightly more sexual harassment than men. Within their department, women more often experience the following forms of expression as harassment: sexually slanted remarks about your appearance or clothes, remarks about your sex life, undressing with the eyes/staring/ogling or leering. Men have more personal experience with remarks about their sex lives, the hanging up of pornography, nude calendars and sexually slanted texts/pictures on the computer.

The organisational culture plays a role in the extent of sexual harassment:
*   social face of the organisation: sexual harassment is experienced less by respondents who feel that in their department attention is paid to the social aspect between colleagues.
*   equal treatment of men and women: respondents who feel that their department has a positive attitude towards the equal treatment of men and women have themselves experienced less sexual harassment.
*   attitude of management towards work/family: sexual harassment is experienced less in departments where the management has a positive attitude towards problems which may arise from the combination of work and family.
*   size of the department: more sexual harassment is experienced in smaller departments than in larger ones.
*   type of department: relatively more sexual harassment is recorded in the sales and administrative departments.

The recent experiences of sexual harassment have mainly been described by women. The dominant pattern that emerges from these descriptions is that of the female employee who is sexually harassed by a male colleague. Most of the occurrences take place at their own work station, at that of the harasser or in the corridor. Slightly less than half of the respondents reacted actively and assertively to the sexual harassment; more often, however, the reaction is indirect or passive: behaving as if you haven't noticed anything, ignoring it, going along with it. Women who have reacted indirectly or passively are more often dissatisfied with their reaction. They would have preferred to have been more openly rejecting. Half of the people who have described a recent experience have talked about it with colleagues or the boss; the other half has not.

Most of the respondents indicated that the sexual harassment has influenced their work: being less able to do the work well, trouble with tiredness, ignoring certain people they have to work with, unpleasant working atmosphere after the event.

3.4   Industrial office workers & secretaries

3.4.1   DEFINITION AND METHODOLOGY

In 1991 a study was carried out by Tijdens and Goudswaard for the Industrial Labour Union. Members of the union distributed almost 5000 questionnaires to female office workers throughout the country (clerical staff, telephonist/receptionist, secretaries) in their organisation. The response rate was 26%. The sample distribution was very close to that of the total population of female office workers in manufacturing in so far as age, weekly working hours, nationality, marital status, and number of children were concerned. Only the educational level was a few percentage points higher than average, and 15% of the respondents were members of a union, whereas only 10% had been expected.

In the study a couple of questions mentioned sexual harassment, but the main subject of this study was the working conditions for office workers in general.

In 1993 a survey was carried out among secretaries concerning the tasks they performed (Sloep and Tijdens). More than 2000 questionnaires were distributed via union groups, advertisements in union magazines, secretarial magazines, via members of two secretarial associations, and the survey was handed out to participants at an annual secretarial fair. The response rate was 25%. The sample was representative as far as the working week and education were concerned, but the respondents were slightly older than the population. A couple of questions were asked about sexual harassment.

3.4.2   RESULTS

According to the industrial office workers survey, sexist jokes and remarks were made in three-quarters of the offices. These remarks were made by colleagues in particular. More than half of the respondents found this 'sometimes annoying/sometimes amusing', and 15% found the remarks 'annoying'. 13% of the women reported their own experiences or colleagues' experiences with sexual harassment. Unwanted touching was reported the most. Reactions to the sexual harassment were not to react or to ignore the harasser, followed by filing a complaint, and making it clear that the behaviour is unwanted. More than half of the respondents did not know where they could report sexual harassment if they should experience it.

In this study it appeared that secretaries run a greater risk of sexual harassment; 16% of secretaries reported having been a victim of sexual harassment, as opposed to 11% of the other office workers. The researchers suggest that the stereotype of secretaries as "office brides" (quite often a sexual relationship is assumed between the secretary and her boss) or "sex kitten" may be one of the causes of a higher incidence rate for secretaries.

The secretary survey reported that 25% of the women had been sexually harassed at work. In particular, colleagues were the perpetrators, to a lesser extent followed by supervisors. The most frequently experienced types of harassment were jokes and remarks with a sexual connotation, and unwanted touching. The responses to the harassment were: making it clear that the behaviour is unwanted, and ignoring the incident.

3.5   Local government

3.5.1   DEFINITION AND METHODOLOGY

Another research at a branch level was a survey among 100 employees (women and men) of a local government in the north of the Netherlands in 1996 (Zaagsma, Landskroon, 1996). Incidence, coping strategies, and policy were discussed. In this study 4 different definitions of sexual harassment were used: from an enumeration of unwanted behaviour, a question about experiences with unwanted sexual behaviour, to a question about experiences with sexual harassment.

3.5.2   RESULTS

Incidence and reactions

The first definition/measurement instrument was an enumeration of sexual harassment behaviour on 4 different levels, from general sexual remarks to serious sexual assault (Fitzgerald's Sexual Experiences Questionnaire). According to this definition, 75% of female and male respondents had been sexually harassed. The second definition was a supplement to the Fitzgerald list, namely: was the described behaviour unwanted. Of the respondents, 52% of the women and 27% of the men felt that this behaviour was unwanted. The third definition was the question 'Have you ever experienced unwanted sexual behaviour/attention?', 45% of the women and 7,5% of the men answered this question with yes. Finally, the last question was 'Have you ever experienced sexual harassment?', 27% of the women and 1,5 % of the men answered yes. The experiences of the men were usually indirect; they were spectators who did not like it when women were harassed in their presence. The way in which experiences with sexual harassment are asked for significantly determines the incidence of sexual harassment. The researchers chose the second definition: an enumeration of actual (sexually tinted) behaviour, which the respondents judged as unwanted. Thus they concluded that 54% of women and 27% of men had reported sexual harassment. The term sexual harassment was used by the respondents for the more severe forms of sexual harassment. The most reported forms of sexual harassment were sexually tinted remarks/behaviour and violent sexual approaches.

The most common reaction to sexual harassment was 'telling the harasser that he should stop his behaviour'. This was the case for 26% of the less severe sexual harassment cases and for 29% of the people who experienced more severe sexual harassment. Other important reactions were 'trying to keep relations good', 'ignoring it/reacting as if nothing had happened' and 'talking with other people about the situation'. Remarkable is that in the more severe cases of sexual harassment, people talked less with others about the situation and tried harder to avoid the perpetrator than in less severe cases.

People with more egalitarian/emancipatory ideas experienced more sexual harassment (or will more quickly give it the name sexual harassment). The questions about behaviour at work were not related to the incidence of sexual harassment.

Policy

The local government had a sexual harassment policy consisting of a confidential counsellor, possibilities for an informal, anonymous or formal complaint, information at work meetings, and a video/lecture. The respondents were satisfied with the information provided about sexual harassment by the personnel magazine, the work meetings, and conversations with colleagues. Most employees knew that there were counsellors, but familiarity with them varied from unit to unit. The employees who experienced sexual harassment did not go to the counsellor. The reasons for this included thinking that it was not serious enough, wanting to solve the problem first themselves, and not knowing that there was a complaints procedure.

3.6   Lesbians and bisexual women

3.6.1   DEFINITION AND METHODOLOGY

In the period 1988-1993 a survey was carried out amongst lesbians and bisexual women. Almost 1300 women reported about their experiences with violence and sexual violence (Van Oort, 1993).

A total of 3800 written questionnaires were distributed by way of mailing lists held by lesbian and gay interest groups and social groups. The response rate was 34%. The questions included four types of sexual violence: non-contact experiences; touching in a sexual way; attempted penetration/sexual assault; and rape.

3.6.2   RESULTS

From the study it appeared that 35% of the respondents had experiences with violence at the workplace. Sexual abuse at the workplace was reported by 23% of the women. Most common types of sexual abuse were the non-contact forms (67%), followed by touching in a sexual way (32%). Most harassers were male colleagues.

4 Foreign women and sexual harassment

4.1 Definition and method

In 1996 a qualitative study was carried out, consisting of 5 interviews with women of Turkish and Hindu descent about their perception of sexual harassment (Tacoma, 1996). During the interview the researcher first asked about wanted and unwanted behaviour in the workplace; at the end of the interview she asked what the women understood by sexual harassment.

4.2 Results

Unwanted behaviour includes physical contact and sexual jokes. The intention of the man is very important: pure, fraternal. The women reported that they took preventive measures in advance in their contacts with men in the workplace: they kept their distance.

The women reacted as follows towards sexual harassment: direct verbal reaction, indirect verbal reaction such as talking about their own relationships, changing the subject, 'body language', walking away, and ignoring the situation. In the long run they would talk to the harasser, let other people mediate, or resign. They would undertake action if they thought that the situation was out of their control. They would only lodge a complaint if there was no other possibility. They would never tell their families, because they would say it was her own fault, she had asked for it, because of the way she had behaved or dressed at work.

A policy against sexual harassment should have a wide/extensive definition because the term sexual harassment only covers the more severe aspects of sexual harassment. Sanctions should be available within the company, this emphasizes that the management is taking the subject seriously. For foreign women there could be other factors hindering talking about sexual harassment because of feelings of guilt and fear of the reaction of their environment. For example, Turkish and Hindu women would rather resign than make a complaint.

References

Amstel R. van, H.J. Volkers, (1993), *Seksuele intimidatie: voorkomen en beleid voeren, Ervaringen bij 50 arbeidsorganisaties*, Onderzoek uitgevoerd in opdracht van het Directoraat-Generaal van de Arbeid door het Nederlands Instituut voor Arbeidsomstandigheden, Den Haag.

Bajema, C.W., M.C. Timmerman (1997), *Sexual harassment in a telecommunication firm*, Groningen (unpublished manuscript).

Diekstra, R.F.W., P. de Heus, M.H. Schouten en I.L.D. Houtman (1994), *Werken onder druk: een onderzoek naar omvang en factoren van werkstress in Nederland*, Den Haag.

Dijkstra, S. (1992), *Ongewenste intimiteiten in de gezinszorg, de noodzaak van een helder beleid*, Stichting tot wetenschappelijk Onderzoek omtrent Sekualiteit en Geweld, Utrecht.

Eikenaar, L. (1993), *'Dat hoort er nu eenmaal bij...', Aard en omvang van ongewenste omgangsvormen bij de Nederlandse politie*, Rotterdam.

Oort, D. van (1993), *(On)zichtbaar. (Seksueel) geweld tegen lesbische en bisexuele vrouwen en meisjes*, Homostudies Utrecht.

Sloep, M., K.G. Tijdens (1993), *Een functie met inhoud, Onderzoek naar de taak inhoud van vier secretaresse functies*. Onderzoeksrapport voor de FNV Dienstenbond.

Tacoma, L. (1996), *Grenzen in de omgang, Turkse en Hindoestaanse vrouwen over hoe zij omgaan met grensoverschrijdend gedrag op het werk*, Onderzoek in opdracht van Pres Emancipatiebureau Utrecht in het kader van het project seksuele intimidatie en zwarte/migranten/vluchtelingenvrouwen, Utrecht.

Timmerman, G. (1990), *Werkrelaties tussen vrouwen en mannen, een onderzoek naar ongewenste intimiteiten in arbeidssituaties*, Amsterdam.

Tijdens, K., A. Goudswaard (1992), *Kwaliteit van de arbeid van kantoorvrouwen in de industrie, Onderzoek naar 'kantoorarbeid van vrouwen in de industrie'*, in opdracht van Industriebond FNV, Amsterdam.

Zaagsma, A.W., A.M. Landskroon (1996), *Onderzoek Seksuele intimidatie*, Groningen.

IX NORWAY

Anne Werner

Several studies of one occupation/branch or region have been carried out in Norway. As yet no national representative survey has been conducted. Unlike in other countries, the government has not been involved in research into sexual harassment at work; the university and labour unions were the initiators of the studies. The first research project was carried out by a research group from the Centre for Women's Studies at the University of Oslo. Most subsequent studies were initiated by one of the labour unions. Compared to other countries, Norway has carried out more qualitative research.

1 Women's magazine questionnaire (Trak*88)

1.1 Definition and method

In 1988 the Trak*88 questionnaire was published in the women's magazine 'Kvinner og Klaer' (Brandsæter and Widerberg, 1992). The magazine has a circulation of 80,000 of whom only 71 responded to the questionnaire. This was a very low response rate. In particular, women with more severe experiences of harassment responded to the questionnaire.

The questionnaire divided sexual harassment into three categories; nonverbal (staring, being eyed up and down); verbal (remarks about body, clothes, private life); and physical harassment (touching, pressure for sexual intercourse).

1.2 Results

Most common were the verbal and physical types of harassment: more than 90% of the respondents experienced unwanted touching, 90% unwanted comments, 65% unwanted proposals or pressure to perform sexual 'acts', and 21% mentioned (attempted) rape.
Sexual harassment caused more negative effects when it was repeated and when the harassee was dependent on the harasser. The sexual harassment experience could have many physical/psychological consequences. The respondents mentioned depression (41%), headaches, muscle aches and sleeping problems (35%), stress (35%), and anxiety attacks (18%). Furthermore, half of the people did not look forward to going to work, 29% have resigned, and 18% have thought about quitting their job.

The individual characteristics age and marital status influenced the incidence of sexual harassment: young women had more experiences than older women, and single or divorced women were more at risk of being harassed than married women. Furthermore, the sex composition at the workplace was important. Women in either female-dominated jobs or male-dominated jobs had more sexual harassment experiences.

The women used several coping strategies: they ignored or avoided the incident (26%), they made jokes about it (44%) or they asked the harasser to stop (73%). Opposed to the fact that many respondents experienced severe forms of harassment, only a minority of 27% had asked for help and about 20% did not tell anyone about the incident. In general, the strategies were not successful. Common to all strategies, according Brantsaeter and Widerberg, is that women behave in such a way that their femininity – their sex and sexuality – turns against them and becomes a social/sexual control mechanism.

Several theoretical explanations were described. One of the theories was the misunderstanding theory. Women and men don't understand each other very well; men interpret the (sexual) signals of women in a way different from what women intend and this leads to misunderstandings. According to the researchers, this is not a good model for explaining sexual harassment because the theory does not include power relations. Therefore the authors use a power model. Sexual harassment has to do with a disrupted power balance between the sexes. Women at work are subordinated to men because of their sex. Sexual harassment experiences are not individual incidents but rather are the result of a social system in which male values have priority over female values. For this reason sexual harassment is a problem of the work environment.

2 Several branches

2.1 Definition and method

Two surveys commissioned by the labour union were carried out amongst employees in several branches. The first study was conducted by Einarsen et al. (1993) into bullying and harassment amongst 4742 members of labour unions (teachers, catering industry, trade, and local government) in the province of Hordaland. Nearly half of the employees who received a questionnaire responded. They were asked about their experiences over the last six months. Einarsen used a more limited definition than other studies: the person exposed must have experienced the situation as unwanted and negative and as sexual, it should have lasted for a certain period of time, and it should have happened during the 6 months before the study.

Another study of the sexual harassment experiences of the members of labour unions was conducted by Almås (1995). The female labour union members of 5 unions in Sor-Trondelag (971 women) were approached with a questionnaire, 53% of whom responded. This study builds on the research of Brantsaeter, Sørensen and Frøberg. The study does not mention the word sexual harassment.

2.2 Results

Einarsen's results confirm that women in particular had experiences of sexual harassment, but contrary to other studies the incidence rate is low (8%). In particular, the incidence of frequent, monthly sexual harassment was low: 1% of the women had to deal with it weekly and 7% occasionally (less than once a month). Women with the following characteristics more often had experiences of harassment: younger than 35, unmarried, secondary school, working in the private sector, and working in male-dominated companies. In addition to these factors, the branch of industry was also of influence. Teachers and local government employees mentioned less harassment, as compared to a higher incidence in the catering and the printing industries. Women who experienced frequent sexual harassment judged their health and work pleasure much more negatively than other women and they more frequently became ill. The results suggest that psychosomatic complaints, muscular pain, and back and neck trouble were the consequences of harassment. Furthermore, women who had had experiences were more negative about the working climate and they were more frequently looking for another job.

The Almås research showed that 8% of the women had experience of sexual harassment. This incidence was highest in the engineering branch. The reactions of the respondents after the incident were angry (49%), insulted (41%) and embarrassed (36%). A number of the harassees had experienced negative effects on their health and personal wellbeing. The respondents reported depression (7%), fear (6%), stress (7%), headaches and sleeping problems (5%), illness for shorter periods (5%), and illness for longer periods (1%). Almås concluded that 4 out of 5 did not speak with others about their experience, and when they did they talked with friends, family or colleagues. Some of the women were harassed by subordinates. Women engineers and women working in health care were to a great extent harassed by clients and patients.

In 3 out of 4 cases the incident had no consequences for the harasser, in the other cases the harasser received a warning or an official reprimand.

3   Branch studies

3.1   Health care

3.1.1   DEFINITION AND METHOD

Two studies were conducted in the health care sector. The first was qualitative research carried out by Frøberg for the Labour Union Norsk Kommuneforbund in 1991. This study consisted of 2 parts. The first part was based on in-depth interviews with 10 employees (8 female, 2 male) who were working on a psychiatric ward. The main subject was their opinions about sexual harassment and sexuality at work. The second part was based on 13 in-depth interviews with 8 female and 5 male confidential counsellors about their experiences in this function.

The second quantitative study was conducted by Moland (1997) and concerned harassment and pressure of work, commissioned by the Norsk Kommuneforbond. The information was gathered by telephone interviews with about 2500 members of the labour union working in health care, the cleaning services, and as salesmen/women. He asked the employees if they had been exposed to unwanted sexual attention at the workplace.

3.1.2   RESULTS

The generally supported idea that sexual harassment was not a problem in the hospital was not confirmed by Frøberg's study. The most important result of the study was that sexual harassment is a normal experience in the workplace and that it can happen between patients–nurses and between superiors–subordinates. In general, nurses are confronted with sexual harassment, but some male nurses had also had experiences (to a great extent with female patients). In particular, young newly arrived nurses reported sexual harassment, but they did not dare to complain about it.

Sexuality regarding patients seemed particularly difficult to handle. For example, when psychiatric patients made sexual comments and approaches this behaviour could be a part of their illness. This made it difficult to define as sexual harassment. Part of the job of a nurse is to determine the boundaries/limits and this also includes sexual advances/harassment by patients. If a nurse was offended by a patient then this implied that the nurse was not capable of handling the situation in a professional way. Nurses said that dealing with sexual harassment from somatic patients was more difficult than psychiatric patients, because these patients were accountable but nevertheless still harassed.

The second section evaluated one of the measures against sexual harassment: the confidential counsellor in the hospital. The counsellors rarely received complaints about sexual harassment at the hospital, in contrast to the experiences of employees reported in the first section of the study. Only 3 of the 13 counsellors interviewed were contacted by victims of sexual harassment. The counsellors observed much more sexual harassment in the work environment, but employees did not report it. Frøberg concludes that the confidential counsellor could be a barrier to publicising sexual harassment because they have the power to define an incident as non-harassing. The most important problem for organisations was accepting that sexual harassment is a problem related to the working climate. The author recommended that counsellors should be educated about the influence of sexuality/sexual harassment in the workplace, in order to take preventive measures against sexual harassment in the workplace.

Moland's study amongst employees working in health care, the cleaning services and as sales(wo)men showed that physical assault, rude insults, and sexual harassment were part of the growing pressure of work. Physical aggression and insults were the most common, followed by sexual harassment which was reported by 15% of the respondents. The growing work pressure was caused to a great extent by patients. Employees working in home care (19%) and the hospital (17%) most often reported

116

sexual harassment. The work environment appeared to have an influence on the incidence of harassment: working at the homes of patients/clients gave the patient a lot of space and the employee had less control over the situation.

The sexual harassment experience had a negative effect on the health of employees: they were ill twice as often as their colleagues.

3.2 Army/Navy

3.2.1 DEFINITION AND METHOD

Two qualitative studies were carried out in the army/navy branch. Research by Vendshol (1993) paid attention to sexual harassment in the navy. This was a qualitative report based on 10 interviews with female and male navy employees.

Werner (1996) describes the wanted and unwanted consequences of sexuality for women in the army. She carried out interviews with 15 women and 2 men, aged 20-30, working on a transport unit, half of them soldiers, half of them officers.

3.2.2 RESULTS

In the navy study it appeared that young women in particular were reluctant to talk about sexual harassment, older women were more open. In spite of this reluctance, the young respondents nevertheless mentioned experiences of sexual harassment. Incidents occurred more often on board than in the office, because of the fact that work and leisure time occurred in the same space on board. Young and new women reported sexual harassment more often. These experiences varied from threats to report badly executed work or to spread rumours if the women did not comply with the advances of a male employee, to constant remarks about body or looks and incidents where men hid in the cabin of a woman while she got ready for bed. The material gathered showed that rumours about women who had apparently slept with a man were widespread and that these rumours had a negative effect on the work position of the women. Vendshol concluded that there was a tendency to hold women responsible for determining the boundaries of sexuality on board and that women should take the negative consequences if they were not successful in keeping to them.

One of the results of Werner's army research was that desired heterosexual attention and contact was quite common in the unit studied. A majority of the respondents had a relationship with a colleague or was married to a colleague. Most employees considered flirting as a positive element in the working climate. However, the sexual intimacy also caused problems for the female employees, especially in the lower ranks. The most frequently mentioned problems were the spreading of rumours about females and their sexuality/sexual affairs. These rumours had consequences for their work: women were put on the spot to justify their behaviour. The strategy the female soldiers used was to distinguish themselves from the 'not serious ladies' in the army.

3.3   Airline

3.3.1   DEFINITION AND METHOD

A study was conducted by Frøberg in 1990 concerning the expression of sexuality at work and the wanted and unwanted consequences for female and male employees in an airline company. She studied an airline unit and an office unit by interviewing 10 employees. Her point of departure was the balance between sexual attention as a compliment (confirmation of sex) and sexual attention as a reprimand (control of sex).

3.3.2   RESULTS

It appeared to be difficult to talk about sexuality and sexual harassment. One of the results of the study was that it depended on the type of workplace whether an incident was defined as sexual harassment or not. In the office, sexuality was part of the informal working climate. It was a personal affair, and therefore it was easier to define sexuality as a problem. At the air unit, sexuality was a more open part of the job: for the stewardesses sexuality was seen as a tool for making contact with the passengers, because the employees and the passengers were not familiar with each other, the only thing known was the sex of a person. The looks and sexuality of the stewardesses were therefore a professional part of the job. This made it more difficult to define incidents as sexual harassment.

3.4   Perception of the sexual harassment incident by victims

3.4.1   DEFINITION AND METHOD

Sørensen carried out a qualitative study of victims of harassment and their perception of the harassment situation. She used the results of the Track'88 research and carried out in-depth interviews with 10 respondents from the Track'88 research.

3.4.2   RESULTS

The Track '88 research suggested that two types of sexual harassment could be distinguished, depending on the type of work: In male-dominated jobs the sexual harassment is more public and is perpetrated by a group of men. In female-dominated jobs the sexual harassment is more hidden and the perpetrator is more often a supervisor who is harassing one or more female employees – who don't know this about each other. The interviews suggest that the harassed women often take the responsibility for what has happened; they are the ones to be blamed. Sørensen states that this can be explained by the morals of women, which is strongly linked to 'body' and 'sexuality'. Sexual harassment can be a threat to the dignity of a women, because she did not manage her body and sexuality in a virtuous way. Because of this, sexuality can function as social control of women at work.

3.5   Heterosexual arrangement at work

3.5.1   DEFINITION AND METHOD

A Norwegian research (Brandsaeter, 1990) investigated the heterosexual arrangement at work. She used the results of the Track'88 research and carried out in-depth interviews with 8 lesbians.

3.5.2   RESULTS

The main result of this study is that heterosexuality is the communication norm at work. Lesbians often find difficulty in expressing their sexual inclination at work. Most of the time they use strategies to prevent that colleagues find out about their lesbianism. Lesbians try to separate private life and work (and sexuality is a private matter) or only talk about their sexual inclination with a small amount of women the respondent trusts. The women interviewed were exposed to unwanted sexual attention at work. Examples concerned the sexual harassment of lesbian women by male colleagues.

4.   Policy measures

4.1   Definition and method

To obtain information about the functioning of confidential counsellors and the extent to which sexual harassment is a secret at work, Dahlen et al. (1989) interviewed 35 people who were involved in this subject: confidential counsellors in companies, key figures in labour unions, employees of the labour inspection, and key figures in the employers' organisation. Furthermore, she analysed 7 legal cases.

4.2   Results

The main conclusion of the research was that the confidential counsellor is not the right person to solve conflicts about sexual harassment at work. The counsellors lacked training and special competence concerning the subject of sexual harassment. In such a situation the personal characteristics of the confidential counsellor were very important for the way that a counsellor handled a complaint. Harassed women rarely contacted assistance. This was one of the main reasons why incidents of sexual harassment did not become 'cases'. The silence of the victims worked as indirect approval of sexually harassing behaviour.

References

Almås, H. (1995), *Seksuell trakassering i arbeidslivet i Sør-Trøndelag.* Universitet i Trondheim, Psykologisk institutt.

Brantsæter, M.C. & K. Widerberg (red.) (1992), *Sex i arbeid(et)*, Tiden, Oslo.

Brandsæter, M.C. (1990), *Om kjønnets logikk - i et lesbisk perspektiv.* Intervjuer med lesbiske kvinner om deres erfaringer i arbeidslivet, Universitetet i Oslo (UiO), Institutt for sosiologi.

Dahlen, T. (1989), *Seksuell trakassering i arbeidslivet*, UiO, Rådet for arbeidslivsstudier.

Einarsen, S., B.I. Raknes, S.Berge Matthiesen (1993), *Seksuell trakassering*: Bøllen og blondinen på norske arbeidsplasser, Bergen, Sigma.

Frøberg, S. (1990), *9-6 Om arbeidsliv og seksualitet*, University of Oslo.

Frøberg, S. (1991a), *De er jo syke. Et forprosjekt om seksualitetens betydning på en psykiatrisk avdeling. Intervjuer med 10 ansatte.* Delrapport 1, Oslo, Norsk Kommuneforbund (NKF).

Frøberg, S. (1991b), *Tillitsvalgte og (be)driftkultur. Intervjuer med 13 tillitsvalgte*, Delrapport 2. Oslo, Norsk kommuneforbund (NFF).

Moland, L. E. (1997), Ingen grenser? Arbeidsmiljøog tjenesteorganisering i kommunene. Oslo, *Faforapport 221.*

Sørensen, R. (1992), *Det gar pa verdigheten los. Om seksuell trakassering pa arbeidsplassen*, University of Oslo.

Vendshol, T. (1993), *I samme båt* - En undersøkelse rundt kvinnelig personells erfaringer med uønsket seksuell oppmerksomhet i Sjøforsvaret, UiO: Kandidatstudium i arbeidshelse.

Werner, A. (1996), *(U)Seriøse damer i forsvaret,* En studie av kjønn, kropp og seksualitet i møtet med en militær avdeling, UiO, Institutt for sosiologi.

X   SWEDEN

Ninni Hagman

With the 1987 governmental report by the Equal Opportunities Ombudsman on the FRID-A project came formal recognition of sexual harassment. Subsequent to this report, six universities have conducted surveys revealing sexual harassment against students, researchers and other employees. Several surveys have been carried out in different branches and at workplaces in the public sector, some of them by the unions. Further, a few surveys have been conducted within the private sector. Revealing the existence of sexual harassment 'everywhere' has resulted in an increasing number of preventive programmes.

1   National surveys

1.1   Definition and method

The FRID-A-research by the Swedish Emancipation Ombudsman was a nationwide survey financed by the Ministry of Employment. About 4000 working women, chosen at random, from 9 Labour Unions in both the private and public sectors received a questionnaire about sexual harassment at work. Half of the women participated in the research, which is a response rate of 50%. For nonresponse the researchers had the following explanations: in general, questionnaires with personal questions produce a lower response rate, this is also true for sexual harassment questions; some of the people with sexual harassment experiences push these experiences away, this group will not respond to the questionnaire; the questionnaire was rather long.

Experiences with sexual harassment were enquired after as follows: "Have you in your working life ever experienced any of the following unwanted behaviour with a sexual connotation?" The possible answer were: repeated unwanted remarks about appearance, body, clothes, or private life; unwanted telephone calls, letters with a sexual content or sexual pictures; unwanted touching of the body; unwanted proposals or demands concerning sexual services or a sexual relationship; and rape or attempted rape.

Additionally, a further nationwide study was carried out by the Central Statistical Office and the Labour Inspectorate about the working climate. Between 10,000 and 15,000 people were interviewed about both the physical and the psychosocial working environment. In the 1993 survey one question was asked about sexual harassment: "Have you experienced sexual harassment at work in the form of unwanted advances or humiliating remarks about sex-related subjects?" Employees could answer as follows: at least a couple of times a month; rarely in the last 3 months; and not at all. In the publication 'Hotad, mobbad eller sexuallt trakasserad pa jobbet'

121

(Arbetarskyddsstyrelsen, Statiska centralbyran, 1995) the answers to this question were worked out in more detail.

1.2   Results

According to the FRID-A survey, an average of 17% of the women indicated that they experienced one or more forms of sexual harassment at work. There were differences between the labour unions; the tendency was that respondents working in male-dominated branches reported more sexual harassment. The most common form of harassment was unwanted touching (71%), followed by unwelcome sexual verbal comments, looks, gestures, jokes, and pornographic pictures (68%). Further, almost half of the harassed women reported unwanted sexual comments about looks, body, clothes, or private life, while nearly a third of the women had received unwelcome requests for sexual favours or sexual relations, and 22% had had unwanted telephone calls/letters with a sexual connotation. Experiences with (attempted) rape were mentioned by 2%.

The responses to this survey indicated that all kinds of women could be victims of sexual harassment, but that young women and women in male-dominated occupations were more likely to be sexually harassed: of the women who experienced harassment 48% worked in a male-dominated job, 24% in a female-dominated job and 22% in a sex-balanced job.

Half of the women were harassed by supervisors or employers. Further, the harassment in male-dominated professions was more often perpetrated by colleagues, whereas in female-dominated jobs the superior is more often the perpetrator. More than half of the respondents working in the health care sector indicated that the harassment was perpetrated by patients.

Feelings at the time of the unwanted sexual attention were anger (61%), feeling uncomfortable (58%) and offended (36%). Scared and threatened were mentioned by 32% of the respondents.

The harassed women used different strategies to react to the harassment: they asked the harasser to stop (55%), they ignored the problem/did nothing (42%), or they made a joke of it (38%). The most effective strategy was the assertive one; for half of the women the situation improved, for 36% it stayed the same, and for 7% the situation worsened. The ignoring strategy had less effect, only in 20% of the cases did the situation improve, while for 73% the situation stayed the same, and for 7% it got worse. The 'making a joke of it' strategy succeeded for 20% of the harassed women and failed for 80% of the women. It appeared that the women in the male-dominated occupations reacted more assertively than in the other occupations. A quarter of the harassed women asked nobody for help. The other women contacted a colleague or 'someone else', in a third of the cases these strategies led to improvement. Women rarely asked for the help of authorities within the work environment, such as the employer (8%), labour union (3%), or personnel manager (3%). Of the women, 5% felt forced to agree with the proposals or demands concerning sexual services or a sexual relationship. This meant that for more than half of them the situation stayed the same, for less than half that it improved.

A third of the harassed women mentioned negative consequences: reduction of duties; no extra remuneration anymore; higher demands on the work performance, unreasonable criticism; and isolation. About a third of the respondents were unable to find any other solution to the problem than to leave the job, either by giving notice or by taking leave of absence or sick leave. Other negative consequences were psychosomatic complaints; 18% of the harassed women mentioned headaches, muscle aches, 16% of the harassed women reported stress reactions such as palpitations, and sleep problems; 12% got depressed and 2% had considered suicide.

The recommendations of the Ombudsmen for emancipation to employers and labour unions were: 1- Make the subject debatable and make it clear that it is a personnel issue and not a personal issue; 2- Carry out a survey amongst the employees about the incidence; 3- Take active measures against sexual harassment: train supervisors, personnel managers, labour union employees, ombudsmen, provide clear information about the issue, and appoint confidential counsellors.

In the survey by the Central Statistical Office and the Labour Inspectorate women reported sexual harassment more often: 1 in 50 women (2%) experienced sexual harassment at least twice a month, whereas 1 in 100 men (1%) reported this.

When distinguishing between the branches of industry, women were harassed more often when working in transport and traffic (3,6%), technical/natural sciences jobs (2.6%) and services (2.7%). It appeared that, in particular, women working as waitresses, as bus or taxi drivers, and in health care had a higher incidence of harassment. For male employees it appeared that men working in health care and social work were relatively more frequently harassed.

Overall, 33% of the women and 37% of the men had an aversion to going to work at least twice a month. Women and men who were exposed to violence, sexual harassment or bullying had a greater aversion to going to work than others. This is especially true for employees who were exposed to bullying in general (80%). Of the sexually harassed employees nearly 60% (both women *and* men) had an aversion to going to work at least twice a month. Overall, 37% of the women and 56% of the men reported that they did not get help in a critical situation at work. Of the harassed women a higher percentage got no help in critical situations (58%). The same tendency was true for the harassed men (65%), but the differences here were smaller.

2   Branch studies

2.1   University

2.1.1   DEFINITION AND METHOD

In 1993 a survey was carried out among the personnel of Gothenburg University. The definition of sexual harassment in the FRID-A-report was used as an introduction for both women and men to the survey of sexual harassment. The questionnaire for women was more extensive than the questionnaire for men. The women's questionnaire contained an enumeration of examples from the definition, asked for the types of harassment, the coping behaviour, and consequences for personal or professional life. The men were only asked to what extent they agreed with the definition and whether they had been exposed to sexual harassment either according to that definition or according to how they themselves defined sexual harassment.

A postal survey was sent to all employees (2558 women and 2559 men) of Gothenburg University. Of the women 85% responded and of the men 67%, resulting in a general response rate of 76%.

2.1.2   RESULTS

15% of the women had experienced sexual harassment and 4% of the men. Women researchers and graduate students were exposed to a higher rate than other categories of employees, for instance women administrators. This and the following results are on the whole in accordance with the results of a similar survey done by Stockholm university in 1992.

Questions concerning verbal harassment such as sexual innuendoes and telephone calls were not separated in the questionnaire from the nonverbal harassment such as gestures, looks, objects, and pictures. Of the 280 women who said that they had been exposed to sexual harassment 37% had experienced more than one type. The most often reported form of sexual harassment was unwelcome sexual touching such as pinching, rubbing, brushing against (62%), followed by unwelcome sexual innuendoes, looks and gestures (48%), unwelcome jokes (39%) and unwelcome sexual comments regarding appearance, clothing and private life (36%). Lower incidence rates were reported for pressure for sexual favours or a sexual relationship (8%), unwelcome telephone calls, letters, pictures, and objects of a sexual nature (6%) and attempted rape (0,5%).No questions were put to the men about what types of harassment they had experienced.

The most frequent reactions to sexual harassment were irritation (43%), embarrassment (42%), anger (30%) or feeling violated (27%). Some were surprised (21%), disgusted (18%) or felt ridiculed (14%), 10% were intimidated and felt themselves threatened. The reaction from 9% of the respondents was shock, and 5% blamed themselves for being harassed.

The most common strategies for coping were: to pretend not to notice (36%), to shun the harasser (26%), to try to joke the problem away (24%), and to ignore the harasser (23%). To a lesser extent the harassed women did nothing at all (14%), asked the harasser to stop (14%), scolded the harasser (7%), paid the harasser back in his own coin (4%). For half of the women who said 'no' the harassment stopped or decreased. Other strategies were ineffective.

The harasser was in 97% of the cases a man. Of the women 1 in 3 was harassed by employees in other occupations than the victim, 32% by employers or supervisors, 28% by colleagues, 7% by students and 10% by tutors. Nearly 40% of the harassed women knew that the man had harassed other women as well, while few of the other women in the survey had knowledge of victims. 24% of the harassed women thought that the harasser was unaware that his behaviour was unwelcome, 21% did not know, 20% thought the man might be harassing on purpose, and 17% were sure it was his intention to harass. According to the harassed women, the reason for the man's behaviour was to vindicate his superiority (31%), to seek sexual contact (24%), to show off his power (16%), to become acquainted (10%), or that he was in love (8%).

More than 40% of the harassed women were aged between 25 and 34 when they were sexually harassed, but all ages were represented. 13% had been exposed for more than 5 years, marital status was irrelevant. The victims were often women in managerial positions, researchers or graduate students. They worked in male-dominated working places to a higher degree than women who were not sexually harassed.

The survey also contained questions concerning 'the erotic climate'. It is notable that many 'exposed men' were of the opinion that flirting and sexual comments, jokes and jargon at the workplace were pleasant. They were more positive towards an erotic climate both during breaks and in the working situation than either 'not exposed' men or women. The difference was especially high when compared to 'exposed women', who found such a climate disturbing to a high degree.

There were several consequences of harassment for the person or the organisation. Of the harassed women, 44% experienced negative consequences at work: isolation (17%), spreading of rumours (10%), uneasiness about going to work (17%), unwarranted criticism, change for the worse in working conditions, loss of tasks, new tasks under the level of competence, no promotion or increase in wages, exhortation to seek another job, and 4% had given notice. Furthermore, 14% said that the harassment had led to physical or psychosomatic problems.

The report stresses the negative consequences for the university: reduced work effort and quality, lessened job satisfaction, costs due to absence from work, loss of good reputation.

2.2 Wood Industry Workers

2.2.1 DEFINITION AND METHOD

The definition of sexual harassment in the FRID-A-report was used in the survey of sexual harassment among members of the Swedish Wood Industry Worker's Union (1993). The questionnaire contained an enumeration of examples from the definition.
Seven local union ombudsmen were interviewed in order to find some suitable companies to be part of the project. Four relatively big companies with a varying mixture of men and women were chosen.

An exhibition on screens showing the results of interviews with union representatives about sexual harassment was used as an introduction to the survey together with a verbal presentation of the subject "sexual harassment". Both the local union and the management participated in the meetings at each company. The local union was responsible for distributing the questionnaire to its members: 640 women and 652 men. The total response rate was 34% (women 36%, men 31%).

2.2.2 RESULTS

Of the employees, 23% of the women and 4% of the men had experiences of sexual harassment. Some of the harassed women had been exposed to more than one type of sexual harassment.

The most frequently experienced types were: sexual innuendoes, looks, gestures, and jokes (57%); unwelcome sexual touching such as pinching, rubbing, and brushing against (36%); and unwelcome sexual comments regarding appearance, clothing, and private life (25%). Other sexual harassment types were pressure for sexual favours or a sexual relationship (11%), and unwelcome telephone calls, letters, pictures, objects of a sexual nature (6%). Of the harassed men, 3 said that they had been exposed to sexual touching, 3 to sexual innuendoes, looks, gestures, and jokes, and 1 to comments regarding appearance, clothing and private life.

The question about reactions was as follows: "How does an exposed person feel?" The answers from both men and women were: embarrassed (45%), offended (33%), angry (28%), intimidated (20%), ridiculed (18%), and threatened (11%). The figures for answers from women were higher for all types of reactions than for men.

To a great degree members of the Wood Industry Worker's Union have different jobs depending on whether they are men or women. No man in the survey reported that he worked in an occupation dominated by women, 9% of the women were in male

126

occupations. A third of the women and a quarter of the men said that their occupation was neither female nor male. The survey does not answer the question whether women in male-dominated working places were harassed to a greater extent than other women.

There was no question about the sex of the harasser. In the case of the seven women and two men who answered that they had been harassed by an employer/supervisor, it was probably a man, since 96% of the labour management were men. The most common harasser was another worker. Almost 20% of the women knew about someone who had been harassed, while 11% of the men had knowledge of victims.

About a third of both men and women thought that the harasser was unaware that his behaviour was unwelcome. Further, 17% of women and 11% of men thought the unwelcome behaviour was intentional. The rest did not know.

2.3   Social Insurance Office

2.3.1   DEFINITION AND METHOD

The definition of sexual harassment in the FRID-A-report was used in the survey of sexual harassment among the employees of the Social Insurance Office of Älvsborg County (1995). The questionnaire contained an enumeration of examples from the definition.A postal questionnaire was sent to all 858 employees, resulting in a high response rate of 86% (562 women and 174 men).

2.3.2   RESULTS

In total, 8% of the employees had experienced sexual harassment; of the women 9%, and of the men 4%. Of the harassed employees - the survey does not separate the sexes further - 26% had been exposed to more than one type of sexual harassment. The following types of harassment were reported by the respondents: unwelcome sexual touching such as pinching, rubbing, brushing against (37%); unwelcome sexual innuendoes, looks, gestures, jokes (35%); unwelcome sexual comments regarding appearance, clothing, private life (22%); pressure for sexual favours or a sexual relationship (3%); and unwelcome telephone calls, letters, pictures, objects of a sexual nature (3%).

Reactions from men and women were: embarrassed (36%), offended (25%), and angry (27%). Strategies for coping were: to shun the harasser (30%); to pretend not to notice (25%); to try to joke the problem away (25%); to ask the harasser to stop (23%). More than half of the harassed employees told one or more people about the harassment: colleague (48%), partner (19%), friend (18%), the union (7%). Very few had turned to the personnel department or to someone in management. Talking to someone helped in two-thirds of the cases.

The harasser was in 97% of the cases a man. Employers/supervisors were harassers in 27% of the cases and another employee in 45% of the cases. 34% of the victims knew about others who had been harassed. Of the victims, 19% thought that the harasser was unaware that his behaviour was unwelcome, 23% of them thought the unwelcome behaviour was intentional, and the rest did not know or did not answer the question. The victims believed that the reason for the unwelcome behaviour was to seek sexual contact (25%), to show off power (18%) or love (10%).

Age played a minor role. People aged between 26 and 35 were slightly over represented. Marital status was irrelevant.

Almost 15% of the harassed employees had experienced negative consequences such as a change for the worse in working conditions, no increase in wages and unwarranted criticism. Furthermore, 16% said that the harassment had caused physical or psychosomatic problems.

2.4   SL Metro Company

2.4.1   DEFINITION AND METHOD

The definition of sexual harassment in the FRID-A report has been used in four surveys of sexual harassment among women employees at the Subway Division of SL Metro Company, which manages local traffic in Stockholm. The questionnaires contained a sample of examples from the definition, some slightly changed.

The Subway Division is a pioneer in the fight against sexual harassment in Sweden. When a sample of women employees showed the highest figures (39%) in the FRID-A report the manager immediately started affirmative action. This has now been in progress for ten years and includes, among other things, seminars for managers, supervisors and union representatives, a contact committee with the aim of providing support, information and advice, a folder, and the four surveys. The fourth survey was conducted in 1997 and the report is not yet ready. The third survey will be described here (1993).

To prepare for the third survey a letter was sent to the homes of women employees who worked as drivers on the underground trains and as ticket staff at the stations, that is 570 women. A postal questionnaire was sent to their homes a week later. The members of the Contact Committee visited the different working places to answer questions about the survey and to encourage the women to take part. The response rate was 69%.

In comparison with the second survey two years earlier, the third survey showed a reduction of the incidence rate from 33% to 27%: 107 women answered that they had been sexually harassed. Many of the respondents had experienced more than one type of harassment.

The types of harassment reported were: unwelcome sexual proposals (93%); unwelcome verbal innuendoes (82%); unwelcome telephone calls, letters, pictures (63%); and unwelcome physical advances (50%).

Strategies for coping were: to shun the harasser (49%); to pretend not to notice (49%); to try to joke the problem away (36%); to ask the harasser to stop (42%). Many exposed women had told somebody about the harassment, in the first place a colleague, their partner or a friend. A fifth had talked to someone in management. Very few had turned to the union or to the safety controller.

For 63 women who had said "no" or talked to someone the harassment decreased or stopped. However, some of the others who had tried to stop the harassment met with ridicule, were given nicknames, etc.

The reasons given for not telling anybody about the harassment were: " I will be ridiculed", "I am afraid of the consequences", "I will get the blame", "No one will believe me", "I did not know whom to turn to".

The harassers were men in all but a few cases. In half of the harassment cases the harassment was perpetrated by colleagues and managers/supervisors of SL Metro Company. This is a reduction since the second study, where a greater number of women reported such harassment. The rest – almost half of the cases – is harassment from passengers and other men whom the women meet during working hours, for instance people from the security service. This figure is the same as in the second survey.

The women among the ticket staff are exposed to sexual harassment from all categories to a higher degree than the drivers.

18% of the victims had experienced negative consequences such as psychical mobbing, changes for the worse in working conditions and the spreading of rumours. Most of the women said that the harassment had affected their health: psychosomatic problems (25%), stress reactions (28%), depression (12%), thoughts of suicide (4%), other examples (34%).

SL Metro Company maintains that sexual harassment at work involves a threat to the health and economy of the harassed employee, but is also "bad business" for the employer, for example, the costs of replacing the woman should she become ill or leave the company.

Since it began to combat sexual harassment the Company has succeeded in solving several cases in a quick and confidential way.

2.5   Health care

2.5.1   DEFINITION AND METHOD

The provincial government of Kristianstad (1993) sent a postal questionnaire to a number of its health care employees: female doctors (119 people), female housemen (106 people), female ambulance personnel (23 people) and male ambulance personnel (87 people). The response rate came to 59%.

Sexual harassment was defined as: 'Unwelcome or unwanted sexual attention. Sexual harassment is any type of unwanted sexual comments or behaviour in the work environment which results in the victim feeling uncomfortable. It could be comments or gestures that are meant to be funny, comments about one's private life, touching, or the request for sexual services'. They used the same questionnaire as the FRID-A research.

2.5.2   RESULTS

Overall, 22% of the respondents reported sexual harassment, with one highlight: the female ambulance personnel. In this occupational group 53% experienced some form of sexual harassment, whereas the female doctors reported 17%, the housemen 13%, and the male ambulance personnel 14%. The researchers mentioned the young age of the female ambulance personnel as a possible explanation for the high incidence rate. As a result of the study the provincial government wanted to appoint trained confidential counsellors in each unit of the organisation, and the management of the ambulance personnel wanted to organise extra training for its employees to change the attitudes towards women.

2.6   Hospital

2.6.1   DEFINITION AND METHOD

In 1996 4000 employees of the 'Sahlgrenska sjukhuset' filled in a postal questionnaire about work climate, flexibility, leadership, development, and effectiveness. This was a response rate of 67%. One of the issues was violence, threats and humiliating treatment, including a question about humiliating treatment by means of sexual comments and/or sexual harassment.

2.6.2   RESULTS

Almost 30% of the respondents had experience of sexual harassment; 20% was perpetrated by patients and 8% by colleagues.

References

Andriansson, L. (1993), *Ett högt pris, kartläggning av sexuella trakasserier vid Göthenborgs universitet.*

Bodén, M., I. Carlsson, B.Å. Ekström, H. Furucrona (1993), *Sexuella trakasserier på arbetsplatsen,* SL Tunnelbanan AB.

Hela Sahlgrenska (1997), *Klimatundersökning för anställda på Sahlgrenska sjukhuset.*

Jämställdhetsombudsmannen (JämO) (1987), *FRID-A projektet, Sexualla trakasserier mot kvinnor i arbetslivet,* Stockholm.

Kristianstad (1993), *Sexuelle trakasserier,* projektledare K. Ekström.

Larsson, S., P. Dittmer (1993), *Sexuella Trakasserier,* Svenska Träindustriarbetareförbundet.

Mellquist, L. and Arvidsson, H. (1995), *Könsdiskriminering, sexuella trakasserier och mobbing,* Försäkringskassan i Älvsborgs län.

Statistika Centralbyrån, Arbetarskyddsstyrelsen (1995), *Hotad, mobbad eller sexualt trakasserad påd jobbet,* Stockholm.

XI UNITED KINGDOM

Cristien Bajema

Sexual harassment has become a legitimate research issue in the United Kingdom. A great deal of research has been carried out into the topic of sexual harassment at work. One of these studies is nationwide, the others concentrate on one or several branches: health care workers, police, retail, and office workers.

Many of the surveys inquire into the incidence of harassment, as well as the sexual harassment policies. Interest groups are important initiators of studies, followed to a lesser extent by labour unions and government.

1 National study

1.1 Definition and method

In the nationwide study, commissioned by the Industrial Society in 1993, the respondents' definition of sexual harassment was the point of departure. The questionnaire inquired about any experiences the respondents may have had or directly observed with respect to unsolicited and unwanted sexual attentions at work from persons of either sex. 27 verbal, nonverbal and physical types of harassment were listed in the questionnaire.

About 1700 responses were received from employees working in several branches: manufacturing, financial services, food services, charities/trusts, non-profit, pharmaceutical soaps/cosmetics/chemicals, health services, government, retail trade. No information was available concerning the response rate.

1.2 Results

According to this study, 54% of the women and 9% of the men reported sexual harassment. The verbal forms 'sexual jokes' (56%) and 'remarks about figure/sexual behaviour' (60%), and the nonverbal form 'staring/whistling' (60%) are the most frequently experienced types of harassment. The physical type 'unsolicited physical contact' is reported by 1 in 5 respondents. Concerning frequently experienced behaviour, around 30% experienced sexual comments, 30% had been looked up and down obviously, and 10% frequently experienced unwanted touching.

The coping strategy most frequently used was asking the harasser to stop (40%), followed by ignoring the behaviour (30%) and requesting investigation (30%). The least reported strategy was the pursuit of a formal complaint (5%). However, this action seemed to be the most effective one; filing a grievance or complaint improved the situation in over 70% of the cases, whereas telling the harasser to stop had improved the situation in only 40% of the cases. In most cases the harassers were male colleagues (around 65%), followed by managers at least one level removed from the harassee's immediate supervisor (30%). Very few respondents reported harassment by customers or vendors.

For a quarter of the respondents the sexual harassment experience(s) did not influence their work situation. For another section of the respondents it did, however: 13% reported an uncooperative attitude, 11% mentioned a decrease in productivity and 6% said that their working assignments or working conditions deteriorated. There were also effects on a personal level, 24% of harassees experienced difficulty in thinking clearly as a result of being harassed, 18% mentioned an inability to concentrate and 13% claimed to have experienced interference with their problem-solving abilities and judgement. On an interpersonal level, 24% of harassees reported experiencing tension which harmed both professional and personal relationships and affected individual performance. 14% of harassees also reported feeling hostility towards others after experiencing sexual harassment.

Furthermore, the research gathered information about the firms' policies against sexual harassment. Overall, 40% of the employers in the United Kingdom had sexual harassment policies: 40% provided swift and thorough investigations of complaints, 20% had counselling services for victims of sexual harassment, and 15% provided awareness training for managers and equal opportunities staff. On the basis of the results the study recommended the following: make harassment unacceptable within the context of organisational culture and practice; take complaints seriously; investigate them informally or formally, as appropriate; make it the managers' responsibility to enforce the procedures, supporting individuals in any grievance cases and instigating disciplinary action where appropriate.

2. Several branches

2.1 Bargaining report

2.1.1 DEFINITION AND METHOD

In 1987 the Bargaining Report, the journal of the Labour Research Department, examined the scale, concern and activity concerning sexual harassment at work by means of a questionnaire distributed to a range of workplace unions, branches and women's representatives. The total number of replies was 157: 44 from the private sector, 109 from the public sector and 4 from the voluntary sector. The response rate was not reported.

2.1.2   RESULTS

Of the respondents, 73% reported that some form of sexual harassment had taken place in their workplace. The most common types of harassment were suggestive remarks or other verbal abuse (48%), sexist or patronising behaviour (45%) and unnecessary touching or unwanted contact (34%). The private sector also had problems with offensive pin-ups and calendars (32%). Physical assault was unexpectedly high (10%). There was a strong link between unwanted physical contact (touching, assault) and harassment by seniors: more than 90% of the perpetrators of this type of harassment were supervisors or members of management.

On the whole, managers are the most common harassers (45%), followed by colleagues (18%). Nearly a third of public sector workplaces reported harassers from the public or from other non employees such as clients, patients and prisoners.

One in five of the workplaces had a union/management agreement covering sexual harassment. Of those who didn't have a specific procedure most (22%) used informal procedures and 20% used an agreed union/management disciplinary procedure.

The most common punishment for someone found guilty of harassment was a warning from management (22%). The next most likely outcome was no action (20%), this was more common in the public than in the private sector. Removal of offensive material came next (15%), and then the relocation or sacking of the harasser (11%). Only 2 cases had gone to an industrial tribunal. About half of the respondents said that their workplace could deal satisfactorily with a case of harassment. These were often the firms with a union/management agreement covering harassment. The most common reason given for feeling that the issue could not be dealt with satisfactorily was that it was not taken seriously by management, or generally in the workplace, often because management, the union or the workplace was male dominated. Despite the high level of incidents among respondents, only 31% said harassment had been discussed as a union/management issue.

2.2   *London School of Economics*

2.2.1   DEFINITION AND METHOD

In 1989 a survey was carried out by researchers at the London School of Economics for the Suzy Lamplugh Trust, concerning the incidence of sexual harassment, physical attack and threatening behaviour at work (Phillips, Stockdale, Joeman). A questionnaire was sent to employees in the areas of professional workers, carers, retail, and office workers. About 1000 questionnaires – 800 women and 200 men – were returned. The sampling procedure was a mixture of both random and non-random sampling.

The employees were asked about incidents they regarded as sexual harassment in their current job, for example unwanted sexual comments, staring/leering, physical contact, requests for sexual favours, or persistent advances. Furthermore, they were given the opportunity to report up to two incidents and to describe the nature of each incident by means of both precoded and open-ended questions.

2.2.2   RESULTS

Sexual harassment was reported by one in seven respondents (14% of the sample). About 16% of the female employees reported sexual harassment, as opposed to 2% of the male employees. The most frequently reported form of harassment involved physical contact (8% of the sample). The majority of incidents of sexual harassment fell into two categories. The first of these comprised sexual comments, innuendo and advances, which in some cases was accompanied by threats or offers of reward. The second involved physical contact, which in some cases was accompanied by comments and advances (44%). Of the 70 incidents involving physical contact, 8 were categorised as assault, and 1 as rape (sexual intercourse against the respondent's will).

There are differences in the incidence rates across the occupational groups. In the professional-out group, as well as those in retail and office jobs, 20% of the women reported sexual harassment. In the professional-in group the incidence rate was 15% and in the caring occupations 9%.

The picture that emerges of the nature of sexual harassment as reported by the respondents is a mixture of isolated incidents and continuous behaviour, initiated predominantly by men towards women. Two-thirds of the reported incidents involved harassment by colleagues, over half of whom held positions senior in status to the person being harassed. Over 70% of the incidents occur in the worker's own workplace, but sexual harassment clearly occurs in a variety of other situations, such as visiting other workplaces, in a clients' homes and especially at conferences.

In half of the cases the reaction to the sexual harassment was 'discuss it with colleagues or friends'. However, only a quarter of the incidents were formally reported and in a further quarter of the incidents the person who was harassed did nothing. Reasons for not reporting included the expectation that their complaint would not be taken seriously. Other respondents said they were too stunned or surprised to do anything. In a third of the incidents the person harassed retaliated or confronted the harasser, but in 6% of the cases the individual left or seriously considered leaving their job.

The importance of having a clear company policy and a sympathetic reporting procedure is highlighted by the fact that in 10% of the cases there was no procedure or union representative available, and in 5% of the cases the individuals concerned did nothing because of the identity of the person to whom they would have to report the incident.

The predominant feeling after experiencing sexual harassment was anger (64%), followed by depression (18%), and the feeling they were less efficient at work (14%). In over a third of the cases, those who experienced harassment avoided certain people at work, or experienced physical symptoms of stress.

2.3 Manufacturing firm, service firm and a public agency

2.3.1 DEFINITION AND METHODS

Di Tomaso surveyed the experiences of 360 workers in 3 companies: a heavy manufacturing firm, a service firm and a public agency (1989). In each company, 120 non-professionals and non managerial workers, equally divided by race and gender, were interviewed on a variety of topics regarding experiences on the job. A number of questions were asked about discrimination and unfair treatment. Nothing was explicitly asked about sexual harassment, but it was one of the issues referred to in the interviews.

2.3.2 RESULTS

The three organisations had differing characteristics. The manufacturing firm was in heavy industry, with 90% of the workforce male. Top management in this firm was exclusively male, with a few women professionals in staff positions, and almost all first-line managers were male. The women were getting paid 'male wages' (higher wages than in the other companies).

The non manufacturing firm was at the other end of the scale for most of these characteristics. The work in the firm was predominantly office work, and 70% of the firm was female. A large proportion of the professional and managerial staff was female, but the very top management was both male and white. About two-thirds of the first-line supervisors were female.

The characteristics of the public agency were in between those of the manufacturing and non-manufacturing firms. Like the non manufacturing company, its work was labour-intensive and fell within the service category. The workforce was about 70% female, but there was much more gender segregation of work within this agency. About 40% of the first-line managers were females, but their assignments were obviously gender segregated: about two-thirds of the females in this agency had female supervisors, but less than a fifth of the males did.

During the interviews it was asked whether the employees had ever experienced sex discrimination on the job. The pattern of response was very uneven across the 3 organisations: 30% of the females working in the manufacturing company had experienced sex discrimination, as opposed to 2% and 7% respectively in the non manufacturing firm and the public agency. Women working in the manufacturing industry experienced unpleasant working conditions. The behaviour of men was offensive: "Women were not treated as co-workers, but as women per se. Sexuality became part of the workplace negotiations". Women felt men were hostile to them whilst at the same time made demands on them.

To sum up, women working in male jobs or women otherwise challenging male authority in the workplace were most likely to become conscious of the sexualization of the workplace in the form of sexual harassment and sex discrimination. In contrast, women who worked primarily with other women or who reproduce their subordination in the workplace in relation to men are less likely to be conscious of the sexualization of their workplaces. By entering the male job market women place themselves in competition with men, who then attempt to secure their dominant role by emphasising the 'womenness' of their female co-workers and subordinates.

According to sexual harassment, management in the manufacturing firm was motivated in two directions. They expressed fear of having to face lawsuits, and so wanted to find some way to end the harassment of women before it reached the grievance level. But they also suggested that such behaviour was 'normal' between men and women. One manager said: "It doesn't happen. If it did happen, the men were probably joking. If they weren't joking, the women probably asked for it".

3   Branch studies

3.1   Police

3.1.1   DEFINITION AND METHODS

The research discussed is a 1993 police survey about aspects of sex discrimination within the police service. A sample was derived from ten police forces in England and Wales. A questionnaire was sent to 1802 policewomen, 510 policemen, 162 civilian support staff, and 86 traffic wardens. The response rate was 65%. The respondents were asked if they had experienced a number of itemised sexually harassing behaviours in the previous six months. These behaviours were defined as unwanted and un-reciprocated by them. Furthermore, it was asked if such unsolicited behaviour had had an impact on the respondents and if it had had negative consequences.

3.1.2   RESULTS

Nearly all the policewomen had experienced some form of sexual harassment from policemen. Nine out of ten women had heard suggestive jokes or comments on a woman's appearance, and for almost 40% of them it had had an unpleasant impact, followed by 66% of the employees who had heard comments about their own figure or appearance, which in almost 50% of the cases had had an unpleasant impact. Furthermore, 3 out of 10 policewomen were themselves subjected to offensive insults or unwanted touching, and 1 in 5 were pestered for unwanted dates. Serious sexual assault was reported by 6% of the respondents, in 85% of the cases this had had an unpleasant impact.

The experience of sexual harassment appears to be similar for probationers and police constables, but is less frequently experienced by women from supervisory ranks. For example, around 60% of probationers and constables received comments on their appearance, as opposed to 34% of the supervisors

Both male and female civilians reported the same incidence of categories of harassment. The most commonly reported form of sexual harassment was hearing jokes or comments about the appearance or figures of other women, which is experienced at the same rate by both men and women. Policewomen reported some experiences of sexual harassment at a greater rate than women civilians: they more often heard jokes about women, comments on their own appearance, comments on the appearance of other women; they were more often touched or pinched and were more often sexually assaulted.

Women police officers as well as male and female support staff indicated that male police officers were the most likely perpetrators of sexual harassment. Both male and female traffic wardens state that the public was the most likely perpetrator.

Consequences of the harassment were: considering leaving, affected work performance and taking sick leave. Evidence from the survey results indicated that a third of the police officers and half of the civilian respondents would use the grievance procedure should the need arise.

3.2   Office

3.2.1   DEFINITION AND METHOD

The third study mentioned is a 1991 research project into the temp. agency Alfred Marks Bureau. This survey investigated the attitudes and behaviour towards sexual harassment in the office of two groups: Alfred Marks temporary staff and Alfred Marks clients. Of the 5000 temporary employees who received a postal questionnaire, 546 participated in the research; of the 5000 clients approached, 521 replied. This is a low response rate of about 10%. About 3 out of 4 respondents were female.

The questionnaire first inquired about the perception of sexual harassment. Respondents were asked what kind of behaviour they regarded as sexual harassment, followed by an enquiry into which of the actions they regarded as sexual harassment had been observed towards themselves or others.

More than half of the temporary employees stated that they had personally experienced sexual harassment: 61% had experienced sexual harassment by the opposite sex and 10% by the same sex. The most common forms of harassment were: being eyed up and down, suggestive looks at parts of body, and bantering about a person's sex life. The victims' reactions included laughing off sexual harassment (51%), followed by remaining cool and uninterested (49%) or pretending not to notice (39%). Emphatic verbal reaction (36%) and physical reaction (8%) were less common. The overall pattern of responses in the past and predicted for the future showed that victims do little in practice (48%), but would like to do much more if harassment occurred in the future (60%). The main effect of the harassment was a feeling of humiliation/embarrassment (54%). The offender tended to be a colleague/person at the same level (46%), other senior member of staff (43%), or immediate boss (34%); men were the main offenders and women the main victims.

Most respondents experienced no threats for sexual favours, although 12% were offered some form of preferential treatment at work. The most common reward was promotion (63% had observed a reward being given). In addition, 9% of the respondents experienced a form of punishment for non-compliance. The most common punishment was dismissal or forced resignation (31%). One in four of those harassed reported this to a friend or relative (48%) or a colleague (33%). Complaints were filed to an immediate boss (12%), other senior members of staff (10%) and colleagues (5%). In other words, victims tend to talk about the incident rather than complain about it.

As a result of reporting the incident to the senior staff, the most common response to reporting the incidents was that the company took no action (43%), followed by resignation of the victim and, less likely, dismissal of the offender (4%).

Although 9 out of 10 of the respondents believed that an organisation should have a grievance procedure, only 12% of the respondents said that their organisation had one. Measures suggested were a clear and well-publicised procedure and an independent counselling service. Of the employees, 19% said that the employers were effective in dealing with sexual harassment and 54% not. Remarkable is the high number of instances of harassment, as opposed to the low incidence of reporting and the low confidence level in the organisations' ability to take action to reduce sexual harassment.

The Alfred Marks clients unanimously regarded several potential forms of sexual harassment as harassment, such as forcible sexual aggression, direct sexual propositions and pinching/grabbing. There was more debate about displays of pornographic material, touching or patting, being asked out on dates despite refusal, suggestive looks at parts of the body, regular sexual remarks or jokes. Most commonly observed were touching/patting, regular sexual remarks or jokes, being eyed up and down, suggestive looks at parts of the body. Overall, 88% of the clients had seen harassment.

The most common reaction to harassment by the victims was to laugh it off (79%) rather than emphatic verbal reaction (52%) and physical rejection (19%). Most victims did nothing/hoped the offender would stop (71%) or they complained to a colleague (60%). Concerning the effects of sexual harassment, victims tended to be humiliated/embarrassed (68%) while offenders either suffered no consequences (42%) or became angry/bad tempered (21%).

The offenders tended to be senior staff other than the immediate boss (59%), colleagues (55%), or the immediate boss (43%). Men were usually the offenders and women were usually the victims. A fifth had observed a bribe or threat to obtain a sexual favour: general preferential treatment was the main bribe and being given menial tasks was the main threat. According to the clients, victims rarely report incidents, mainly because of fear or embarrassment. Where incidents were reported it tended to be to a colleague or friend/relative. The most common outcome was that the offender was disciplined (43%) or that the incident was reported but the company took no action (32%). A grievance procedure was available in 34% of the companies (22% had a formal written and 12% an informal, unwritten procedure).

Asked about their own experiences, 38% of the client sample had been sexually harassed: 47% of females, 14% of males. Touching, pinching, and grabbing are the most common (43%), followed by suggestive remarks/innuendoes (41%) and direct sexual proposition (32%). About 1 in 4 considered the employers effective in dealing with sexual harassment in the office and about 60% found them not effective.

3.3   Health care

3.3.1   DEFINITION AND RESULTS

The labour union The Confederation of Health Service Employees (COHSE) carried out a survey in 1991. They received 140 replies to a questionnaire published in the union journal.

3.3.2   RESULTS

A great majority of the respondents reported sexual harassment; 98 women and 16 men. Of the respondents 86% stated that harassment took the form of unwanted suggestive looks or remarks, 67% had been subjected to unwanted pressure for dates and 16% to pressure for sexual favours. In addition, some people had been locked in a room with the harasser, and experienced physical assault and attempted rape.

The survey showed that men also suffer harassment, but it was a qualitatively different experience from that of women. Many of the women's responses were accompanied by detailed comments about their experiences, revealing the pain and suffering caused by harassment. The effects of sexual harassment can be more devastating and longer lasting for women than for men.

Student nurses seemed to face much more harassment than anyone else in the health service, and they all feared that reporting incidents could affect their assessment and therefore their prospects for qualification. Complaints were mainly against senior staff and doctors. Many complaints were also against members of the public.

The effects of harassment were the following: adverse effect on emotional well-being (86%); adverse effect on their feelings towards work (59%); adverse effect on their relationships with family, partners or friends (39%); deterioration in the quality of their work (33%); adverse effect on their physical health (20%).

More than a third of the women did not report the incident, over half had reported the incidents, most of these did so verbally and informally. Of those who did report the incidents over half felt that they had been dealt with appropriately.

3.4   *Lesbians and gay men*

3.4.1   DEFINITION AND METHODS

The lobbying group Stonewall did a survey about discrimination and sexual harassment against lesbians and gay men in the workplace (1993). They drew up a questionnaire addressing experiences with discrimination and harassment, equal opportunities policies, and concealment of sexuality at work. Questions were also asked about age, sex, job, income to provide a social profile of the respondents. Respondents were invited to 'tell their story' by attaching written accounts of the problems they had faced.

To reach as many sections of the community as possible the researchers wanted to circulate the questionnaire very widely. A total of 20,000 copies of the questionnaire were distributed by way of mailing lists held by gay businesses and social groups. Nearly 2000 completed questionnaires were received, a response rate of 10%. The questions asked about harassment were: have you ever been harassed at work because you were known or suspected to be lesbian or gay?; If you have been harassed at work, please indicate the form this harassment took?

3.4.2   RESULTS

The researchers found that 48% had experienced some general form of harassment at work. Of the 881 who had suffered harassment, 79% had experienced jokes or teasing, 51% had been subjected to homophobic abuse and 41% to aggressive questioning. Sexual harassment was not asked about in particular, but the respondents reported their experiences in the category 'other': 20 persons described experiences of sexual harassment. In most cases this was from men, both lesbians and gay men were sexually harassed by men.

All in all, 46% of the respondents were covered by an equal opportunities policy which included sexual orientation; in the private sector this was 14%, in the public sector 58% and in the voluntary sector 76%. It appeared that respondents whose employers had an equal opportunities policy including sexual orientation were less likely to conceal their sexuality at work. This suggests that a good policy helps to make it easier for lesbians and gay men to come out at work. Alternatively, it could be possible that in a more accepting environment it is easier to lobby for inclusion in the equal opportunities policy.

4   Policy measures

4.1   Definition and method

Research into sexual harassment as seen through the eyes of management was conducted by Davidson and Earnshaw (1991). They sent a questionnaire to the Personnel Directors of 500 organisations, a sample of The Times 1000 (a rank order of UK organisations). The response rate was 22%. The incidence of sexual harassment was measured by the number of complaints made.

4.2   Results

The questionnaire was divided into five main sections. The first section concerned knowledge about the legal responsibilities of the employer; 74% of the personnel managers were aware that as employers they may be liable for acts of sexual harassment perpetrated by their employees.

The second section concerned attitudes towards sexual harassment. About 65% of the respondents regarded sexual harassment as a serious management issue. All personnel directors regarded unwanted physical contact and demands for sexual favours in return for promotion as sexual harassment. There was less agreement about jokes with sexual connotations and pin-up calendars; about 40% is of the opinion that this amounts to sexual harassment. A majority of the personnel directors were in favour of certain preventive measures and support systems, such as publicity given to legal and other remedies currently available to victims of sexual harassment (86%); measures to promote awareness of the problem of harassment (80%); support given to women's organisations and others providing skilled assistance to victims of sexual harassment. Only 30% was in favour of stronger legislation.

The third section was about the incidence of harassment in their organisation. The number of complaints of harassment was very low (total of 41 incidents), with 65% of respondents reporting no incidents at all during the past year. Furthermore, not one of these complaints of sexual harassment had led to a Tribunal Hearing, even though 71% of Personnel directors believed the complaints were well founded. On the whole, the respondents believed that the problem was underreported, whereas 65% believed that between 70 and 100% of sexual harassment incidents were never reported.

The fourth section concerned the methods of dealing with the complaints and the harasser. A majority of the respondents maintained that complaints of sexual harassment were treated seriously and sympathetically and as a disciplinary offence which is dealt with under normal grievance procedures: 63% had no specific procedure to deal with complaints of sexual harassment or a specific person to receive complaints. The most common punishment for someone found guilty of harassment was either an official or unofficial warning. The next most likely outcome was no action whatsoever. Furthermore, the victim of sexual harassment had a greater likelihood of being relocated as compared with the harasser.

The last section concerned preventive measures. About 90% of the Personnel Directors had not issued a policy statement of any kind regarding the management's attitude towards sexual harassment. When asked whether procedures for dealing with sexual harassment were included in the grievance and disciplinary procedures, 32% replied in the affirmative.

4.3 Industrial Relations Services

4.3.1 DEFINITION AND METHOD

Research into the evaluation of policies was carried out by the Industrial Relations Service in 1996. In this study 65 public and private sector organisations were asked about their sexual harassment policies. In the survey the following subjects were dealt with: incidence of complaints, incidence of employers with a sexual harassment policy, and the kind of policy measures implemented.

4.3.2 RESULTS

Sexual harassment is a common problem right across the working population: 54% of organisations said that cases of sexual harassment had been reported among their employees during the past year.

Of the surveyed organisations, 72% had a sexual harassment policy. In 1992 only 33% of employers said they operated an explicit policy and 38% reported they had no policy but were considering introducing one. So, in this 1996 report over twice as many employers have a sexual harassment policy. The public sector as compared to the private sector more often has a policy: 86% of the public sector as opposed to 65% of the private sector. These figures suggest that more and more employers have recognised the importance of providing explicit procedures for dealing with complaints.

The survey examined the reasons why employers introduced sexual harassment policies. The vast majority of employers with sexual harassment policies (95%) said that ensuring equal opportunities was one of the main reasons for introducing a policy. The next most important reasons were to avoid legal and potential costs such as increased absenteeism, higher sickness levels and lower productivity, reported by two thirds of organisations with policies. Just under the fifth of respondents (18%) said they had introduced policies in response to EC developments.

One of the prerequisites for a successful policy is communicating the policy to all employees, in order to raise awareness of the issue and the company's procedures for tackling the problem. The researchers state that regular publicity and discussion of the subject will also serve to remove misconceptions many managers and employees have about sexual harassment and enable more people to raise the issue without fear of embarrassment. It appears that more than 90% of respondents have taken steps to publicise their sexual harassment policy: publication of the policy in staff manuals, company handbooks, issuing copies of the policy to all employees, distribution of leaflets, or the display of poster and notices.

Furthermore, just over half of the employers with policies provide training for staff expected to deal with complaints of sexual harassment. Training programmes vary according to whether an employee acts as a first-line recipient of complaints or whether they are responsible for investigating and determining the complaints' validity.

Cases were reported among all sizes of organisation and in firms where women represented either the majority or the minority of the total workforce. An obstacle to the reporting of harassment complaints is that the number of complaints appears to be linked to the existence of sexual harassment policies: organisations with a policy have a higher number of complaints, suggesting that harassed persons are more willing to come forward in organisations that adopt specific procedures for resolving sexual harassment complaints.

A vast majority of complaints of sexual harassment (70%) were upheld following an internal investigation. Furthermore, a significant number of organisations failed to provide any information about the outcomes of complaints and one can safely assume that a significant proportion of these would have been upheld. The most common actions taken were formal warnings or disciplinary action against the harasser reported by 50% of the employers. The next most common were informal warnings to the harasser (34%) and the transfer of the harasser (32%). In cases where complaints of sexual harassment were not upheld, just over half of the employers said that no further action was taken. Where employers took action, the most common measure was an informal warning to the employee making the accusations, followed by dismissal of the employee who made the accusations.

Employers were asked what channels would be available to employees to forward a complaint of sexual harassment. In the vast majority of cases where no policy existed a victim of sexual harassment is expected to lodge a complaint through the organisation's formal grievance procedure, and the line manager is the person employees are expected to approach in the first instance. A limitation of a regular grievance procedure is the embarrassment the women involved feel when raising a complaint with their line manager (usually a man) and the fear some women have of not being taken seriously may dissuade them from pursuing a complaint. Moreover, the immediate supervisor is often the accused harasser and in these cases it is highly unlikely that the victim will pursue a

complaint through this channel. Consequently, procedures need to provide for alternative channels of complaints.

In organisations with sexual harassment policies, around 70% has a formal procedure relating specifically to sexual harassment. Half of employers with explicit sexual harassment policies reported that complainants could approach either their line manager or a personnel/human resource manager. In some cases an equal opportunity officer, a harassment officer, or a counsellor were potential contacts.

In general, senior management levels have the ultimate responsibility for deciding whether a complaint of sexual harassment is valid. In some organisations a investigatory panel or committee has the final say over the validity of a complaint. All the employers with sexual harassment policies reported that written notes would be taken at all stages of any complaint. Around 70% of the surveyed organisations said they set out guidelines on how quickly any complaint should be investigated. Some employers prefer to follow a clear time period, while others stress the need for enquiries to be dealt with as quickly as possible.

Monitoring and review procedures were operated by half of the organisations with a policy. Mostly, this is a system where all cases of sexual harassment are recorded centrally by the organisation's personnel human resources or equal opportunities department. Also 16% of the companies said that attempts had been made to measure the extent of sexual harassment in their organisation. The most common method for gathering this information were confidential staff surveys.

The following measures were recommended by the Equal Opportunities Commission and leading commentator Michael Rubenstein:

* Policy statement: the policy statement should expressly prohibit sexual harassment; take the form of either a separate part of a general equal opportunities policy or a written policy statement dealing specifically with sexual harassment; state that employees have the right to be treated with dignity and respect; define what is unacceptable behaviour, appropriate disciplinary action for those found guilty, provide details of the procedure to be followed by harassed employees.

* Complaints procedure: the procedure should give employees the confidence that their allegations will be taken serious; complaints should be dealt with promptly, and there should be a possibility for informal procedures.

* Confidential counsellor: employees should be able to seek confidential advice on their case. Employers should consider the appointment of designated counsellors to assist complainants.

Furthermore, the IRS researchers recommend that a successful policy should involve the following 3 components: communicating the policy to the whole workforce; training staff and managers involved in upholding the policy; and setting up monitoring and review procedures to help develop and improve the policy.

References

Alfred Marks Bureau (1991), *Sexual harassment in the Office. Report 1: A quantitative report on client attitudes and experiences. Report 2: A quantitative report on employee attitudes and experiences,* Richmond-upon-Thames: Adsearch.

Anderson, R., J. Brown, and E. Campbell (1993), Police research group, Home Office, *Aspects of sex discrimination within the police service in England and Wales,* Hampshire Constabulary.

Confederation on Health Service Employees (COHSE) (1991), *An abuse of power: sexual harassment in the NHS.* Banstead, Surrey: COHSE.

Davidson, M.J., S. Earnshaw (1991), Policies, Practices and attitudes towards sexual harassment in UK organisations, *Women in Management Review and Abstracts* 6, 15-21.

Her Majesty's Inspectorate of Constabulary (1993), *Equal opportunities in the police service.* London: Her Majesty's Inspectorate of Constabulary.

Industrial Relations Services (1996), Sexual harassment at work 1: incidence and outcomes. In: *IRS employment trends,* September 1996, London, 4-10.

Industrial Relations Services (1996), Sexual harassment at work 2: developing policies and procedures. In: *IRS employment trends,* October 1996, London, 7-10.

Industrial Relations Services (1996), Sexual harassment at work 3: policy developing policies and procedures. In: *IRS employment trends,* December 1996, London, 7-11.

Industrial Society (1993), *No offence? Sexual harassment, how it happens and how to beat it.* London: Industrial Society.

Labour Research Department (1987), Sexual harassment at work. In: *Bargaining Report,* December 1987, 4-11.

Phillips, C.M., J.E. Stockdale and L.M. Joeman (1989), *The risk in going to work.* London School of Economics & Political Science, commissioned by the Suzy Lamplugh Trust, funded by Reed Employment.

Comments on the Dutch Study

The study carried out by the Dutch experts aimed at gathering the information available on the issue in 11 countries (Austria, Belgium, Denmark, Finland, Germany, Ireland, Luxembourg, the Netherlands, Norway, Sweden and the United Kingdom). It presents an overview of all research projects conducted in those states between 1987 and 1997, i.e. 74 surveys and qualitative studies.

The study is divided into two parts. In the first part, the researchers try to draw conclusions from the overview made, as regards in particular the types of sexual harassment, the profiles of harassers and harassed employees, the costs and consequences of sexual harassment. On that basis, they then suggest explanations of sexual harassment and examine the policies carried out at national level to combat sexual harassment. The second part is devoted to an analysis, country by country, of the surveys and studies conducted during the last ten years.

A. Necessary keys to interpret the study

1.Some preliminary statistical remarks about the studies

It is to be noted from the outset that the number of surveys and studies conducted considerably varies from one country to another : from 1 in the last 10 years in Luxembourg to 14 during the same period in Sweden. Is also to be noticed that nearly 90% of these studies were conducted at the branch level and that several of them were restricted to one single occupation or profession (police, secretaries, local government). Save in Belgium and Finland, there was only one national survey made in each country. As regards the response rates to the surveys and studies, the average was between 45% and 60% (extremes 10% and 100%).

2.How to measure sexual harassment and its influence on the results

The Dutch experts indicate that most studies measured sexual harassment by asking respondents about their experience with actual behaviour. However, they note that a complicating factor when measuring sexual harassment is that perception of what behaviour constitutes sexual harassment differs greatly among respondents.

* In fact, almost 50% of the studies asked respondents about "unwanted actual behaviour" without mentioning sexual harassment. Questions are thus, for example, phrased as follows : "Have you in your working life experienced any of the following unwanted behaviour with a sexual connotation: repeated unwanted remarks about appearance, body, clothes, or private life, or rape or attempted rape"

* A very small group of studies inquired about actual behaviour and then about the respondents' perception of sexual harassment ("Does the behaviour experienced constitute sexual harassment according to the respondent" ?).

* A third category of studies (almost 25 %) first asked about sexual harassment. The next question concerned the kinds of behaviour the harassment consisted of, ranging from sexual jokes or unsolicited physical contact to rape.

* A final category (almost 25%) exclusively asked about experiences with sexual harassment without mentioning actual behaviour. Questions are thus, for example, phrased as follows : "May I ask you whether you have ever been exposed to sexual harassment in the workplace yourself" ?

* *A preliminary conclusion* : The absence of an universal method to measure sexual harassment makes it difficult to interpret correctly the results of the surveys and studies. But it cannot be ignored that this absence merely reflects the varying perceptions of the harassed employees of what constitutes sexual harassment.

3.The problem of the definition
- The Community definition of sexual harassment
The Commission Recommendation (92/131) gives a comprehensive definition of sexual harassment. It includes unwanted conduct of a sexual nature or other conduct based on sex affecting the dignity of women and men at work. The EC definition includes three conditions:
(a) unwanted, improper or offensive behaviour
(b) refusal or acceptance of behaviour influences decisions concerning a job, and/or
(c) the behaviour creates a working climate that is intimidating, hostile or humiliating for the person.

- The definition used in the studies
The Dutch researchers found that much research only included some of these conditions. For instance, the (b) condition appears in 50 % of the studies. The (a) condition is the one most frequently used, although the definition in the questions only mentioned the word "unwanted", and did not cite the two other words ("improper" - "offensive").

B. About sexual harassment

1.Its incidence and frequency

Although the results vary depending on definition and methodology, sexual harassment appears to occur in virtually all workplaces to a varying degree. In general, the studies found that approximately 30% to 50% of women, and 10% of men have experienced some form of sexual harassment.

According to the experts, the divergence in the degree of occurrence of sexual harassment can be linked to the way questions are asked, the representative nature of the research, the fact that it was a national or a branch study.

- Incidence of sexual harassment of women
Highest rates (70%-90%) were generally found in national surveys and where a comprehensive definition of sexual harassment was used, i.e. including, for example, sexist behaviour in the definition. Medium occurrence rates (25%-60%) generally concern branch studies, while low occurrence rates (2%-25%), which were found in a couple of national surveys and some of the branch studies, can be attributed to the small

number of questions concerning sexual harassment and the length of time taken into account.

- Sexual harassment of men

It can be noted that only 15 (of the 74) surveys included that issue. The incidence rate varies greatly (1%-30%).

2. Types of sexual harassment

Three categories of sexual harassment can be identified: verbal, non verbal and physical. The most common one is the verbal type (i.e. verbal conduct such as remarks about figure/look, jokes and verbal sexual advances) and the most frequently experienced (around 60%) seems to be the "sexual joke".

Within the non verbal forms, "staring and whistling" is the most frequently reported form (almost 60%).

Within the physical forms, the most commonly experienced form of sexual harassment is "unsolicited physical contact, touching", although big differences in the incidence are to be noted among Member States. High percentages (between 55% and 90%) were found in Austria, Denmark, Germany, the Netherlands and Sweden, while low percentages were found in Finland (7%) and in the UK (20%). The most severe form, "sexual assault/rape" is reported by 1% to 6% of female employees.

A fourth category (called "quid pro quo harassment", i.e. threats of disadvantage (or advantage) if sexual involvement is refused (accepted)) was identified by three national surveys (Austria, Germany, the Netherlands) and experienced by 3% to 16% of female employees.

3. Responses of sexually harassed employees

Experts identified four types of responses :
* non-intervention responses. The person acts as if nothing happened
* personal responses. The harassed employee avoids the places where harassment is possible, for instance
* informal responses. The person seeks the assistance of friends
* formal responses. The person seeks the aid of professionals

Most of the harassed employees respond in several ways. The non interventionist response is used by around 40% persons (fear of negative consequences, idea that a complaint would not be taken seriously), although the rate is lower in branch studies. The personal response is used by 18% to 73% persons (highest rates in branch studies). The informal response is used by 33% to 75% persons. The formal response is the less used one (average 5% to 9%). The reason given was generally a lack of confidence in a counsellor or the will to solve the problem personally or with the help of friends. Surveys also indicated that filing a complaint was the most successful response in some Member States but not in others.

It is also to be noted that surveys showed that harassed employees do not necessarily feel satisfied by the way they respond to sexual harassment and that they would like to react more openly and more actively.

C. About the harassers and the harassed employees

1. About the harassers

In general men are the perpetrators of sexual harassment. They are mostly colleagues (on average 50%) or supervisors (on average 30%). Patients and clients were found to be the harassers in 15% of the harassment incidents. This rate is higher in branches where employees have more frequent contacts with them (health sector, hairdressers,...). Subordinates were also sometimes found harassers (on average less than 5%).

Only two surveys collected data on harassers of male employees. They tend to indicate that in this situation the harasser is younger than the harassed, is more frequently of the same sex and more likely on the same hierarchical level.

2. About the harassed employees:

   -personal characteristics. Overwhelmingly women. Characteristics influencing the likelihood of harassment are age (between 20-40) and marital status (single or divorced). Studies also showed that women with a lower level of education are more exposed to sexual harassment.

   - Job related characteristics. The type of job exercised is influential too. The incidence of sexual harassment appears to be related to the sex ratio of the occupation. Women in male-dominated jobs are more frequently harassed. Other characteristics were also identified, such as the size of the undertaking (more experiences of sexual harassment in firms employing over 50 people), the sex of the supervisor (sexual harassment is less frequent where the supervisor is a woman), organisational culture (higher incidence where "suggestive remarks" are daily routine or where more permissive norms regarding social-sexual behaviour exist) or the unequal power distribution (fewer experiences of sexual harassment in workplaces characterised by a relatively equal distribution of women and men throughout the hierarchical structure of the workplace and the sex ratio).

D. About the costs and consequences of sexual harassment

Negative consequences of sexual harassment on the well-being of harassed employees are obvious. The lowest rate reported is 46%, but the rate goes up to more than 80% in two surveys.

   - Private consequences.
Are in particular mentioned emotional and psychological consequences, psychosomatic symptoms, interference with private life.

   - Effects on jobs and ability to work.
On average 11% of harassed employees experienced a negative impact on their career (decreased motivation, left their job, took sick leave, were fired,...).

E. Explanations of sexual harassment at work

The main purpose of the 74 surveys conducted between 1987 and 1997 was to document the prevalence of sexual harassment. Less attention has been paid to the explanation of sexual harassment. Some researchers have attempted to interpret their empirical findings in the context of existing theoretical perspectives. However, few theories are empirically grounded.

Major views which have been considered include individual power perspectives (sexual harassment is an abuse of power), organisational power perspectives (sexual harassment is more common where the organisational context permits of facilitates such behaviour: sexualized work environment, sex segregation of jobs,...), "the established and the outsiders", i.e. unequal power relationships between social groups (both groups then commonly believe that the unequal power balance is just and natural), misperception theory (sexual harassment would result from men's misperceptions of women's behaviours and intentions) and the "token theory" (the theory of tokenism refers to discrimination and marginalisation of members of a group in a minority position. It considers that members of any social group will be discriminated against if their group makes up less than 15% of an organisation).

F. About policies

Evaluation studies into sexual harassment policies were carried out in 4 countries (Belgium, the Netherlands, UK and Norway). According to the Dutch experts, although few research projects have been conducted to evaluate the effectiveness of sexual harassment policies, it appears that most policies usually consist of the same components: information activities, such as publicising a policy statement, confidential counsellors and grievance procedures.

1. Information and training activities

The study indicates that a substantial number of companies have taken steps to develop their information policies about sexual harassment (brochures, staff magazines, meetings,...). A policy statement is also often used to inform staff about sexual harassment.

2. Confidential counsellors

The appointment of a confidential counsellor is the method the most commonly used, save in the UK. It appears that confidential counsellors are selected among staff managers or health professionals. Their tasks vary from one country to another. Another difference is the sex of the counsellor. In the Netherlands for example, almost all counsellors are female, while in Belgium a small majority of them are male.

- Problems as regards the person of the counsellor

Many problems are identified as regards facilities granted to confidential counsellors to exercise their role: no specific protection, no extra time for that activity, a lack of training or of competence concerning sexual harassment. Further, the fact that the counsellor is often a manager, i.e. someone linked to the employer, has a deterrent effect on contacting him. Another reason for not contacting the counsellor can be the fact that he is relatively unknown or is not trusted.

3. Grievance procedures

This is another measure frequently used by companies (up to 70% of the UK organisations surveyed). However where a grievance commission exists, the same problem of independence arises as the staff manager is almost always one of its members.

According to several studies, between 20% and 50% of sexual harassment cases give rise to a complaint. It also seems that the rate of complaints is higher where companies have developed a specific policy to combat sexual harassment. The main problem with the grievance procedure is the sanctions, or in fact the absence of sanctions, taken. The most common punishment seems to be an official or even an unofficial warning.

Different studies have thus shown that there is a widespread feeling among harassed employees that employers are not effective in dealing with sexual harassment.

G. Some conclusions

Some obvious conclusions can be drawn from the studies made during the last ten years in these 11 countries.

* Sexual harassment is a plague affecting all countries and all kinds of companies.

* Its measurement is however very difficult. A comparison of the studies show that the methods used in the surveys and studies are different and that the results are more or less dependent on the methods used and the questions asked. It is even more so if one keeps in mind that the percentage brackets are generally very wide.

* Further, there is no universal perception of what constitutes sexual harassment, which makes it even more difficult to interpret the results. In this respect it should be noted that the EC definition is not necessarily used in the surveys or studies.

* Information policy in companies in order to prevent sexual harassment has been developed in the last ten years.

* Conversely means to combat sexual harassment (confidential counsellors, grievance procedures) are still rather ineffective as punishment is in general limited to a warning of the harasser.

SPANISH STUDY

SEXUAL HARASSMENT AT WORK IN FIVE SOUTHERN EUROPEAN COUNTRIES

February 1998

Presentation

This document was complied by a tram of six people who were responsible for the following countries:

* Spain: Maria-Carme Alemay (CEDIS)
* France: Juliette Boyer (AVFT) and Nathalie Cattaneo (GEDIOSST)
* Greece: Catherine Paparriga-Costavara
* Italy: Myriam Bergamaschi (Centro Richerche G. Directive Vittorio)
* Portugal: Maria Mauela Campino (CITE)

The national studies were co-ordinated by Maria-Carme Alemany, who drew up the summary report.

Introduction

This study on sexual harassment at work in Southern Europe was carried out at the request of DG V.

It was based on studies conducted in Spain, France, Greece, Italy and Portugal, covering the following points:

a) study of the legal situation with regard to sexual harassment at work based on existing legislation in each country;

b) analysis of the scale of the problem on the basis of existing figures;

c) in-depth examination of the nature of the problem on the basis of existing qualitative research;

d) analysis of industrial relations strategies to cope with the problem;

e) study of action which the European Commission could take to deal with the problem.

The surveys carried out in the five countries show that sexual harassment at work is not something that occurs sporadically but is a fairly widespread and common problem. However, most of them date back to the end of the 80s or the beginning of the 90s and it would be of interest to determine what the situation is today, as we now know more about sexual harassment than before. In France too legislation has been in force since 1992 and it would be interesting to find out what impact it has made.

The term "sexual harassment" also leads to confusion because when women are asked whether they have been harassed, the ones who say they have refer only to the worst types of harassment, i.e. tend to interpret this concept restrictively, whereas if they are presented with a list of unwelcome types of male behaviour, the percentage of women who count as victims of some form of sexual harassment increases very significantly. This shows that, in a sexist environment, women tend to put up with unwelcome male behaviour without regarding it as harassment and do not dare come out against it openly because that are afraid of how people around them will react, of ruining the atmosphere at work, etc. The studies also show that sexual harassment has grave repercussions on the victims' working and personal lives and on their health.

Although women now complain more than in the past, the professional and personal risk which complaints involve lead many women to keep quiet, which means that there are still many areas where the reality of sexual harassment at work is obscured.

The European Commission's policy has had the merit of bringing the problem out into the open in the five countries of Southern Europe and leading some countries to legislate on this matter. It has also prompted a considerable amount of debate which helped to alert public opinion and industrial relations players to the issue. Nevertheless, the total absence of preventive measures shows that there is still a long way to go.

The fact is, however, that the roots of sexual harassment at work lie in the fact that women are not on an equal footing with men at work and in society in general. In other words, women are the main victims of this form of pressure because they are at the lower end of the hierarchy. What is needed is for equal opportunities programmes to be implemented effectively in enterprises. Although occupational equality exists *de jure,* it is virtually a dead letter.

What is more, the employment crisis and increased job insecurity, which mainly affects women, are liable to aggravate situations where there is an abuse of power and, hence, sexual harassment.

Given this situation and the large number of social factors which mask sexual harassment and legitimate complaints about it, the proposals addressed to the European Commission are mainly intended to promote a policy based on **prevention**, since this is better than a cure. However, preventive measures will be ineffective unless they are accompanied by a stronger policy for equal opportunities and for creating and consolidating measures against job insecurity.

1. THE DEBATE ON SEXUAL HARASSMENT

Sexual harassment at work started becoming an issue towards the end of the 80s, especially in France and Italy; in the other countries it was not yet really on the agenda. Nevertheless, that does not mean that the scale of the phenomenon was any smaller, merely that there was very little interest in, information about and awareness of it.

In France and Italy, the role of the information media in publishing "exemplary cases" and explaining what the situation was in the Community was the deciding factor in launching the debate on this issue.

However, the nature of the debate conducted in the two countries differs considerably. Whilst in France it focuses on the need for legislation, in Italy it has taken on a more ideological note and concentrates more on research into the causes of the phenomenon and political discussion of the concept used by European documents.

French feminist associations were the first to call for legal sanctions against sexual harassment in 1990, putting forward a definition inspired by European Community texts and North American ideas. As a result, the phenomenon quickly moved on to the parliamentary agenda, which steered the debate along more traditional political lines.

Surveys carried out whilst the debate was going on were also confined to establishing the impact or scale of the phenomenon, without any attempt being made to reveal its true complexity. At that time too, the women's movement in France was more of a hostage to the parliamentary political system than in Italy.

In 1990, the AVFT presented a penal code to combat sexual harassment to the Secretary of State for Women's and Consumers Rights, the Vice-President of the Committee for Social Affairs at the national parliament and to some twenty members of parliament. The code covered all types of sexual harassment, irrespective of the hierarchical relationship, place and circumstances.

The code, which was distributed widely, was amended and incorporated in a draft law by the Secretary of State for Women's and Consumers Rights, elicited proposals mainly from the socialist and communist parliamentary groups and was supported by the CGT and CFDT trade unions.

In 1991, the *Union des Femmes Françaises* (Union of French Women) proposed a penal code for any sexual behaviour constituting an affront to a person's dignity exclusively in working relations and irrespectively of the hierarchical relationship, which was incorporated in a proposal for an anti-sexist law.

These two texts described all the types of behaviour which ought to be banned which was completely different from the approach adopted by the women's movement in Italy where the debate focused more on women's policy, as we will see later.

During the parliamentary debates in France, there was a constant fear that a law similar to that in the United States would be adopted. Most parliamentarians found that the American law reflected the puritan moral code in the United States, where advances could not be made without risking a complaint of sexual harassment, and that there was no place for seduction *à la française* in this model. The American concept of "environmental" sexual harassment, i.e. harassment by colleagues not just by a superior, was criticised as being too wide, imprecise and open to abuse. It was also criticised for leading to different interpretations of behaviour, depending on the victim's personality, since it was up to the victim to decide subjectively what was offensive and what was not. It was also pointed out that spurious complaints might be caused by somebody misinterpreting the "harasser's" intentions when the person in question was only joking or being friendly.

The spectre of the legal proceedings instituted in the United States, portrayed as an abuse of the system by the media, thus had an impact on the debate in France and contributed to a definition ultimately being adopted which was based solely on abuse of authority with a view to obtaining sexual favours.

A consensus was thus reached on the need to sanction sexual blackmail by a person using the power associated with his or her position. As a result, "environmental" sexual harassment was excluded from the scope of the law as it was considered liable to constitute a ban on seduction. Unwelcome and unpleasant sexual behaviour between colleagues was therefore not defined as forming an integral part of sexual harassment, as the victims were thought to be free to defend themselves since there was no difference in power or dependent relationship involved.

The parliamentary debates also emphasised that sexual harassment was not confined to one sex and thus concluded that sexual harassment could not be defined as a form of sexual discrimination. Although the victims were found to be mainly female and the harassers mainly male, parliament refused to regard sexual harassment as violence against women and as an expression of discrimination.

In actual fact, the idea was less to avoid abuses of the system when the law was invoked than to deny the social relationship between the sexes and to reach a consensus for safeguarding the way men viewed seduction.

In Italy, however, the government's insensitivity to the problem – it had not even provided the European Union with statistics or data on the scale of the phenomenon - brought greater involvement in the debate for the women's movement, which gave it a completely different tone.

The search for "exemplary cases" first conducted by the communication media claimed to be intended to make up for the lack of knowledge and analysis on the subject as it was so new. This led women journalists and programme presenters to ask about the deeper motives for the spread of harassment and women's tendency to keep quiet about their traumatic experiences. Many of them wondered whether the problem of sexual harassment should not be placed in the historical context of the only very recent emancipation of women in Italy. For them "finding work was like winning the lottery" and being tolerant towards "male gallantry", as long as it was not disagreeable or vulgar, seemed to be one of the rules of the game (Crispino, 1986).

Other women journalists, who were also looking at the problem from the point of view of the labour market and particularly the recent integration of women at work, explained the phenomenon by comparing the situation in the past – when women who worked were considered as having lax morals – with the current situation - where a woman was no longer criticised (at least not openly) for abandoning her role of spouse and mother - which unleashed a symbolic struggle to reappraise the value of individuals and led men, who felt threatened, to fall back on and even to reinforce the old stereotypes (Beccalli, 1991).

Finally, others focused on the fact that women were discriminated against at work. Here, proper recognition for work done by women was said to be needed to combat inequality between the sexes and prevent women having to cope with blackmail linked with sexual harassment, and also to form healthier working and legal relations in a wider perspective (Galli, 1990).

It was in this context that the need for a law to protect against sexual harassment emerged. Three different positions vis-à-vis the law could be identified:

* there were those who thought a law was vital as a means of protecting women;
* those who, on the basis of the American experience, feared that a law would trigger a sort of war between the sexes, and;
* those who regarded it as more important to see how women could cope with the conflict with men without being obliged to play the part of victims.

The women's movement expressed its opposition to a law to protect against harassment using similar arguments to those put forward in the debate on the law against rape.

Their reservations were not very different from those expressed on the advisability of promoting legislation on sexual harassment based on the definition in the Michael Rubenstein report. According to this report, sexual harassment is verbal or physical sexual behaviour which the perpetrator knows (or ought to know) is an affront to the victim, i.e. is unwelcome.

This definition (male intentions faced with a refusal expressed by a woman) excludes one fundamental aspect of harassment: the woman's subjective perception of it.

The assumption that behaviour can be identified as sexual harassment only when it is defined as such by a woman turns the current legal thinking on its heads and focuses attention on the unquestioned legitimacy of the female experience, irrespective of men's stated intentions.

In this sense the results of the research show clearly that the harasser's and the victim's perceptions of harassment always differ. The fact is that men perceive, justify and present such behaviour completely differently from women. "As a result, what men regard as legitimate, natural, inevitable and even agreeable for a woman, women feel to be illegitimate, arbitrary, displeasing and an affront to their freedom and dignity" (Ventimiglia, 1991).

The debate surrounding the definition of sexual harassment proposed in the Rubenstein report showed not only that it was necessary to find a more precise definition but above all that the definition of harassment was crucial in identifying legal solutions and standards to be adopted to cope with this problem. It was then obvious that more in-depth knowledge of and information on the subjective perception of sexual harassment was needed in order to find ways of solving the problem by legislation.

This was why the establishment of gendered legislation intended to promote women's self-determination occupied the stage from the beginning of the 90s, lawyers, trade unionists and politicians being involved as well as researchers.

The definition drafted by the European Commission in 1991 (Recommendation 92/131 to which the Code of Practice is appended) identifies sexual harassment as "unwanted conduct of a sexual nature, or other conduct based on sex affecting the dignity of women and men at work. This can include unwelcome physical, verbal or non-verbal conduct.". This definition gave rise to various proposals for laws and helped to standardise public administration collective agreements. It also influenced the law on positive action of 1991 which covers discrimination.

The debate which took place in Italy after the EC Recommendation was not confined to legal sanctions and focused mainly on the definition of sexual harassment.

The definition in the European Recommendation gave rise to differing views from legal specialists.

Some regarded it as a major step forward in terms of the guidance it gave to the courts, since it placed the emphasis on the "undesirability" of the conduct and made no attempt to give an objective typology because it could be interpreted differently by the person it is aimed at.

However, other specialists said that the "undesirability" aspect did not take due account of the complexity of the relations between the sexes, since there were cases where, despite the fact that the victim did not object to certain actions, it could be shown that she was not consenting to them. Others too thought it was non-specific and vague and did not constitute a clear legal definition, which was contrary to the principle of the certainty of law.

In a proposal for a law presented by a group of women belonging to the *Codi* (helpline for the protection of harassed women), sexual harassment was defined as "unwelcome behaviour referring objectively to the sexual sphere". This definition incorporated both the subjective criterion and an objective appraisal of the unwelcome conduct (Ianiello, 1994).

However, the law approved by the Senate on 26 September 1995 incorporated the definition in the European Commission's Recommendation. The decision therefore went in favour of the woman's perception in determining whether behaviour was disagreeable or note.

From the 90s onwards in Italy, the discussion on the definition of sexual harassment and on whether a law was needed to combat it showed no signs of abating. Its intensity was such that the legislative procedure was blocked. At the beginning of the 90s, members of parliament said that there were profound differences of opinion, not only between the various political parties but also in the ranks of the progressives. The debate mainly centred on adoption of the subjective viewpoint because, even though it could well be a reliable means of plotting a course for women's policy, it might also prove inadequate as a yardstick or standard in judicial proceedings. The fear was that in practice –in order to eliminate potential conflicts of legal interpretation – "correct" behaviour, i.e. rules on normal sexual behaviour, would have to be defined precisely. Since such a definition would be governed by the authority "which historically had patriarchal leanings", the law would end up backfiring on women (Zuffa, 1993).

Another key issue was the unlawfulness of sexual harassment. There were many doubts and conflicting opinions about including sexual harassment in criminal law but they did not differ greatly from those expressed with regard to the law against sexual violence. The main reservation hinged on the effectiveness of prosecution, since legislation alone could not resolve a problem of such a scale and with such complex origins. This point of view was shared fairly widely by women, even from a variety of political and cultural factions.

Other specialists pointed out, however, that it was incorrect to penalise and punish interpersonal communication and feared that sexuality would become the target of increasingly widespread condemnation. They were particularly reluctant to see the complexity of communication between the sexes subject to criminal law.

Another issue was whether punitive legislation helped to assert women's rights to freedom. Despite negative reactions and doubts as to the advisability of a law on sexual harassment, those who participated in drawing up the proposal for a law did not think that it could be seen as infringing the principle of self-determination for women, as it guaranteed protection for it. Their argument was that offering protection – even under criminal law – was not a sign of weakness but, on the contrary, could make women aware of their rights and empower them instead of being a disincentive to standing up for them (Ianello, 1994).

Others, without denying the importance of a law on sexual harassment at work, pointed out that an effective technical means of defending women's rights when they have been infringed was vital. In civil law, a change in women's favour has, in fact, already been seen, namely the reversal of the burden of proof, which can be applied to sexual harassment where it is regarded as an instance of discrimination (Gandus, Hoesch, 1993).

European policy on sexual harassment has therefore definitely had a considerable impact in France and Italy because it has alerted not only public opinion but also industrial relations strategists to the problem.

Two different approaches emerged and subsequently informed the activities of the feminist and trade union movements:

> In France, the main objective was to have a law enacted. The consensus required for promulgating it meant that it was flawed, from the point of view of the women's movement at least, but this legal half-victory stifled the debate, prevented the matter from being examined in more detail and made practical action more difficult.

> In Italy, however, the legal framework was not changed but the in-depth discussion which took place within the women's movement led to a greater awareness of the problem amongst all those involved in industrial relations, as we will see later.

2.   THE SCALE OF THE PROBLEM

2.1   Overview

The European Parliament's resolutions in 1984, acknowledging that sexual harassment was a major problem which was an affront "to women's dignity and rights", and the Council of Ministers' request to the Commission to undertake research into this matter led some countries such as Spain to conduct surveys to assess the situation.

Others were induced to carry out studies on this matter by the results of the Rubenstein report published by the European Union in 1987.   Hence, towards the end of the 80s, a whole set of surveys was conducted more or less simultaneously for the first time in the various countries of southern Europe.

Henceforth, all the countries had information from surveys or samples which supplied them with information on the scale of the problem, although only two countries (France and Portugal) carried out nation-wide research.

However, no international comparison of the surveys conducted in the countries could be made, as the methodology used to measure the scale of the problem was not uniform and, for some countries, there were no nation-wide surveys.

The results of the surveys carried out in the five countries of southern Europe show that the percentage of women who claim to have received unwelcome sexual propositions or attentions is between 30 and 84%.

However, this figure falls to between 25 and 45% when women are asked whether they have been harassed and whether sexual advances or propositions have been made to them.

If women are presented with a list of unwelcome sexual behaviour, comments and looks, the percentage of women who say that they have experienced such things goes up to 84% (according to the survey carried out in Spain).

It should be emphasised too that in the surveys with questions on various types of behaviour (comments, looks, invitations, bodily contact, pinching, touching and rape) which ask women to identify those which they **regard as sexual harassment**, we see that all the women interviewed say that direct sexual propositions or bodily contact, touching or sexual assault constitute harassment but fewer classify less crass behaviour (such as unpleasant remarks on women's physical appearance or clothing and unwelcome winks or glances) as such. This shows that social pressures and pervasive sexist attitudes make women play down their experiences and place a restrictive interpretation on sexual harassment.

There are therefore several kinds of unwelcome behaviour which women accept or put up with and regard more or less as part of normal relations between men and women at work. Other more detailed studies show that women say that they feel uncomfortable with certain types of male behaviour but do not dare to say so because they are afraid of how their colleagues might react, of spoiling the atmosphere at work or being called intolerant or even frigid.

These results show that in the countries of southern Europe, sexual harassment at work is not an episodic phenomenon but, on the contrary, is a regular occurrence which women come to see as normal and accept as something which they have to put up with because it is part of being a woman.

Results of the surveys				
Country	Year in which the survey was carried out	Area	Sample	% of women harassed
Spain	1986	Madrid	772 women	84% Not severely 55% Non-verbal
France	1985	National	958 women	36%
Greece	1988	Athens area	1 500 women and men	60%
Italy	1989	Piedmont and Rome	5 500 women	35%
Portugal	1988	National	1 032 women	34.2%

2.2 The initial research work carried out in the various countries

As the methodology used for the surveys differs from one country to another, the results are presented by country in more detail below.

SPAIN

Spain is one of the countries where the least research on sexual harassment has been carried out and there are not even any nation-wide studies.

The only survey in Spain was conducted by the Women's Department of the trade union UGT in Madrid in 1986 and covered the municipality of Madrid only. The number of women surveyed was 772.The occupations chosen for the survey were as follows: cabin crew, administrative work in public service, hotels, journalism, production work in the metallurgical and chemical sectors, and health.

For the purposes of this survey, sexual harassment was taken to mean "any unwelcome sexual behaviour, verbal or non-verbal, or using physical or mental pressure to obtain sexual favours from the person harassed at work".

It incorporated a series of questions on behaviour - subsequently classified depending on the level of sexual harassment - designed to identify the behaviour involved in sexual harassment and to determine the scale of the problem.

Level I – Slight

Questions:

1) *Has any man at work whistled at you suggestively?* Replies in the affirmative, 30%.

2) *Have lewd comments, conversations or stories been addressed to you against your wishes by any man at work?* Replies in the affirmative, 63%.

3) *Has any man at work made unwelcome remarks of a sexual nature to you during working hours?* Replies in the affirmative, 78%.

Taking the three questions together, 84% of women have been exposed to one of these types of behaviour against their wishes.

Level II – Moderate

Questions:

1) *Have you had the feeling that any man at work has undressed you with his eyes?* Replies in the affirmative, 39%.

2) *Have unwelcome sexual gestures been made to you at work?* Replies in the affirmative, 21%.

3) *Has any man at work winked at you suggestively during working hours?* Replies in the affirmative, 33%.

55% of the women replied in the affirmative to at least one of the questions.

Level III – Medium

Questions:

1) *Have you received unwelcome telephone calls or letters about sex from any man at work?* Replies in the affirmative, 4%.

2) *Has any man at work made unwelcome proposals to go for a drink or dinner with a view to having a sexual relationship?* Replies in the affirmative, 25%.

3) *Have you received unwelcome invitations to sex parties from any man at work?* Replies in the affirmative, 6%.

All in all, one in four female workers has suffered from one of these three types of sexual harassment.

Level IV – Severe

Questions:

1) *Has unwelcome physical contact been made in corridors, lifts, offices, etc.?* Replies in the affirmative, 14%.

2) *Have you been the object of physical pursuit by any of the men at work?* Replies in the affirmative, 8%.

3) *Has any man taken advantage of a situation to put his arm around your waist against your wishes?* Replies in the affirmative, 16%.

4) *Has any man at work pinched you against your wishes?* Replies in the affirmative, 6%.

27%, i.e. one in four women, replied to one of these questions in the affirmative.

<u>Level V - Very severe</u>

Question:

1) *Have you been pressured to have sex by any man at work?* Replies in the affirmative, 4%.

The results can be summed up as follows:

Level I	-	Slight 84%	
Level II	-	Moderate	35%
Level III	-	Medium	27%
Level IV	-	Severe 27%	
Level V	-	Very severe	4%

The average profile of the harasser is as follows:

Age:	31 to 45
	Physical appearance: Normal
Level of education:	Similar to the person harassed
Marital status:	Married
Seniority in the company:	Over ten years

Harassers are mainly colleagues (47%) followed by immediate and higher superiors (28%) and, finally, subordinates (24%).

As regards the profile of the victim, divorced, separated or widowed women are those who are harassed the most often and most severely. Harassment also decreases with age. Low-level harassment mainly affects the youngest women (under 20) whilst severe or very severe harassment mainly affects women of between 26 and 30.

The enquiry also shows that physical attraction and frequency of all levels of sexual harassment are directly related. The frequency and intensity of harassment thus increases with physical attraction, 13% of attractive women having been exposed to very severe harassment.

FRANCE

Between 1985 and 1991, four surveys sought to measure the scale of the phenomenon in France.

(1)   In collaboration with the *Liege des Doritos des Femmes* (Women's Rights League), the magazine *Bib* published, in issue No 68 of October 1985, a survey carried out between 19 and 29 July 1985 by the *Institut Quotas* on a representative sample of 958 women who were working or had worked. 36% of the women replied in the affirmative to the question "*Have sexual advances been made to you at your place of work?*". Of these, 66% said that they did not "yield to these advances" and 26% said that "their refusal had consequences".

2)	On 13 April 1988, the *Institut Louis Harris* submitted a report entitled *"Us prime noxious* at work" to the magazine *Maxi,* giving the results of a survey carried out between 7 and 9 April 1988 on a national sample of 313 working women of 18 and over. The question was *"Have any of your superiors made sexual advances to you during work?"*. 9% of the women replied in the affirmative.

3)	In 1990, the trade union CFDT commissioned a survey from the CSA on "The situation of working women in France". This was carried out between 12 and 17 February 1990 on a representative national sample of 804 women aged 18 and over with the following question being put to them *"Since you have been at work have unwelcome sexual advances been made to you?"*. 8% of the women interviewed replied in the affirmative.

4)	On 7 January 1992, the Secretary of State for Women's Rights and Consumer Affairs published a survey carried out by the *Institut Louis Harris* between 9 and 13 December 1991 on 1 300 persons, i.e. a representative sample of 1 000 persons and an individual sample of 300 working women of between 18 and 40. 9% of the women in the sample had "encountered fairly or highly unpleasant situations at work which according to the *Institut Louis Harris* represented a statistic of 19% of working women or women who had worked. Although the individual sample was confined to working women and to a single age group (18 to 40), this survey, which was focused exclusively on sexual harassment and contained a large number of questions, was the first to provide results from a large sample and also signalled a change in the interpretation of sexual harassment. It was also the first to cover a wide range of types of sexual harassment: advances accompanied by blackmail, renewed advances despite a refusal, dubious comments and gestures, an unpleasant working atmosphere, pinning up of pornographic drawings and photos, etc.

*a)	The characteristics of sexual harassment*

12% of the victims reported advances accompanied by blackmail, 63% dubious proposals and gestures, 60% renewed advances despite a refusal and 48% an unpleasant working atmosphere.

*b)	The situation of harassed women*

At the time when they were harassed, the vast majority of the women involved said that they were not:
* 	in a difficult emotional situation:	82%
* 	in a difficult financial situation:	19%
* 	in an insecure employment situation:	77%
* 	in a situation of personal isolation:	80%

which shows that it is not only women in vulnerable situations who are affected.
The age group involved most often was the 25 to 40 group.

*c)	The harassers*

The most frequent harassers were: the boss (28%), customer (26%), a superior (25%), and a colleague (21%).

The vast majority were married and had children. The age group involved most frequently was the 40 to 54 group.

d)   *Professional consequences*

38% of the victims said that harassment had damaged their prospects and in 14% of these cases they were forced to resign or were dismissed. In 19% of the cases, it was the harasser who had suffered the consequences.

e)   *The sectors affected most frequently*

The sectors affected most were: trade and crafts (18% of women in this sector were victims of sexual harassment), industry (17%) and hospitals (14%).

GREECE

A survey was carried out in 1988 by the Women's Rights League in the Greater Athens area on a sample of 1 500 women and men, which makes it the largest one carried out in this country.

The definition of sexual harassment used was as follows: any form of sex-related behaviour (ranging from verbal provocation to sexual violence) which is unwelcome from the women's point of view and which can have consequences on working conditions (promotion, career, working atmosphere, etc.). Such behaviour may be perpetrated by an employer, a superior, a colleague or even a customer. A list of male behaviour was used to measure the level of harassment without it being described as sexual harassment.

The survey showed that 60% of women had been victims of sexual harassment at work. Widows (82%) and divorcees (70%) were the main victims, followed by single women (59.5%) and married women (56%). As regards level of education, 72% of the victims had a low level of education. The sectors most affected were those where men were in the majority and the supervisors were also men.

ITALY

In Italy there are no nation-wide surveys, only ones confined to certain geographical regions or certain occupational categories. But Italy is the country where the most studies have been carried out on this question. The various surveys conducted towards the end of the 80s were promoted by the trade unions. These helped to bring the phenomenon to light and document its spread.

1)   Survey carried out by the trade union FIOM-CGIL in the Piedmont region covering various factories in the metallurgical sector. 2 500 questionnaires were distributed to women in eight production units. The results obtained were as follows: 32% of the women were subject to sexual blackmail or knew of similar cases and 9.9% were victims of sexual harassment. The study carried out in the Piedmont showed that women regarded recruitment and promotion as the most critical times when they were most exposed to sexual blackmail. It also showed that harassment was tolerated by heads of enterprises as a means of control over female workers (Oct, 1990).

2)	Study carried out by the women's co-ordination unit of the CGIL in the central Rome area in sectors where there was a high proportion of female labour (2 000 questionnaires were distributed).

36.7% of the female workers in the area replied to the questionnaire According to the survey, 35% of the women had encountered some form of sexual harassment. The most frequent complaints came from the health sector (60%) and from other ministries (43%) and the women affected mostly were separated women, single women or widows aged between 30 and 40. It is important to point out that 12% of the victims or persons who knew that their colleagues were being harassed made a complaint. On the other hand 14% said that the situation had been to their advantage and had had no negative repercussions.

3)	Survey carried out in 1990 by women in the postal workers department of the CGIL in the Labium area. The aim of this survey was to build up a picture of harassment in this sector. The questionnaire was filled in by 4 887 female workers in central post offices in Rome employing a total of 12 213 women. The results showed that:45% of the women declared that they had been victims of sexual harassment or had immediate knowledge of cases amongst their female colleagues but only 0.5% of the victims lodged a complaint;28% said that they had rejected advances from their superior or colleagues. Of the women who were victims of sexual harassment but did not complain about it, only 0.5% said that the situation was beneficial to them.

4)	Survey carried out by women in the CGIL in Creme in 1990.

This survey was carried out in what were regarded as key sectors of the local economy, i.e. health, metallurgy and the food industry1. 560 questionnaires were distributed and over 50% of the women replied. The results obtained were as follows: 20.1% said that they had been harassed, the youngest women being harassed most severely or frequently. Only 11.8% had lodged a complaint whilst 64.7% had rejected advances but without making a complaint. Of those who did not reject such advances (23.5%), 17.6% said that the situation had been to their advantage. The sector affected most was the metallurgical sector.

In the four previous studies, women were asked for their opinion on complaining about sexual harassment and whether they thought that collective agreements should contain clauses on the problem. The replies obtained in the four surveys were similar:

* between 60 and 70% of women thought that collective agreements should have provisions on sexual harassment and;
* between 54% and 67% thought that a complaint should be made when it occurred.

It should be emphasised that the above results reflect what people think, not what they do; in actual fact, very few complaints are made. We should remember that harassment isolates the victim and that there are many personal factors which come into play, such as the victim's social environment and financial circumstances.

PORTUGAL

The first national survey dates back to 1988 and was conducted on a sample of 1,022 women using a questionnaire at work. The distribution by sector was as follows:

industry 40%, trade 9%, services 24% and public administration 27%. The variables were age and level of education.

The results showed that 34.1%, i.e. one woman in three, had been harassed at least once. For 19.1% of the victims, this was a rare occurrence, for 9.4% not so rare and for 5.6% it happened frequently. 25.5% of the women said that they had been harassed by their colleagues, 13.6% by their superior and 7% by customers or suppliers of the company.

73.9% of the victims said that they had relations of trust with the colleagues who harassed them and in the case of superiors, 49.6% said that the relationship was good. However, when the harasser was a customer or a supplier, 90.3% of the victims said that no relationship of trust existed.

Single women and divorcees were harassed most severely and most frequently. 56.4% of the harassed women said that the situations occurred without witnesses, 31.3% said that they were harassed in the presence of persons of both sexes but other situations were rare, 7.7% being in the presence of other women and 4.6% in the presence of other men.

The survey listed types of behaviour in order to identify what women regarded as sexual harassment. The replies showed sexual harassment to be defined as follows:

* 30.7% identified "unwelcome comments on dress" as harassment,
* 37.1% "unwelcome comments on physical beauty",
* 50% "unwelcome comments on a part of the body",
* 49% "unwelcome glances or men undressing women with their eyes",
* 76.5% "proposals or invitations with ulterior motives",
* 100% "sexual propositions, touching or pinching, bodily contact, lewd gestures and rape".

The results showed that the phenomenon might be on a wider scale than the survey suggested, since almost half of the women did not regard certain types of behaviour which ought to have been included under this heading as harassment.

As we can see, the results vary from one country to another, depending mainly on the questions designed to measure the level of sexual harassment. This is why the surveys in France indicate a level of harassment which is lower than in other countries because the questions are restrictive and cover only sexual advances or propositions or, in other cases, refer only to cases where the harasser is the superior. However, when the behaviour is described in detail without the expression sexual harassment actually being used, and when women are asked to indicate whether they have been subject to such behaviour, the percentage increases very considerably (Spain and Greece).

The results also suggest that the concept of sexual harassment is not clear-cut for the majority of women because they interpret it as being only the worst types of behaviour (physical advances or assault).

For the purposes of an international comparison, therefore, the term sexual harassment should not be used because it has been found to be interpreted restrictively by the majority of women. Instead, the phenomenon should be measured on the basis of a list of practices taking into account the specific situation in each country.

2.3   More detailed studies in the 90s

The 90s mark a new stage in studies in sexual harassment because surveys and samples to establish the scale of the phenomenon were abandoned and research focused on analysing its roots and the consequences of sexual harassment on the victims' working and private lives. Another novel aspect was that men were included in some studies, enabling other aspects of the problem to be tackled for the first time.

These new studies were carried out using various methodologies:
*   methodology of the qualitative type based on interviews or group discussions (Spain);
*   more detailed surveys (Italy);
*   use of statements from victims and specialists on the question (Greece and Italy), or;
*   analysis of the files on women who have made a complaint (France).

The studies of the 90s certainly all provide a more accurate picture of the phenomenon and prompt thought on measures which could be taken but what is missing are studies showing how harassment and attitudes to it are developing. Nor are there any recent data which enable us to assess the results of measures to combat sexual harassment at work, especially in France where legislation introduced in 1992 has not been assessed.

SPAIN

A qualitative study was carried out in Barcelona in 1996. It was commissioned by the *Institut Cattalo de la Dona* (Catalan Women's Institute) of the *Generalist* (regional Catalonian government). The study took the form of discussions in groups of men and women from various economic sectors and occupational groups about how men and women see issues relating to work and sexual harassment.

The work-related topics were integration of women in production work, equal opportunities, promotion for women, men's and women's work and the relationship between men and women at work.

The sexual harassment-related topics were: what was understood by sexual harassment, episodic or daily sexual harassment, the idea of female provocation and men's and women's sexuality.

The main results of the research showed that sexual harassment at work was more frequent than might be imagined and that it was regarded as normal. This meant that instances of sexual harassment at work were not a pathological phenomenon, since they were not exceptional but day-to-day occurrences. This almost invariably prompted the victims to end up by accepting sexual harassment as a normal situation which was part of being a woman.

A figure which inhabited men's imagination - and women's too, particularly if they were poorly educated - was that of the "provocative" woman, which often led women who had frequent contact with men at work to attempt to go unnoticed and not to attract attention by their dress or manner. This was why harassed women rarely received support from their female colleagues since they tended to put the blame on the victim out of prejudice. This atmosphere at work led women to keep quiet about harassment for fear of the judgmental reaction of their colleagues and many women said that it took a lot of conviction to complain about it.

Men, however, thought their conduct was natural and were convinced that women "liked it that way". For them, provoking women was natural and justified the way they treated them. It was almost as if they thought that sexual harassment was often a result of the attraction between the sexes. Men also complained that women could not take a joke and justified this by saying that they did not have the same sense of humour, playing down the effect which sexual jokes or proposals might have on women.

These two points of view were mutually reinforcing and prevented a critical stance to male behaviour being adopted at work by either men or women. The eldest or most senior women in a company therefore often covered up for male behaviour.

The groups at risk were vulnerable women, such as those working in sectors with low social or economic status, single women and those who were ill-equipped to defend themselves or were not economically independent. So far, sexual harassment has been hidden from view even though the number of complaints is now on the increase and the facts are being published by the media. Moreover, the insecurity of women's situation in the labour market (temporary work and fixed-term contracts) and the high rate of female unemployment are creating a climate which was conducive to sexual harassment.

FRANCE

In France there is an association to combat violence against women at work (AVFT) which, at the request of the Secretary of State for Women's Rights and Consumer Affairs, analysed some 100 files on complaints made to them between 1985 and 1990.

a)   The main types of sexual harassment

This qualitative study indicated that 62% of cases of harassment were verbal, 30% physical and 8% non-verbal, but that these types of behaviour were not mutually exclusive.

The type of behaviour described could not be interpreted as an attempt to seduce for it was unwelcome and repeated (the victim having spurned the initial advances in vain, or the harasser being in a position where he should have known that his attentions were unwelcome) and was therefore obviously forced upon the victim, revealing the harasser's desire to subjugate the victim by deliberately humiliating her.

Harassment sometimes comprised a single act, such as sexual blackmail, and sometimes a combination or repetition of various types of behaviour. It was a long-term phenomenon and could subside for periods, depending on the victim's reaction, or become worse as time progressed.

Verbal harassment mostly constituted requests for sex, which were addressed to more than one in two women. A quarter of the women interviewed complained about sexual or sexist remarks about their appearance or about women in general, vulgar or obscene comments, and uncalled for and unwelcome sexual jokes which are forced upon women. Next came, in order of frequency, uncalled for questions and comments on the victim's sex lives, invitations – generally to a restaurant – or requests to be invited to the victim's home, unsolicited confidences from the harasser about his sex life in order to arouse the victim's compassion (explaining that he has marital problems) or desire (by recounting his "sexual exploits") and to create an atmosphere of intimacy and finally, sometimes, offers of money in exchange for sex.

More than one in three women reported physical harassment. This mainly comprised bodily contact, touching, pinching and kissing. The harasser would claim that these were involuntary or friendly and seek to make a habit of them. Such contact could turn into deliberate sexual and physical aggression, such as surprising the victim with a kiss or forcing a kiss upon them, pulling away the clothing to touch the breasts, thighs, buttocks or genitals, bodily contact, attempts to force the victim to touch the penis, etc. Some women also complained that they had been pushed or hit and finally, one in ten women reported rape or attempted rape.

Non-verbal harassment was mentioned least frequently and comprised sexual exhibitions by the harasser and the use of pornography, mainly in magazines which were shown to the victims to embarrass, intimidate or upset them. Prolonged unwelcome glances or looks which "undress" women were mentioned less frequently, probably because harassed women who did make a complaint reported only the most severe and the most tangible instances of harassment.

b)   *Effects on the victim's job*

Sexual harassment was damaging to the victim's job and career:
   * The harasser often ended up by using any means of applying pressure, force or penalties at his disposal to overcome the resistance of the victim or to take revenge when his advances were rejected.
   * The harasser made it much more difficult for the victim to do her job by not replying to questions, by withholding information, giving contradictory instructions and increasing the workload.
   * The harasser criticised and devalued the victim's work, particularly in front of colleagues, which sometimes led to her being isolated and sidelined. There was little the victim could do, particularly if she was forced by her position to keep her own counsel.
   * If the harasser was the victim's superior he could use the working conditions as a means of attack by changing working hours, working tools or the work load, all of which could affect the victim's pay or responsibilities. The harasser could also use a whole range of disciplinary penalties accompanied by measures to make life difficult for the victim.

Under these conditions sexual harassment often caused the victim to lose interest in her work and to make less of a long-term personal investment in the job as a result of her disappointment at work and a feeling of persistent mistrust vis-à-vis her colleagues and superiors.

According to the study, 71% of people reporting sexual harassment lost their jobs, either because they resigned (because it was difficult for them to do their job), because they were dismissed or because their contract expired. Those who kept their jobs, i.e. 29%, were mainly in the public sector where it was exceptional for an employee to be dismissed, unlike in the private sector. Some employees in the private sector only kept their jobs for a while, since dismissal sometimes came several months or even years after they had complained about sexual harassment.

c) *Occupational consequences in the short and medium term*

Sexual harassment also had a negative effect on a victim's career because it made it difficult for her to find a new job for a variety of reasons: the effects of the violence she had been exposed to, her poor state of health, lack of self-confidence, fear of men, fear of being a victim of sexual harassment again, distrust of employers and embarrassment at having to explain what happened in her previous job and disappointment with working life. Some women refused to work under the same conditions again, in particular with men, and went back to traditionally female occupations. Those who were able sought self-employed work as freelance workers or started up their own businesses, etc. In the longer term, some even withdrew from the labour market altogether by taking early retirement, going back to being a housewife or stopping work when they become pregnant.

d) *Effects on health*

This study also highlighted the effects of sexual harassment on the victims' health. They frequently took sick leave, which can last for several months and sometimes had to go into hospital. It was rare for no negative effects on health to be detected.

The problems reported most often by women were problems sleeping, nightmares, headaches, bulimia or anorexia, losing or putting on weight, fatigue, spasmophilia, vomiting, anxiety and sexual problems. The psychosomatic symptoms of stress, anxiety and depression were often reported by women and diagnosed by doctors. Suicidal behaviour had also been observed which in some cases unfortunately culminated in suicide attempts.

e) *Repercussions on the victim's personal life*

Harassment disrupted the victims' working and private life. Psychologically they were torn between their desire to do something about it and their reluctance to do so because they were afraid of ruining the atmosphere at work and losing their job, because they are ashamed, because they were afraid of aggravating the problem or because they felt isolated at work or in the family. Moreover, sexual harassment reflected badly on women, as they saw themselves first as sexual objects and second as incompetent. They felt devalued, and lost their self esteem, all the more so when they did not feel that they could resolve the problem.

f) *Groups at risk*

The study revealed that women who complained about harassment were not, on the whole, vulnerable, either socially, personally or at work. The majority of them had a good education, experience, seniority in their job, pay which was considerably higher than the minimum income and had permanent contracts. The majority of the victims were French and were neither very young nor very old.

Nevertheless, during the study, many women who complained to the AVFT reported economic constraints due to their husbands' unemployment, debts incurred by purchasing housing or a car or the fact that they were single parents, and pointed out that the harasser knew about the situation. Moreover, more and more foreign and young women were turning to the AVFT for help.

Whilst any employee may be sexually harassed, the effects will be greater on people who are economically or psychologically vulnerable. In fact, such people, who are less well-equipped to defend themselves, can be subjected to long-term harassment which may escalate, taking the form of physical sexual aggression and, in some circumstances attempted rape or rape.

GREECE

The most recent studies were carried out in certain towns or sectors of activity and supplied more information on the phenomenon of harassment, despite the small samples.

a) A survey carried out in the course of a thesis on harassment. Place: Patras. Sample: 123 persons (65 women and 58 men of over 17).

When asked "W*hat do you think sexual harassment is?"*, 90% of the interviewees replied that it was when people had to bow to sexual demands to further their careers. When asked *"Who might be the harassers?"* they replied the superior (72%), colleagues (55%) and sometimes clients.

The replies showed that 84% of the persons interviewed knew of cases of sexual harassment although the victims had not spoken about them. The reasons given for the victims' silence were fear of dismissal or isolation at work and also the fact that there was no law penalising harassment. As regards the psychological effects of sexual harassment, the replies indicated that 47% of the victims were furious and 22% felt insecure. The majority (78%) thought that sexual harassment affected working capacity.

b) Survey carried out in the health sector

Sample: 158 women of between 20 and 55 from various occupations in the health sector. Level of education: 2% elementary education, 35%, secondary education,63% higher education.

According to the survey, 73% of the women interviewed knew of cases of sexual harassment and 35% described it as widespread. In 47% of cases the harassers were superiors and in the remaining 53% of cases patients or customers. Of the women interviewed, 19% said that if there was someone who was responsible for this problem they would complain.

c) A collection of testimonies

In 1994 in Athens the NGO "Women's democratic movement" organised a congress on sexual harassment. Over 150 women attended the congress, representing all the regions of the country and pooled their knowledge on this matter, either from their own experience or through written testimonies. There was also a round table of experts where they exchanged notes.

The conclusions of the congress were as follows:

* Sexual harassment is fairly widespread in Greece;
* the victims are generally women (under the same circumstances, men are not exposed to similar conduct);
* the perpetrators are men (of all ages and all social strata);
* sexual harassment is an expression of the harasser's presumed social superiority, even if he does not occupy a higher position in the hierarchy. The act of harassment is used to keep women in their place and in their traditional role;
* men have problems understanding the problem. Exceptions are rare;
* employees do not complain about sexual harassment, mainly because of the lack of legal protection which makes them think that a complaint would be pointless or, worse, might cost them their job, make conditions at work more difficult or cause damaging remarks to be made about them at or outside work.

ITALY

Following the surveys described above, a new phase emerged in Italy with three other surveys seeking to examine the problem in more depth and one study based on testimonies.

a) Surveys

These surveys varied with the concept of sexual harassment used - either the Rubenstein report or the American concept drafted by Fitzgerald and Schulman. They were carried out in the following geographical areas: Lombardy (Milan) Emilia Romagna (Modena) and the North-East (Padua).Although the surveys were carried out using different methodologies, one thing they all reveal is that sexual harassment is not a sporadic phenomenon but a systematic one. It does not constitute isolated incidents but a series of them caused by various types of behaviour.

The surveys show that sexual harassment is a major phenomenon and that the verbal form is most widespread, followed by physical harassment. Another fact which is confirmed in all three surveys is that it is more severe when it is perpetrated by superiors.

As regards the victims' behaviour, the strategies vary depending on the survey's theoretical approach. Those which follow the Fitzgerald model break them down into two types: active solution-driven strategies (talking to the harasser, avoiding him or seeking support) and passive strategies (denial and patience). According to the results of the surveys, the victim's behaviour differs depending on whether the harasser is a superior or a colleague. In the first case, the strategies adopted are active (they talk about it or file a complaint), but in the case of a colleague they adopt passive strategies. The latter proves more harmful for the victim's well-being.

The Milan and Modena surveys also showed that women's reactions to sexual harassment may be "to legitimise male behaviour " (they pretend not to understand), or "to talk about it rationally" (they asked to "be left alone"). Women often find themselves in a situation where they "play down men's behaviour and their responsibility for it".

The men's replies show that women are perceived as being responsible. It is women who provoke male behaviour. As a result, aggression is seen as a simple response to provocative female behaviour. In cases where it is definitely male behaviour that is responsible, they say that it pathological or a departure from the norm. The schematic figure of the "provocative" woman is a construct of male fantasy to which an exclusively male world view seeks to reduce women as individuals. The violent interaction stems from men's ambition to reduce interpretation of the other (female) world view to their own interpretational, linguistic and relational codes (Ventimiglia, 1991).

b) Other research

Other research was carried out using testimonies and personal accounts of women who had been harassed.

In this research, the main motivation for the sexual harassment seemed to be the superior's narcissistic impulse to exercise power over a subordinate or job seeker by taking advantage of the fact that they might be open to blackmail as a result of their economic straits and desperate need of a job or because of they were afraid of losing their job. In these cases, flattery and promises to improve the post or to find a job alternated with intimidation and persecution when a superior could not come to terms with his advances being rejected. In cases where a superior could not dismiss his victim he sometimes took revenge for years by placing obstacles in the path of her career and creating an intolerable climate of persecution.

Such situations were mainly encountered by very young women or single or separated women. The advances started with verbal flattery, followed by unwelcome caresses and went as far as sexual aggression in the worst cases, all of which took place against a background of indifference and acceptance of sexual harassment as if it was a "normal" type of human conduct which was accounted for by the reciprocity of the sexual roles and the instinct to court a mate.

The research showed that it was rare to find gestures of solidarity from women. In most cases they were silent observers of abuse suffered by their colleagues at work since they feared that the same thing would happen to them or because they thought that the women concerned "were asking for it".

When women complained to their employers about being harassed by their superiors they reacted by conniving at or "covering up" such cases, particularly in small enterprises where contacts with the staff were very close. In large enterprises, however, conflicts increasingly ended up with the person most likely to disrupt the enterprise's operations being dismissed.

The accounts of female manual workers revealed that harassment by their male colleagues, whose camaraderie made them feel superior, was much more frequent than in other occupational categories. This was also a typical abuse of power born of male solidarity which took advantage of the divisions between women. Reports from women trade unionists also revealed resistance in trade union organisations to movements to incorporate some form of regulation against abuses into collective agreements. This was because it was a low-priority issue for these organisations and was considered less important than other general matters, no doubt because men feared having to face accusations.

Other research is in progress in Italy particularly the three or localised studies promoted by trade unions and a local authority's equal opportunities commission. The interest in examining the issue in more detail shows that there is greater awareness of it.

PORTUGAL

A new survey was carried out in 1994, this time restricted to the public administration at national level, and included men in the sample.708 questionnaires were distributed by mail, 54.9% to women and 45.1% to men. The results of the survey show that 7% of men and 7% of women have been sexually harassed at work. Because of the specific nature of the survey and the methodology used this can not be compared with the results of the study carried out in 1988. Hence, even though fewer people were found to be harassed in 1994, there are no grounds for concluding that the phenomenon has diminished in Portugal.Moreover, the two surveys suggest that the victims' attitude is passive due to the lack of the institutional or legal support structures to combat harassment.

The results confirm that it is still a taboo subject and that therefore the solution for the victims is to ask for sick leave or to leave their jobs, since they find no support amongst their colleagues, in the trade union or in the company. The conspiracy of silence which they encounter often leads them to take various periods of sick leave. It should also be emphasised that there are normally no witnesses to sexual harassment, particularly severe harassment, which prevents the victim from proving that it has occurred. Moreover the perpetrator is never punished since there is no labour law which covers this type of behaviour nor is their a definition of sexual harassment at work. This is compounded by the insecurity of employment contracts for a large proportion of the female labour force which makes it very difficult for a women who has been harassed to take her complaint to existing institutions.

2.4   Research carried out under the terms of this study

Greece and Portugal carried out two small studies on sexual harassment since very little had been done in this field. Greece carried out a study which took the form of discussion groups with women and Portugal organised a small survey in various sectors.

GREECE

The research was based on information collected from 10 discussion groups. The results are presented by discussion topic.

1. Knowledge of the subject and, possibly, information on Community policy

None of the women had received any information at work. The majority had found it through the media. The women in Group 3 (banking) said that they were well informed, although they had not received any information. Some women knew that Community documents existed, but had not read them and the women in Group 9 (Thessalonika) were familiar with them. Only one women admitted that she knew nothing about them.

2. Knowledge of the term sexual harassment

All the women knew what harassment was but some interpreted it as being restricted to action by a superior and often the term was defined by the effects of such behaviour on women (affront to personal dignity, violence, humiliation, etc.). The women in Group 3 (banking) did not think the term was suitable and said that was why women did not dare to make complaints. Some women said that it was due to "men's sexual desire" but the majority said that it was a question of power. Group 7 (cosmetics) thought the term was confusing. They thought it was a question of individual relationships and hence did not understand why sexual harassment affected the working atmosphere. Group 9 (Thessalonika) accepted the EU definition.

3. Behaviour of men – superiors, colleagues and subordinates – with regard to women

The majority described behaviour of colleagues at work and superiors as being "typical" or "normal". The women in Group 3 (banking) all reported types of harassment which they had had to put up with. The women in Group 7 (cosmetics) said that the atmosphere was friendly but that their colleagues did not like it when they were promoted (discrimination). The women in Group 9 (Thessalonika) said that their male colleagues were "protective" of them. Group 10 (tourism) say that they did not have male colleagues and that their superiors did not trust them.

4. Knowledge of the existence of harassment

All the women said that the phenomenon existed. Some said that it was especially rife in enterprises in the private sector. Others said that it went unremarked. The women in Group 3 (banking) all knew of cases and emphasised that it was a widespread problem which was tolerated and that there were women who took advantage of it to obtain jobs. They quoted the case of a well-known director who harassed women systematically. The women in Group 10 (tourism) also knew only too well that sexual harassment existed.

5. Knowledge of cases and whether they themselves had been victims. If so, how did they react.

Apart from two groups where nobody had been sexually harassed, there were women who admitted to having been victims. The women in Group 9 (Thessalonika) said that they were all victims, describing how their colleagues behaved and saying said that, when challenged, the harassers replied that their feelings were paternal. The youngest in

180

the group remembered the days when they were looking for work and when advances and propositions were clear: the outcome always depended on their attitude. If they did not accept the advances they didn't get the jobs.

The women in Group 10 (tourism) found it difficult to acknowledge that they had been victims. Nevertheless, from their description of cases it was fairly clearly that they had encountered such situations. They reported all types of sexual harassment by superiors, customers, etc., taking the form of oblique and direct advances, humiliating compliments, even offers of money to spend the night together. They said that all they could do about it was resign. But that was a problem, because it was not easy to find work.

6. Do women find it easy to talk about these matters? If not what is the reason for their silence?

The majority said that women did not talk about it and some added "especially if they were still working". Others thought that it was easier to talk about it now. The reasons for their silence were: fear of prejudice (being considered the guilty party or having provoked the harassment), fear of losing their jobs and shame at what was happening to them. Other women added that "they were afraid of becoming victimised again by other people's comments and innuendoes". Finally, others said that "that they were afraid of being blamed by other employees who were jealous because their boss now fancied someone else". The women in Group 10 (tourism) said that they had to remain silent.

7. What would you do if your were unfortunate enough to be sexually harassed? Would you make a complaint and what else would you do?

The majority opted in favour of an individual strategy. Many of the others said that they would approach the head of the enterprise and the trade union. Some women said that they would take legal action and would go to women's organisations. Group 3 (banking) said that it was difficult because there was no proper procedure and there was the threat of unemployment. They said that they could not leave a job in banking because they could not find as good a job elsewhere and there was a whole family depending on it.

8. Discussion of the need for a law or legal clauses and other measures to combat sexual harassment

All the groups but two were in favour of a law or legal regulations. Some women said that the law should include severe penalties. Those who disagreed included the majority of Group 6 (insurance) who did not think a law was indispensable. However, everybody thought that information is needed and that this matter should also be dealt with at school. Group 10 (tourism) was not sure that a law would improve the situation but called for measures against violence to women.

As regards measures to combat harassment, the majority called for information. Others were also in favour of a person who enjoyed women's confidence and had the ability to solve the problem being given responsibility for it. Others said that women should be helped to get rid of prejudices which did not allow them to react or defend themselves against harassment. Others called for psychological support and assistance to victims to help them make a complaint. Group 9 (Thessalonika) called for preventive measures to be taken with seminars being held to train people to be aware of their rights and responsibilities.

The results of the discussion groups show that sexual harassment is a major problem in Greece, particularly in banking and tourism. Banking is a sector which offers good employment opportunities for women but, according to the participants, the way to obtain such work is to put up with sexual harassment. In the tourism sector, however, job insecurity and the unemployment situation in the island of Crete make women more vulnerable in a sector where sexual harassment is the norm.

Since there is no organised protection or legislation, many women try to solve the problem by themselves or become resigned to it. What is more, prejudices about male sexuality and women who "provoke" men, prevent the person who is to blame from being identified and as a result women keep quiet about harassment because they are afraid of the reaction of those around them, even when they are women, because they feel guilty and shame for what is happening to them. This situation isolates the women and induces them to keep quiet. In order to cope with the situation, women think that they need legislation but also preventive measures such as information, training and support structures.

PORTUGAL

The survey was carried out in the Lisbon area on a sample of 170 people, 100 women and 70 men. The sectors were as follows: a) Public sector: health, airports and justice, b) Private sector: banking, financing, insurance, water, electricity industry, electronics industry, telecommunications, textiles, commerce and services.

Of the population interviewed, 70% of the women and 71.4% of the men had positions of responsibility. The population was broken down as follows: 53% managers, 5.8% head technicians, 5.8% technicians, 11.8% administrative employees and 11.8% unskilled workers. 64.6% of the population had a university education and 11.8% secondary education or incomplete higher education. The survey also included questions on the post occupied, training and promotion in the enterprise and on discrimination but only the questions relating to sexual harassment are presented.

The results are as follows: 41% of the persons interviewed, i.e. 43% of the men1 and 40% of the women, said that they had been harassed. In 42.8% of cases the harasser was a colleague, in 42.8% of cases a superior and 14.4% of cases a subordinate. If the replies are broken down by sex the results are as follows:

Women: 25% harassed by a colleague and
                75% by a superior
Men: 33% by subordinate
                66% by a colleague.

90% of women gave three reasons in response to the question "*Why do victims of sexual harassment not do anything about it*":
*   they were ashamed;
*   they were afraid for their jobs;
*   they did not wish to appear in a bad light if the news got around,
and 10% of women said "because nobody does anything in such cases".

When men were asked the same question, 71.4% gave the same reasons as women and 28.6% said that "because nobody would support them". When asked "*Why do you think that a man who is being harassed will do nothing about it*"?

> 28.5% of men replied "because they do not wish to appear in a bad light with regard to their job if the news gets around".
>
> 14.5% said it was because "no-one would support them"
>
> 57% replied that "nobody considers it to be of any importance". This reply was given by all the men who said that they had been harassed, the reason being that men tend to play down the issue and adopt an attitude of superiority with regard to women, doing nothing about it or making light of it.

In reply to the question "*If you were harassed what would you do*"?,
the women replied as follows:

> 40% "immediate and vigorous defence";
>
> 30% "request to change to another department";
>
> 30% "talk to other colleagues in the same situation to undertake collective action";

and the men replied as follows:

> 43% "immediate and vigorous defence";
>
> 28.5% "request to change to another department";
>
> 28.5% "attempt to take advantage of the situation".

In reply to the question "*If you were sexually harassed who would you talk to about it?*",
the women replied:

> 30% "with my husband or with women colleagues";
>
> 20% "with institutions or with a lawyer";
>
> 40% "with friends (male or female)";
>
> 10% "nobody";

and the men replied:

> 57.0% "with friends (male or female)";
>
> 28.5% "with male colleagues";
>
> 14.5% "nobody".

When asked about pornographic photographs at work, 11.7% of the sample said that they existed and 88.3% said that they had never seen any. However, 94.2% said that they had never thought that such photos could be a form of sexual harassment and 5.8% knew that it was.

75% of harassed women had fixed-term contracts whilst the men who were harassed all had permanent contracts. Both the men and women who were harassed received sexual propositions or had sexual remarks addressed to them.

In reply to the question "*How would you describe the working relationship with the harasser*"?

> 25% of harassed women said that the relationship was good and 75% said "neither good nor bad".
>
> 33% of men said "neither good nor bad" and 67% said that it was good.

When asked whether they were subordinate to the harasser or whether he or she could influence promotion, a pay increase or the renewal of their contract, they replied as follows:

        Women: 25% partly and 75% completely (the harasser decided on promotion and on the contract)

        Men: 33% partly and 67% not at all.

In reply to the question: *"Were there witnesses?"*

        25% of women said that there were (men and women) and 75% said that they were alone.

        33% of the men said that other men and women were present and 67% that they were alone.

In reply to the question *"How did you feel during the days that followed?"*

        all the women said "nervous and depressed"

        33% of the men replied "normal" and 67% "depressed".

The replies by sex to the question *"How did you feel about work?"* were as follows:

Women:	25% lacking in motivation
	25% experiencing difficulties in concentrating
	50% not wanting to go to work.
Men:	33.3% experiencing difficulties in concentrating
	33.3% inattentive
	33.3% normal.

The replies to the question *"Do you think that the incident had any consequences?"* were as follows:

Women:	50% "it jeopardised my job"
	50% "it harmed my professional career"
Men:	33% no consequences
	67% "I had problems with the company".

This survey shows that the majority of harassed women had fixed-term contracts and were dependent on their harasser for promotion and renewal of the contract whilst the men who were harassed had permanent contracts and were mainly harassed by colleagues. What is more, the men were not dependent on the person who harassed them which was why they could reply that the matter did not have any significance and that they did not wish to attach any importance to it.

The men's replies show that sexual harassment has a less profound impact on them than women, none of whom are left unscathed by the experience. Some of the men even say that they would try to take advantage of the situation.

Women attach more importance to it, unlike some of the men, who prefer to play it down. It also hits women harder as one in every two are reluctant to go to work and the others lack motivation or have problems concentrating. This reluctance is no doubt due to the fact that three women in every four are dependent on the harasser because he is their superior. Although some of the harassed men felt depressed, none of them felt like missing work.

The consequences of harassment were also different for women as their jobs and careers had been put in jeopardy following the conflict, whilst the men's contracts were not at risk and only some of them had any problems with the company.

However, the results of the survey show that the question of harassed men needs to be gone into more in more depth, because when their replies are compared with women's, it is clear that in some cases they are not talking about the same thing.

3.   THE LEGAL SITUATION WITH REGARD TO SEXUAL HARASSMENT

As pointed out already, it is in France alone that there is a specific law on sexual harassment. In the other countries there are only articles in various laws which can be applied to sexual harassment. This report describes the situation in each country.

SPAIN

The various laws which govern sexual harassment do so only in as far as it is perpetrated by a superior. Nevertheless, the case law has included harassment by a person with the same rank as the victim. In order to do something about this restrictive legislation, the Women's Institute of the Social Affairs Ministry conducted an awareness-raising campaign against sexual harassment in 1997 and is currently preparing a proposal for an article to be included in the penal code banning sexual harassment caused by any person working in the enterprise who has the same rank or a lower rank than the victim.

1. The laws governing sexual harassment at work are as follows:

*   The Constitution
*   The Workers' Statute (Labour Code)
    *   The Law on Infringements and Sanctions in the Social System (LISOS)
    *   Procedure Labour Law
    *   Penal Code

A) THE CONSTITUTION

Article 14 of the Spanish Constitution guarantees the right to equality and hence not to be discriminated against on the grounds of sex. Article 18.1 guarantees the right to dignity and privacy for oneself and one's family, and to one's own identity. Article 40.2 guarantees that the public authorities will safeguard health and safety at work, hence guarantees the right to physical and moral integrity.

B) THE WORKERS' STATUTE

Article 4.2 c) defines the scope of the term sexual harassment as follows: *"In their working relations, workers have the right to respect for their privacy and due consideration for their dignity, including protection against verbal or physical affronts of a sexual nature"*.
For the purposes of Article 1.2, the agent of harassment is the head of the enterprise and anybody who represents him at work or who provides significant decision-making input, such as: production heads, personnel heads, foremen, valued customers, etc. with sufficient authority to decide on key elements of a contract such as duration, pay and job classification. However, a worker of the same or lower rank as the victim is not classified as an agent, even though case law tends to do so. The agent may be the harasser himself or, for example, a head of an enterprise who does not take sufficient measures in the employment contract to guarantee the protection of a worker. Heads of enterprises must therefore adopt preventive and corrective measures to guarantee protection against sexual harassment.

The Statute refers to physical or verbal affronts of a sexual nature but it leaves many points unanswered and as a result offers judges and the courts very wide scope for interpretation. For example, does the affront have to be objective or is it sufficient for the victim to regard it as such? Is a proposal for a stable relationship or a request to dress in a given manner commensurate with the type of service being rendered capable of interpretation as being "of a sexual nature"? "Environmental" sexual harassment is not sanctioned under the Statute.

The passive subject is a person who is bound to the enterprise by a contract of employment. However, this criterion does not include officials, relatives, transport workers who have their own means of transport, etc., even though they may be dependent on those benefiting from their work.

Article 54 includes instances of serious misdemeanours on the part of a worker which may be grounds for dismissal. The article includes physical and verbal offences against the head of the enterprise, workers in the enterprise or relatives living with them. Such offences can give rise to dismissal. Although there is no actual mention of sexual harassment, it can be subsumed under this article.

C) LAW ON INFRINGEMENTS AND SANCTIONS IN THE SOCIAL SYSTEM (LISOS)

Article 8.11 of Law 8/88 on infringements in enterprises, currently incorporated in Article 96 of the Workers' Statute, describes as serious misdemeanours *"Acts by the head of the enterprise which are contrary to respect for privacy and due consideration for the dignity of workers"*. In accordance with the provisions of Article 37, this may result in a fine which, depending on the seriousness of the offence, may range from 500 000 to 15 000 000 pesetas.

D) PROCEDURAL LAW FOR LABOUR DISPUTES

The incorporation, with the Amendment of 27.4.90 in the Procedural Law for Labour Disputes, of a specific procedure to deal with any infringement of a fundamental right is an example of positive legislation worth mentioning. Article 181 of the Law cover all applications relating to the protection of fundamental right, including a ban on discriminatory treatment in working relationships. According to Article 179.2, the burden of proof falls upon the accused, which is an exception to the general rule on the burden of proof established in Article 1214 of the Civil Code.

E) PENAL CODE

Article 184 of the new Penal Code refers to sexual harassment in the following terms :
"Any person taking advantage of their superior position at work in teaching or in a similar situation in order to solicit sexual favours for themselves or third parties with a clear or tacit intention to disappoint the victim's legitimate expectations of this relationship, will be punished as a perpetrator of sexual harassment by a prison sentence of between 12 and 24 weekends or a fine amounting to between 6 and 12 months' pay".

2. A missed opportunity: the Law for the Prevention of Risks at Work

For a person who is being harassed there is certainly a causal link between the conduct or action which constitute sexual harassment and their repercussions on health. The recent law on the prevention of risks at work (1995) did not include or mention sexual harassment. However, the case law reveals that in most cases harassed persons are on sick leave or have stopped work or have consulted the social security doctor or a psychologist, etc.

Article 15 of the Law establishes the principles of preventive action and states in section g) *"that the head of an enterprise has an obligation to plan prevention, seeking a coherent combination of technical equipment, organisation of work, working conditions, social relations and the influence of environmental factors at work"*. Article 4 defines what is meant by working conditions as *"any feature of work which may have a significant influence on generating health and safety risks for the work"*.

Obviously the incorporation of sexual harassment in this Law would have been a step forward, particularly for the purposes of prevention. This omission, for which there appears to be no good reason, shows the Spanish legislators' insensitivity to the problem.

FRANCE

The Law of 22 July 1992 created the offence of sexual harassment which is defined as sexual aggression (Article 222-33 of the Penal Code). The Law of 2 November 1992 created a provision to protect workers (Articles L122-46 and L123-1 of the Labour Code). However, the only scenario covered is abuse of the authority associated with a job in order to obtain "sexual favours". The occupational repercussions for the victim are regarded as instances of discrimination. The scope of the Law goes beyond the working environment and applies also, for example, to doctor/patient or teacher/pupil relations1.

1. The Penal Code defines sexual harassment as sexual aggression

The offence of sexual harassment which was originally provided for in the section of the Penal Code entitled "Discrimination" in the chapter "Affronts to personal dignity", ended up being incorporated in the section "Sexual aggression" in the chapter on "Violations of physical or mental personal integrity". As has already been pointed out, parliamentary debates highlighted the fact that the victims of sexual harassment were not confined to one sex, thus refusing to regard it as violence against women and as a type of discrimination.

The Penal Code defines the harasser as a hierarchical superior who abuses the authority his job confers upon him in order to exercise sexual pressure on an employee. This abuse of power is defined by the expression "orders, threats or pressure".

Labour law defines the abuse of power more widely because it also covers "all types of pressure". The following, on the other hand, do not constitute sexual harassment:

* sexual blackmail by a person who is of the same rank or lower;
* unwelcome sexual behaviour which affects the working atmosphere, especially sexist remarks, obscene jokes and pornographic pin-ups which are not aimed at any person in particular;
* verbal or physical behaviour of a sexual nature, especially sexist insults and contact, the intention or effect of which is to humiliate a person. But non-sexual contact is also humiliating if it is unwelcome.

2. The Penal Code and labour law regard the occupational repercussions of sexual harassment for the victim as sexual discrimination

Labour law therefore covers measures affecting a person's job and career in order to protect a victim of harassment. The same applies to decisions taken in consideration of the fact of sexual harassment *"especially regarding recruitment, remuneration, training, place of employment, qualifications, classification, promotion, redeployment, termination or renewal of the contract of employment or disciplinary sanctions"* (Article L123-1 of the Labour Code). The general provisions on sex-related discrimination apply to cases of professional reprisals against an employee where they are motivated by sexual harassment, even though no explicit mention is made of sexual harassment (Article L225-2-3 of the Penal Code). Labour law has wider ranging provisions on discrimination.

3. Labour law bans any decision on the grounds of sexual harassment which might affect the contract of employment

Article L123-1 paragraph 3 at the head of the chapter on equality for men and women at work thus provides that *"the fact that the person concerned has been subjected to or has refused to tolerate action defined under Article L112-46 or has testified to such action or has reported it may, under no circumstances, be taken into account to decide on matters of recruitment, remuneration, training, place of employment, qualifications, classification, promotion, redeployment, termination or renewal of the contract of employment or disciplinary sanctions"*. Civil servants are protected by Article 6 paragraph 4 of the amended law of 13 July 1983 which states *"No measure concerning, in particular, recruitment, establishment, training, promotion, place of employment and redeployment may be taken with regard to a civil servant which takes account of (sexual harassment) (...)"*. These articles also protect witnesses against discriminatory measures.

4. Penalties and compensation for sexual harassment

a) Under the Penal Code the offence of sexual harassment is punishable by a prison sentence of a maximum of one year and a fine of FF 100 000 (Article L222-23).
b) Labour law provides for the possibility of disciplinary action being taken against the harasser.

The law does not define such action nor is it mandatory but is taken at the employer's discretion. Here, the Law abides by the general principle in France that the head of an enterprise is responsible for management and discipline. The rule does not apply to harassment by a colleague, since this is not against the law. Article L122-47 refers explicitly to the legal definition of harassment given in Article L122-46 of the Labour Code. An employer who harasses his staff is, by definition, immune from any such penalty as he has sole responsibility for exercising disciplinary authority.

c) Labour law provides that any punishment or dismissal of a harassed employee is automatically void (Article L122-46 of the Labour Code). The same protection is afforded an employee who has testified to sexual harassment.

Labour law has not considered the possibility of reprisals against a third person close to the victim of harassment who might be employed in the same enterprise. A spouse who is punished, reassigned or even dismissed is not entitled to the above protection under the Labour Code.

5. Legal penalties and compensation for discrimination in connection with sexual harassment

Penalties are provided for under both the Labour Code and the Penal Code.

a) Under Article L152-1-1 of the Labour Code, infringement of Article L123-1 is punishable by a prison sentence of one year and a maximum fine of FF 25 000. Under this Article the judgement may also be posted in the enterprise and published in the newspapers.

b) Under Article L225-2 of the Penal Code, refusal to recruit, punishment or dismissal of a harassed person is punishable by a prison sentence of a maximum of two years and a fine of FF 200 000.

Legal persons, i.e. enterprises, except the State in its capacity as an employer, can also be sanctioned under the Penal Code, their responsibility coming on top of that of the perpetrator of the discrimination. The maximum fine of FF 200 000 for physical persons is then multiplied by five. Provision is also made for optional additional penalties, such as a suspended sentence, posting and dissemination of the judgement, a temporary or permanent ban on exercising the occupational activity involved, exclusion from public contracts, temporary or permanent closure of the establishment and placement under legal supervision.

6. The employer's legal responsibility

The employer's civil responsibility may be invoked on various grounds. The law of 2 November 1992 stipulates that it is up to the employer to prevent sexual harassment. Article L122-48 of the Labour Code gives grounds for a claim for civil liability in the event of no action being taken when a case of sexual harassment is brought to the employer's notice. The employer may also become liable under general civil liability rules for damage caused by his own deeds or negligence or the deeds of persons for whom he is responsible. The employer may also become liable under the penal code on the grounds of complicity in the offence of sexual harassment and in the event of discrimination linked with sexual harassment (Articles L1382, L 1383 and L1384-5 of the Civil Code).

7. Prevention of sexual harassment

The law of 2 November 1992 places the initial obligation for prevention on the employer, leaving staff representatives free to propose preventive measures to the employer through the CHSCT (committee on health, safety and working conditions). The occupational physician can also take part in prevention.

THE EMPLOYER'S ROLE

1) First of all, he must provide <u>information</u> by including in the establishment's employment regulations – a mandatory written document for enterprises employing at least 20 people – the provisions of the Labour Code on the abuse of authority in sexual matters. The Labour Inspectorate monitors the legality of the employment regulations, which must be sent to it for the purposes of information.

2) The employment regulations must be posted at places of work and recruitment on pain of a fine. Article L123-1 is also posted at places of work and recruitment offices.

This is mandatory, irrespective of the size of the enterprise or whether employment regulations for it exist. The Labour Inspectorate monitors whether employers meet their obligation to post this information.

3) The employer's main, general task in preventing sexual harassment is set out in Article L122-48 of the Labour Code "*It is up to the head of the enterprise to take any necessary measures to prevent action covered by the above two articles*". This rule does not impose any specific prevention policy or measure. Everything depends on the employer's attitude, i.e. whether he is indifferent to the problem of sexual harassment, connives at or is himself responsible for it or whether he is convinced that sexual harassment is detrimental to personnel management and the smooth running of the enterprise, in which case an effective prevention policy can be put in place.

The employer's general obligation to safeguard his employees' health and safety, provided for in Article 230-2 of the Labour Code, might also apply to sexual harassment and thus force the employer to adopt preventive measures in this area. This Article stipulates that the head of the establishment must take measures to prevent health and safety hazards that he must "*avoid*" them and "*evaluate*" them "*when they cannot be avoided*" and "*plan prevention, integrating in a coherent overall plan, organisation of work, working conditions, social relations and the effect of environmental factors*". The case law interprets this is a real obligation to produce the desired results.

The laws on sexual harassment are now an integral part of the social landscape because they have given rise to a significant body of case law (complaints, legal action and verdicts against harassers), whereas when they were promulgated it was feared that they would remain dead letters. However, they have still not produced the results expected of them and the legal provisions adopted (which pursue three aims: enforcement of penalties, protection of employees and prevention) are still inadequate.
Moreover, contrary to public opinion, these laws only protect a small proportion of the victims. The definition of sexual harassment in French law therefore needs to be expanded because it ignores "environmental" sexual harassment, i.e. harassment which affects personal dignity and working conditions and does not involve an abuse of authority, such as harassment by a colleague.

GREECE

There is no legal definition of sexual harassment in the legislation. However, there are some provisions in the laws on equal opportunities in the Civil Code and in the Penal Code which can be applied to cases of sexual harassment at work. Up to 1997 there was no case law in this field. We may therefore conclude that up to this date, the problem of sexual harassment had not been brought before the Greek courts.

The laws in force which can be invoked are as follows:
Law 1414.30.01.84 on equality. This bans any discrimination of either sex at work.

Civil Code:
* Article 57: Any person whose personal dignity has been affronted unlawfully can demand that such affronts cease and are not repeated in the future.
* Article 59: The court can condemn the guilty party to pay compensation for any non-material damages.
* Article 281: Provides for penalties for any abuse of rights.

191

* Article 662: Provides that the employer guarantees the safety and health of employees at work.
* Article 932: Provides for compensation of an employee who has suffered damage to his or her health or mental well-being or has been deprived of his or her freedom.

Penal Code:
* Article 337: Provides for penalties for acts which are an affront to personal dignity with respect to a person's sex life.
* Article 343: Provides for punishment of any State employee who sexually abuses a subordinate.

ITALY

As pointed out above there is no specific law covering sexual harassment at work. At present there are only draft laws which have been submitted to Parliament but which have come up against a number of problems.

Article 660 of the Penal Code bans harassment but only in cases *"where it is committed in public or in places open to the public or by telephone"*. Harassment can involve injurious behaviour which is an affront to personal dignity and respect, regardless of whether the perpetrator is known to the victim (Article 594 of the Penal Code). In Italian law, the offences under which proceedings can be instituted against a harasser apart from those mentioned above are set out in the following articles: private violence (Article 610 of the Penal Code), obscene acts (Article 527 of the Penal Code) and sexual violence (Article 609a of the Penal Code). However, according to some specialists in favour of a specific law on sexual harassment at work, these laws cover too many different areas.

The Resolution of the European Parliament played a key role in creating this legal situation, since sexual harassment was defined as an infringement of the principle of equal opportunities in access to work and a career and for conditions of employment. Subsequently, the Recommendation of November 1991 stated that sexual harassment had to be regarded as indirect discrimination, because sex was the determining factor.

The concept of indirect discrimination is covered in Italian legislation by Law 125/91 on equal opportunities and positive action.

In labour law, harassment is covered under three headings (Vettor, 1996):
1. Disciplinary action
2. Compensation for misdemeanours
3. Compensation for discrimination

1. *Disciplinary action*

Sexual harassment can be covered by the enterprises' employment regulations. But penalties for sexual harassment have not been included in the disciplinary codes of collective agreements, except in the national collective agreements for employees in the public sector, ministries and local authorities, where provision is made for sexual harassment to be punished by suspension without pay.

2.   Compensation for misdemeanours

Compensation for misdemeanours requires the offence to be assessed in economic terms. Article 2043 of the Civil Code provides for compensation for any unlawful behaviour. Article 2087 of the Civil Code also provides for compensation for misdemeanours under the terms of employment contracts.

A victim of harassment is entitled to claim damages, since the head of the enterprise is obliged to take all the measures necessary to safeguard the physical and mental health and well-being of his employers. In the latter scenario, compensation can be sought irrespective of whether the harasser is the head of the enterprise, a colleague or a superior of the victim.

The case law covers both material and non-material damages caused by unlawful behaviour, physical damages and damages for infringement of the right to physical and mental well-being (Vettor 1996).

3.   Compensation for discrimination

According to the EU, sexual harassment comes under the heading of discrimination on sexual grounds. In Italian law action can be taken under the laws on discrimination (Law 903 of 1971 and Law 125 of 1991).

PORTUGAL

The absence of any legal definition of sexual harassment poses problems in analysing and handling the phenomenon in legal and social terms. This vacuum in Portuguese law makes it impossible for the labour administration or the courts to tackle this problem properly, particularly when it affects fundamental rights like the right to work and the right not to be discriminated against at work on the grounds of sex.

References to the issue of sexual harassment are to be found in labour law:

Article 19 of Decree-Law 49 408 of 24.11.1969 on the *"obligations of the enterprise"* where one paragraph is devoted to *"c) the obligation to organise good working conditions for workers, from both the physical and mental point of view"*.
Article 40 states that: *"Work must be organised and carried out in conditions of discipline, safety, health and moral conduct"* and *"the employer is under an obligation to institute disciplinary penalties or to dismiss workers of either sex who, by their conduct, cause or threaten to cause demoralisation of their colleagues, especially women and minors"*.
Article 3 1) of Decree-Law 392/79 of 20 September also deserves a mention: *"The right to work assumes the absence of any discrimination at all based on sex, be it direct or indirect, principally with reference to marital status or family situation"*.

Reference should also be made to more recent labour legislation on this matter, namely Decree-Law 64-A/89 of 27.2.1989, which obliges the head of an enterprise to take disciplinary measures against anyone who: infringes the rights or guarantees of the workers in the enterprise (Article 9-2b); is responsible for physical violence, abuse or other offences prohibited by the law against workers in the enterprise (Article 9-2i).

Decree-Law 64-A/89 permits workers to terminate their employment contract without notice if they are the victims of unlawful violations of their physical integrity, liberty, honour or dignity caused by a head of enterprise or his legal representatives (Article 35 1 e and f). In such cases a worker has the right to compensation (Article 36).

In the Penal Code (Decree-Law 48/95 of 15/3) in force since 1 October 1995, there is a chapter (V) on *"violations of sexual freedom and self-determination"* broken down into two sections, the first on *"violations of sexual freedom"* and the second on *"violations of sexual self-determination"*.

However, neither of these articles mentions, governs nor defines sexual harassment. Nevertheless, the articles of the Penal Code do enable sexual harassment at work to be punished. Article 154 provides that: *"Forcing a person into an action or an omission or support of an activity by means of violence or threats of grievous harm, shall be punished by a prison sentence of three years or a fine"*. In direct connection with this article, the following (Article 155) provides that: *"Where pressure is brought to bear...b) By a civil servant abusing his authority, he shall be punished by a prison sentence of between one and five years"*.

Articles 181 and 182 of the Penal Code, which cover abuse or its equivalent and verbal defamation, are also laws which may include sexual harassment. Article 181 thus provides that:*"1. Causing injury to a person by addressing remarks which are an affront to his or her honour and dignity shall be punished by a prison sentence of three months or a fine amounting to 120 days pay"*. Article 182 provides that: *"Defamation and verbal abuse are comparable with those made in writing, by gestures, pictures or any other means of expression"*.

Article 70 1 in Book I, Title II, Chapter I, Section II on "the rights of persons" in the Civil Code provides, with respect to the "general protection of persons" that: *"The law protects individuals against any unlawful offence or offensive threat to their physical or mental integrity"*. Article 483 1 of Book II, Chapter I, Section V, Subsection I on *"responsibilities in connection with unlawful acts"* provides that: *"Anyone who unlawfully infringes the right of others or any legal provision designed to protect the interests of others shall be obliged to compensate the person for the damages resulting from such infringement"*.

Finally, reference should also be made to Articles 13 and 59 of the Constitution of the Portuguese Republic which guarantee all citizens (men and women alike) the same social dignity and equality before the law and oblige the State to guarantee organisation of work in socially dignified conditions.

From this presentation of the situation in each country, we can see that there is no country which has an effective legal system for dealing with this question. This suggests that there is a need for a directive from the European Commission to improve the legal protection against sexual harassment at work and especially to reinforce coercive measures to prevent it.

4. THE POSITION OF ENTERPRISES WITH REGARD TO SEXUAL HARASSMENT

4.1 Methodology

In order to find out how enterprises stood with regard to sexual harassment we had decided to conduct a small survey (six enterprises) in each country on the following questions:

* their interpretation and definition of sexual harassment
* their position as regards sexual harassment (if they have had cases in the enterprise)
* their prevention policy
* their knowledge of EC rules and the Code of Practice
* the effects of sexual harassment on productivity in the enterprise.

We had also defined the criteria for the sample on the basis of two variables: the size of the enterprise and the composition of the workforce in terms of sex in order to obtain enterprises with a high, medium and low proportion of women in the services sector and in industry. This survey was to be carried out by a semi-structured interview in Spain, France and Italy by interview and questionnaire in Greece and by questionnaire alone in Portugal. Unfortunately, the methodological criteria finally had to be abandoned, especially in Spain, France and Italy, because there were problems in finding enterprises willing to discuss this issue. We were forced to present the subject of the interview differently in order to obtain appointments but still did not obtain better results. We therefore had to choose enterprises on the basis of other criteria, such as geographical ones for Italy or quite simply to interview any enterprises which were willing (France and Spain).

The interviews had to start off with more general questions on the enterprise's policy on equal opportunities or working conditions in general (France and Spain). However, we got a similar reaction when, during the course of the interview, we broached the subject of sexual harassment and the enterprise's policy for preventing and combating it.

We often came up against a wall of silence, which was much the same in all five countries, the questionnaires not having received a better response. In Greece, the results were very disappointing because the enterprises did not reply to the most important questions.

The reluctance of directors and people responsible for human resources to discuss the subject took different forms which can be classified as follows:

a)   a categorical refusal to consider the issue and to accede to our request for an interview, saying that they had no comments to make – the most frequent reply (in France and Spain) – because they had never encountered this sort of problem and had not given it any thought. In these cases, the people in charge described the atmosphere in their enterprise as "quiet" or "calm" or quite simply "normal". This was the case in enterprises in the banking sector in Italy. Other heads of enterprises said that the atmosphere was "very good" which meant that sexual harassment did not take place. In other cases, heads of companies said that they did not feel that the phenomenon was relevant since they had a low proportion of women on their staff. We thought it useful to analyse this refusal to comment because it is significant. We therefore treated it as an interview forming part of our own research which we tried to interpret on the basis of the attitudes and replies obtained from those who agreed to be interviewed.

b)   acceptance of an interview by telephone (in France). In these cases the people in charge said that there were in-house rules which prohibited sexual harassment and therefore there was no need for a prevention policy. They mentioned that a law existed in France, the impression being that the enterprise was at pains to execute the letter of the law but to deny the existence of sexual harassment in the enterprise. This justified not commenting further on the problem and for not feeling obliged to shed any light on the problem which, they said, did not concern them.

c)   acceptance of the interview at which they distanced themselves to the problem. This was the case in the majority of the interviews carried out. In order to facilitate matters we were obliged to justify our research by referring to the request from the EU, which showed heads of enterprises and management that this was a pan-European problem, and to be very careful in presenting questions about sexual harassment in the enterprise (Spain). The fact that this was necessary showed that this was an issue which managers and people in charge of human resources were not comfortable with.

One of the main questions we decided to study was, therefore, why enterprises should be so ill at ease.

4.2   The outcome of the interviews

4.2.1 Interpretation and definition of the concept

The question "how do you define sexual harassment?" elicited the same two replies from all the persons interviewed

1)   that the behaviour was "unwelcome" and
2)   that it was an abuse of power on the part of a man vis-à-vis one or more women.

However, opinions differed more when it came to defining the type of behaviour which should come under the heading of sexual harassment.

Although nobody suggested excluding physical action or aggression, some heads of enterprises tried to play down the importance of verbal harassment, saying that they were reluctant to accept the wider interpretation including psychological pressure, sexual comments or jokes which were not addressed at a specific person but which spoiled the working atmosphere.

Many men in positions of responsibility sought to play down the importance which might be attributed to certain sex-related comments, stressing the danger of classifying somewhat high-spirited male behaviour, which could be regarded as banter or gallantry, as sexual harassment .

An argument frequently deployed was that nowadays women who might be upset by such behaviour were better able to defend themselves and did not hesitate to make it plain that they did not appreciate such comments (Spain). However, they emphasised that the perception of sexual harassment was subjective and that it was difficult to find a universally acceptable definition. Such an attitude on the part of managers and people in charge of personnel gave us to understand that in many enterprises some types of sexual behaviour was still being played down and interpreted as camaraderie and jokes which were all part of the enterprise's customs and culture. However, when we interviewed women managers or women in charge of human resources they all mentioned such behaviour and did not hesitate to classify it as sexual harassment (Spain). They evidently had a better understanding of the problem than their male counterparts, even though at other times during the interview they also tried to keep the subject at arm's length.

4.2.2   *The situation in the enterprise*

In reply to the question *"Have you had to cope with sexual behaviour in your enterprise?"* the interviewees distanced themselves considerably from this question and the majority replied that there had been no sexual harassment in their enterprise, particularly in Portugal where not a single manager interviewed said that he had had to deal with such matters. Even those people in charge who did have to cope with such problems sought to present them as exceptions or problems which were things of the past.

There was even a case where the trade unions said that there had been a major conflict requiring action on their part, whilst the management denied having had to deal with any instances of sexual harassment (Italy).

However, women responsible for human resource management were far more willing to admit that there had been cases in the enterprise and gave the interviewers to understand that such problems might crop up again in the future, male behaviour being as it was. They admitted that they had heard young women in their own departments commenting on or warding off what many men were keen to describe as "banter or suggestive talk". They also pointed out that there were women who liked and even invited such behaviour.

They said that human resource departments were not always informed about what was going on in the enterprise as a whole (in large enterprises), except in the most serious cases, and that it was difficult to broach the subject. They said that their departments did not take "official" notice of the facts unless the person affected lodged a written complaint (which required a certain amount of resolution, conviction and courage) or the situation was serious, but that was not often the case.

However, in some cases (in Italy), the points of view and responses varied with the position and job occupied more than with the sex. Heads of enterprises who were not directly involved in dealing with sexual harassment on a day-to-day basis frequently condemned it far more openly, whilst at the same time remaining ambivalent in their attitude towards the situation in their own company. Mostly they admitted that they did not know exactly what the position was in their company and preferred to leave their reply vague. Managers or heads of enterprises in close contact with their staff tried to make light of the situation, their main objective being not to disclose any conflict but to uphold the image and reputation of the enterprise, especially when the most frequent cases of sexual harassment were caused by people in positions of authority.

Managers or heads of enterprises definitely tried to play down the importance of this problem by concealing or not admitting to the facts because they did not wish to admit in public that sexual harassment could be a problem in their enterprise.

4.2.3 *Measures taken to deal with the conflict*

The majority of managers and heads of human resources said that these were problems which were handled with great discretion and that they tried to find solutions which did not publicise the conflict in order to protect the reputation of both parties.

Generally speaking, cases of sexual harassment were solved by transferring the victim and it was very rare for the harasser to change jobs (in Spain and Italy), except following a case of physical harassment or a previous warning. In such situations, the transfer was meant as a punishment (particularly when it was a man in a position of responsibility) or a warning of possible dismissal.

At first sight, the transfer might appear to be a defeat for the victim, because it is a measure which may mask a certain amount of tolerance towards the harasser and abuse of power by men vis-à-vis women (as pointed out in the Italian report). However, it would appear that the problem is not always easy to solve.

According to the interviewees, it was often the women who asked for a transfer to escape "the shame of the assault" and said that they wished it to be kept secret. In such cases, the transfer of the harasser and publication of punitive measures would make it necessary to reveal the conflict, which was not what the victim or the enterprise wanted. And this was not only to prevent a negative image of the enterprise being propagated but also for fear that revealing the conflict could lead to criticism from the trade unions or other forces outside the enterprise. In effect, if the enterprise solved the problem publicly, it would open its in-house operations up to external scrutiny, which was a risk it was unwilling to run. In other cases some enterprises preferred to negotiate a mutual agreement to dismiss the victim but the researchers were not able to establish whether that was what the victim wanted.

In regions untouched by unemployment it was often the victims who preferred to leave the enterprise and seek alternative employment rather than remain in a working atmosphere with unpleasant associations (in the region of Veneto in Italy).

The care with which managerial staff weigh their words when talking about the situation in their enterprises in order not to say too much and the lengths they go to deal with any conflicts in complete secrecy so that they pass unnoticed or without remark only highlight the potential for embarrassment this problem holds for enterprises on the following counts:

a)   the risk of questions being asked about the role of the head of human resources;

b)   unwillingness to call attention to any dysfunction within the enterprise;

c)   the desire to keep things secret.

A) THE RISK OF QUESTIONS BEING ASKED ABOUT THE ROLE OF THE HEAD OF HUMAN RESOURCES

Revelations of sexual harassment cause a crisis in human resources departments. Indirectly, the department is responsible for the harasser, to whom it has delegated authority, but it also feels directly involved because the conflict reveals problems in choosing the right staff, especially those entrusted with responsibility. What is more, the human resources department might be indirectly to blame for contributing to or tolerating such behaviour. This explains why human resource departments try to keep quiet about and cover up any cases that do occur or pretend unconcern or detachment vis-à-vis this problem, in order to avoid external scrutiny of their work and their powers which might ultimately put their jobs in jeopardy.

B) UNWILLINGNESS TO CALL ATTENTION TO ANY DYSFUNCTION WITHIN THE ENTERPRISE

In some enterprises sexual harassment is known to be a hidden factor which is often involved in promotion, recruitment and pay increase policy. The system is based not solely on constraint but also on sex as a means of obtaining advantages at work. High-profile cases of sexual harassment call into question the working conditions imposed by the organisation, which is why managerial staff are unable to adopt a critical stance and say that they have had to deal with this problem because this would be an admission of functional weaknesses in their enterprise and would challenge its (injudicious) delegation of authority, (poor) work organisation and would hence constitute a challenge to their own authority.

C) THE DESIRE TO KEEP THINGS SECRET

Affronts to women's dignity are a familiar problem in enterprises but also a new one in the sense that harassment has now been defined as a concept, identified as a problem and outlawed with a view to eliminating very long-standing types of behaviour which were "legitimate and tolerated" at the workplace until just recently. However, it is not the novelty of the conflict surrounding abuses of power which is at the root of the enterprise's unease but men's collective desire to disguise types of behaviour that have been outlawed and not to disrupt the established order which is, of course, a male order. As a result, the managerial approach to sexual harassment is not always even-handed.

It is also the desire to protect male privilege which very frequently leads enterprises to cover up for harassers under the guise of discretion, demonstrating solidarity on two fronts, with both management (in the case of a person in a position of responsibility) and men closing the ranks. This also explains why complaints are more likely to be damaging to those who lodge them, as the normal reaction is for the woman to be transferred, dismissed or to resign.

However, complaints also backfire on women because they have dared to lift the veil on something which is supposed to be kept secret and the management's strategies to deal with the conflict are merely warnings to the others that it should remain so.

The "pact of secrecy" surrounding sexual harassment is also reinforced by administrative dictates to hold back information so that nothing is leaked to the outside world for fear of the consequences that a public revelation of sexual harassment could have on the enterprise's image and reputation. This is why employers oblige people in positions of responsibility to filter and hold back information so as to maintain a sort of corporate confidentiality in order to hide dysfunctions from the external observer and give the appearance of the enterprise operating in perfect harmony with management strategy.

4.2.4   The enterprises' prevention policy

The survey also set out to assess the measures adopted by the enterprises to prevent sexual harassment and protect the dignity of men and women at the workplace. One aspect of this policy is training which is as an indirect indicator of the desire to get to grips with the cultural roots of the problem. We found only one enterprise (in France) which had undertaken preventive action against sexual harassment through information and training of people in positions of responsibility and workers but this was an exception. This approach to prevention is unknown in the other four countries. What is more, occupational safety and health training (which developed very rapidly in all five countries as a result of the Community Directive) does not include prevention of sexual harassment either.

Of the five countries involved in the study, France is the one which places the greatest emphasis on prevention because in French law a manager or supervisor is the only person who can stop sexual harassment by deploying his disciplinary authority and is the only person who can be identified as a harasser and punished, as sexual harassment is punishable only when it also constitutes an abuse of power.

It is therefore understandable that the interviewees were extremely careful not to reveal that they were doing nothing in terms of prevention1 apart from including a reference to the law in the enterprise's employment regulations. They thought that the penalties for infringing the employment regulations were enough of a deterrent to restrain possible harassers – which the researchers felt was a very naive point of view.

In Italy, a services enterprise in Lombardy covered by the national collective agreement, which included provisions on equal opportunities and the law on positive action in training, had introduced courses for its staff. In Spain, not even the enterprises covered by collective agreements which included references to the ban on sexual harassment at work felt that prevention was a matter for them or made any effort to include the subject in training. One of the enterprises interviewed had not even incorporated the ban on sexual harassment in the enterprise's employment regulations.

It should also be noted that regular organisation of training activities in an enterprise is a relatively new development in some countries (Spain, Greece and Portugal) and is mainly found in medium and large-sized enterprises. However, training is also perceived by enterprises in these countries as a directly operational matter linked to problems of production, the market or organisation, while sexual harassment is a general social problem which heads of enterprises do not feel to be an immediate concern of theirs.

Some Greek heads of enterprise also think that information and prevention should be a matter for the family or education, since it is mainly about changing attitudes.

Another important aspect to be underlined is that expenditure on training has been cut drastically due to the economic and financial problems facing enterprises (in Italy), whilst training is reserved to cope with more practical problems which are essential for the smooth running of the enterprise.

Finally, the most powerful argument and the one which we have already stressed is that if enterprises decided to introduce preventive measures or incorporate prevention in their training programmes, this would prompt discussion of harassment and would bring it out into the open, which is precisely what heads of enterprises are reluctant to do for fear of leaving themselves open to questions about relationships between superiors and subordinates, especially between men and women at work and, finally, the position of women in the enterprise. Hence, many enterprises are very reluctant to disseminate information on the importance of equal opportunities (Spain, Italy) and see no point in doing so, as this is obviously something which has to be respected. Any discussion of the issues could sow doubts as to whether the enterprise lives up to the idyllic image which it is at pains to present. For others (in Italy), disseminating information also provides an opportunity to refute it and gives the enterprise's trade union delegates ammunition which they could use to expose the discrepancy between what management says and what it does, which is a risk they feel they would be ill-advised to take.

All this explains why many enterprises refuse to take preventive action and others prefer to wait until the case arises before looking at the problem and possibly putting preventive measures in place. This means that, as long as sexual harassment does not become a public scandal which threatens to damage the enterprise's or its management's reputation, the problem does not exist, particularly as the vast majority of them have been able to cope with it so far without the true scale of the problem being revealed.

4.2.5   Knowledge of EC rules and the code of practice

Generally speaking, EC rules and the code of practice are a closed book to enterprises, since virtually none of them knew about the EC Recommendation, the contents of the code of practice or the "confidential counsellor". However, in the case of Italy, this was in contrast with the fact that some enterprises had said that they would welcome an external consultation service.

The code of practice had not been circulated in the five countries' enterprises and some Portuguese enterprises said that EC provisions should be disseminated by the communication media, through employers' organisations or the relevant national bodies. However, some were at pains to point out that just because they were not familiar with the EC code of practice did not mean that they did not take suitable steps to deal with harassers (Spain, Italy). Managers said that when they had proof they took firm action but any penalties were contingent on their being able to prove the facts of the matter. Not all enterprises were in favour of adopting a code of practice because they thought that each country was properly equipped to deal with the problem and that each enterprise should look for the best strategies for curbing harassment. In some countries, such as Spain and Italy and, to a lesser extent, Greece, there was a growing number of collective agreements which incorporated clauses on sexual harassment. In Spain, some of these agreements restricted themselves to questions of principle. The majority of heads of enterprises were reluctant to accept such clauses because they did not see what use they were.

Opinions differed with regard to a specific law on sexual harassment (in Greece and Italy) or incorporation thereof in labour law (in Spain), because some people saw it as a positive measure to discourage possible harassers whilst others were not sure that a law would solve the problem. One Greek enterprise came out openly against a law on sexual harassment because it could ruin human relations between the staff.

4.2.6 The effects of sexual harassment on productivity

Harassed women, the trade unions, occupational physicians and labour inspectors point out that sexual harassment is detrimental to an enterprise's productivity and has an impact on costs due to:

* loss of interest in work
* reduced efficiency and performance
* loss of motivation
* problems doing and completing work
* sick leave and resignations which cause additional personnel management costs
* deterioration in the working atmosphere.

However, in our survey we did not find enterprises to be sympathetic to such arguments. In this report we will first try to analyse the reasons which prevent enterprises from factoring in the costs which sexual harassment can incur and will then look more closely at the facts revealed by our survey in order to see where enterprises stand.

A) THE REASONS WHICH PREVENT ENTERPRISES FROM FACTORING IN THE COST OF SEXUAL HARASSMENT

As we have pointed out, sexual harassment is still a hidden phenomenon and it is only because of the complaints that have been lodged that we can see the tip of the iceberg.
As things stand, enterprises would have to take organisational steps to monitor cases of sexual harassment closely in order to become aware of the impact of the costs or losses of productivity it causes. However, existing cases of harassment are covered up and, what is more, it is often the harassers, i.e. the superiors, who are supposed to trace or measure losses of productivity or the impact on the enterprise's costs, which makes things all the more difficult. Moreover, as an Italian manager said, sexual harassment is not a "sport for the masses" and it is not a large enough problem to produce statistically measurable data on productivity. It would certainly be more expensive for enterprises to introduce arrangements to monitor its cost.

Finally, we would be forgetting the links between sexual harassment and the balance of power between the sexes in a hierarchy if we thought that enterprises would be able to cultivate an awareness of the costs, which are difficult to measure, of a problem which they are not necessarily keen to eliminate but merely wish to control.

B) THE TYPE OF ENTERPRISE SURVEYED

Other aspects of the problem emerge if we look at sexual harassment in relation to the size of the enterprise, the type of organisation and the jobs occupied by women in the enterprises surveyed. The first thing we should ask is how an enterprise can measure productivity. If we take absenteeism as a parameter in service enterprises, we see that women's absences as a consequence of sexual harassment come under the heading of "sick leave", which is nothing out of the ordinary and will not prompt an enterprise to ask any further questions. Should an enterprise ask itself what the causes of sick leave amongst women are? This would appear to be a fairly questionable approach and could only be successful if personal privacy was invaded. In practice, as far as enterprises are concerned, the rate of absenteeism as a whole, amongst both men and women, is too high and their efforts are directed towards reducing it right across the board and not only amongst women.

If we look at the size of the enterprise, we see that, in the majority of the southern European countries, it is mainly small enterprises which employ a lot of female labour. In these enterprises there are only one or two superiors and productivity is monitored closely. In such a situation harassed women can hardly reduce output or stay off work repeatedly to the point where productivity is reduced without measures being taken. It is mainly in such enterprises that the head of the enterprise abuses his power to harass women who suffer in silence until the situation becomes intolerable and they are forced to resign, especially in areas where there is no lack of work (in north-east Italy). In such cases sexual harassment takes place out of the public eye and resignation eliminates all traces of it.

In such small enterprises where there are no trade unions, a woman who dares to raise her voice will quickly be dismissed without having her case heard as the enterprise has no interest in keeping her, especially as she is probably doing an unskilled job and can easily be replaced. In large and medium-sized production companies, women are employed in unskilled jobs, most often in assembly lines where the quality and quantity of the work are monitored closely. Any shortcomings are quickly spotted and remedied which means that women can easily be blackmailed or threatened.

In administrative posts held by women in service enterprises or in industry, individual productivity is very difficult to measure, because the work is broken down into departments and between several people In service enterprises where work calls for far more intellectual input, it is often organised in terms of projects and goals and it is difficult to attribute delays or difficulties in meeting deadlines to problems with the work itself or to other causes. The working atmosphere would have to deteriorate very considerably for the impact of sexual harassment to be measurable in terms of output.

Because of the way work is organised and the type of work which women do, especially in the services sector or in the administrative services of other sectors, it is impossible to monitor individual productivity closely, which means that the impact of sexual harassment on an enterprise's costs loses some of its force as an argument for remedying the problem. As regards the costs of replacing labour following resignations, we should note that in general, women are in jobs for which replacements can easily be found, which also explains why it is women who are transferred to other departments when there are cases of sexual harassment.

In the final analysis, we were not able to establish any concern on the part of managers or people in charge of human resources with regard to the effect of sexual harassment on the functioning of their enterprises nor could we adduce any arguments to increase enterprises' awareness of the problem by looking at it in terms of its effects on productivity.

5.   THE TRADE UNIONS' POSITION

5.1   Raising awareness of the problem

Most of the trade unions acknowledge that this is a major problem and that it is an obstacle to the integration of women in the labour market and equality for men and women at work. But this does not mean that sexual harassment is one of their main concerns. Feminists in the various countries agree that sexual harassment is sexual discrimination, as it is mainly women who are affected by the problem. Feminists interpret sexual harassment as a manifestation of power over another person which, at the workplace, may escalate to take the form of an abuse of the power conferred by rank.

This feminist interpretation of the problem, which has also been adopted by women's committees in the majority of the trade unions in the five southern European countries, has created tension in all the trade union organisations in southern Europe. The trade unions are used to defending workers (men and women) against employers but they are not used to taking action on behalf of women alone. So although the trade unions condemn sexual harassment, the measures they are supposed to take to combat the problem are often moved down the agenda to accommodate more general problems.

However, trade union organisations' awareness of sexual harassment varies considerably from one country to another, because their perception of it depends greatly on the clout that women trade unionists wield in the organisation and the awareness of the problem in society.

If countries were to be classified in terms of how actively women trade unionists combat this problem, **Italy** would take first place for promoting intensive discussion within the trade union organisations and for the many surveys carried out in various regions or sectors to define the problem more precisely and to gather information so that the scale of the problem could be publicised more widely.

At the same time, it was also very important to involve men in discussing this issue in order to prompt them to start thinking about their sexuality. As the women in an Emiliano trade union point out "If it is men who are committing rape, there is no way that women can be the only people who are still talking about it; men have to consider what might cause it without taking refuge behind the excuse that it is deviant behaviour". The input of Italian women trade unionists was crucial in persuading the male members of their organisation to face up to the problem, see sexual harassment from a different point of view and even to look at their relationships with women in the unions in another light. As some trade unionists point out "relationships are less frivolous and less superficial" when this problem is discussed with women in the trade union. In other words the policy conducted by the women in the trade union has led to a fresh awareness, particularly amongst the youngest members, which is slowly gaining ground.

It was also the women trade unions who introduced "hotlines" in women's groups and in centres for helping harassed women. They also pioneered the inclusion of this issue in collective agreements. In Italy, too, the role of equal opportunities committees was vital in supporting harassed women and in introducing the figure of the "confidential counsellor" (suggested in the Code of Practice) in enterprises or at regional level. In conclusion, the action and discussion prompted by women in trade union organisations have created an attitude which is conducive to dealing with the problem.

Spain is also a country where women trade unionists were aware of the problem at a very early stage. It was the Women's Department of the Regional Union of the UGT in Madrid which conducted the first and only survey of harassment in 1987 in Spain1. The women's committees of the two major trade unions (CC.OO. and UGT), which were aware of the scale of the problem, tried to raise its profile by means of statements and publications. The influence of the women's committees in the CC.OO. trade union led the national confederal body to organise a congress entitled "A trade union for men and women" in 1991. This congress represented a significant commitment by trade union leaders to women's problems and to adopting feminist theory as part of trade union doctrine. The decisions taken at the congresses of 1991 and 1993 helped to put equal opportunities and the right to dignity on the syllabus for training trade unionists in legal offices and trade union delegations.

The fact that sexual harassment is now being included as a hazard in the training programme for hazard-prevention delegates (health and safety at work) is also another step towards raising awareness of the problem amongst CC.OO. trade unionists. The current campaign against sexual harassment launched in Catalonia by the Women's Secretariat with the agreement of the regional confederal body is designed not only to raise awareness of the problem and to persuade women to lodge complaints about harassment but also to persuade trade union leaders in regional federations to become actively involved in this issue.

The Federations' Women's Secretariats' desire to conduct an internal discussion on sexual harassment between the negotiators of collective agreements was also responsible for this matter being incorporated. For their part, the UGT published a pamphlet on sexual harassment for trade union delegates which illustrates the women's department's concern to raise awareness amongst men in the trade union. The UGT and the CC.OO. also prepared a document on this issue for presentation to the employers' organisations in order to come to an agreement for the harasser to be redeployed or transferred to another work post, unless the victim wishes otherwise.

In **France** it was the CFDT which became aware of the problem earliest. In 1990 it conducted a survey to find out more about its extent and took part in drafting the proposal for a law. However, the advent of a specific law on sexual harassment in 1992 completely stymied any action by the French trade unions in this area. The effects of the legalistic approach to solving the problem can still be felt today, as it is only recently that the CGT and the CFDT have changed their strategy. The remaining trade unions, although they are minority ones, are still silent on this issue, except the trade union Sud which has made its views known.

The CFDT explain that they were operating on the principle that there was a law, which should have enabled them to combat the problem. Finally, however, as the person responsible for this issue in the organisation explains: "you realise that the law does not enable you to deal with the problem and that there is a need for places where concerns can be voiced, which the law does not provide for". Although the CFDT has been concerned about the problem for several years, it is only recently that it has started to tackle it more practically. The debate on this issue in 1996 revealed that the trade union needed to be able to get to grips with it rather than just muddling through, and that ways of getting trade unionists actively involved had to be devised. The declarations in 1997 by the National Secretary illustrate the trade unions' desire to adopt a proactive approach: "Although the legislative measures adopted in 1992 enable women to have their case heard more widely and to institute judicial proceedings, legal action is only one of the tools that trade unions can use. We should also develop prevention and negotiation procedures. The goals of the CFDT today are to lift the taboo on sexual harassment at work, give the victims a voice, organise effective action on their behalf by the trade unions, raise the awareness of and train players in working life and develop preventive measures". The union is obviously keen to do more than just resorting to legal proceedings. A variety of measures has been implemented to this end: a brochure addressed to trade union activists, a guide, posters to be put up in trade union offices and a pamphlet for workers have been produced and two training centres for trade unionists in enterprises and conciliation board chairmen have been set up.

CGT guidelines on combating sexual harassment for the whole confederation have now just been issued after isolated, empirical action had been taken for several years. The last congress (December 1995) was a landmark, with feminist issues being enshrined in the trade unions' value system: "the CGT must make its presence felt in any areas where women want it to". Statements made during the discussion organised on 8 March 1996 emphasised the fact that "it is now up to the trade union to make every effort to deal with this problem which is ruining many women's lives at work". These declarations were followed by more practical action, such as training on sexual harassment at a course for members of conciliation boards on sexist discrimination (other courses are to follow), articles appearing in the confederation's publications, "success stories" on action taken by local trade unions being circulated, a confederal women's committee on harassment being formed and also the issue being included in legal training for the heads of departmental unions or federations.

The fact that the CFDT and the CGT have taken a stand marks a sea change in the French trade union movement, but it is too recent to draw any conclusions from it.

The trade unions in Greece and Portugal are in a very different situation because virtually nothing has been done to tackle this issue. They are actually unwilling to accept that this is a serious and widespread problem.

In **Portugal**, it has not been a subject of discussion for very long. Women trade unionists feel that this is something which female workers know very little about and their willingness to lodge complaints depends on their level of education and social status. In 1992 the UGT approved action against sexual harassment in its statutes. Nevertheless, it did not figure in recent negotiations with the government and the employers which shows that there is a gap between declarations of principle and practice. There is very little awareness of the problem and hardly any progress has been made. Moreover, in the absence of a women's movement, seminars or discussions on the subject are unlikely to be organised, which explains why sexual harassment still goes entirely unnoticed by the public. But one aspect which could also account for trade unions' insensitivity to this issue is that there are cases of sexual harassment trade unionists. This is therefore not a problem in enterprises alone but in workers' organisations too.

In **Greece** too the trade union organisations show little awareness of this problem, even though cases of sexual harassment are very widespread and complaints are on the increase. However, there is a women's committee at confederal level in the GSEE trade union which is very active. The committee took charge of the four complaints lodged in 1997 and there are high expectations of the judgements in these cases. The committee also made its presence felt during negotiations of the general and national collective agreement in 1993 when a special article on dignity at work was introduced. This initial agreement prompted the Federation of Bank Employees (OTOE) and the Federation of Insurance Employees (OASE)1 to include similar articles as well. This committee and the women's movement are obviously enabling trade union organisations to make some progress in this area.

However, it should also be pointed out that trade union involvement in cases of sexual harassment is also a major problem in Greece which deprives the trade unions of any credibility they may have had in combating this problem.

This description of how trade union organisations stand with regard to sexual harassment indicates that there are great differences between the five countries, although the scale and nature of the problem do not differ much from one country to another, as the surveys and studies conducted in each of them show.

However, one important point is that, even in the countries where women trade unionists have long been active in raising awareness within their organisations (in Italy and Spain), sexual harassment cannot be described as being one of the unions' prime concerns because it is still regarded as being a matter for women trade unionists.

There are various reasons for this:

a) The trade unions' power base. Although women are well integrated in the labour market and their numbers in the unions are on the increase, they are still not constitute a sufficiently strong pressure group, as Italian trade unionists point out. The trade unions' battle plans still reflect the concerns of the majority groups amongst card-carrying members with good jobs and, as far as sexual harassment is concerned, they say that "men are not particularly keen on talking about such matters". Moreover, women's claims are made on behalf of the most marginal groups which do not account for a large proportion of union members.

b)The lack of women in positions of responsibility. Positions of responsibility in the trade unions are mainly occupied by men whilst women's jobs are usually in women's committees or carry less responsibility which prevents the problems which really interest women being moved up the organisation's agenda. We should also add that, according to Italian trade unionists, the women's group is weak and does not pursue its interests consistently and constantly but waits until an **opportunity** presents itself. And the trade unions only take action when a problem arises and "if it does not arise it is not a problem".

c)The problem's lack of profile. Sexual harassment is still a problem which has too low a profile and which female trade unionists have difficulty unmasking and as a result the effort that needs to be made to combat it does not offer much of a political return for trade union organisations. This explains why statements of principles by trade unions are not always matched by the commensurate level of activity and commitment within the organisation and action is still left too much to the initiative of women's committees.

5.2 Trade unions' strategies

The trade unions' approach to combating sexual harassment follows two main courses of action. The first strategy combats it with penalties and the second focuses more on changing the way people act.

a) Penalties

Here, women's committees have sought to highlight the problem by publishing information and facts whilst alerting women to the issue in order to persuade them to lodge complaints. This is the strategy adopted by the Spanish trade unions and the one emerging in Greece and Portugal, though there is less impetus behind it there. It is also in these countries that the lack of a legal framework in which the problem can be addressed is felt most keenly. In Spain, the absence of legislation is offset by clauses in collective agreements under the heading of misdemeanours and penalties but even in more recent collective agreements which deal with the problem far more fully, the emphasis is on procedures for rectifying the situation and for penalties and there are no preventive measures.

This strategy assumes that a potential harasser will refrain from action because of the penalties that can be imposed on him, but women still have to make complaints otherwise it will be relatively ineffective. Even though such a strategy serves to alert opinion to the problem, it comes up against the obstacles which stop women from lodging complaints (the risk of losing their job, being blamed by the people around them, a lack of support structures, and the absence of any law which protects them, etc.) and it is only women who are very sure of themselves and highly aware who embark on a complaint. Ultimately, the majority of women who have been harassed consider the cost of a complaint to be too high and it is only women who are very sure of their rights who dare to complain. As a result, the effort put into this strategy has not borne much fruit. What is worse, it has unfortunate side effects which ultimately backfire on women instead of the harassers, because the strategy's failure is blamed on women not complaining in sufficient numbers as they were meant to.

b) Changing the way people behave

This is the approach which the women's committees in the Italian trade unions have adopted where they try to change attitudes rather than concentrating on punitive measures. In the collective agreements on this subject, most of the proposals are for studies and research designed to introduce preventive measures. The equal opportunities committee adopts the same approach, introducing the "confidential counsellor" to help harassed women to cope with the situation and to deal with the problem with more tact than a male trade unionist would, particularly as the organisations still have not provided their delegates with in-depth training.

Giving women the wherewithal to defend themselves also seems a more suitable means of combating the problem than concentrating on punitive measures and this is the main thrust of the Italian trade unions' approach.

However, in Italy the discussion on the introduction of standards and penalties in collective agreements is not yet at an end, because there are people who feel the need for a law providing protection in this matter. Others, however, do not feel that penalties are the right way to diminish or discourage sexual harassment. The jury is still out on this question.

There is a third approach now gaining ground whose main thrust is prevention. This is the strategy which the Greek Women's Committee is opting for, which the French trade unions CFDT and CGT are starting to embrace and which some Italian women's committees are considering. It is certainly appears the most effective, because in the case of sexual harassment, prevention is better than a cure.

6. JOB INSECURITY: AN IDEAL BREEDING GROUND FOR SEXUAL HARASSMENT

As we have seen above, the best way of dealing with sexual harassment seems to be prevention, but any attempt to establish a coherent prevention policy at work will clearly have to come to terms with the enormous incidence of increased job insecurity in the five countries of Southern Europe. According to the interviewees, waxing insecurity creates ideal conditions for abuses of power and harassment of female workers who have been made more vulnerable by under-employment.

In an employment situation increasingly racked by uncertainty, instability, the retreat of labour law and growing exploitation of power, especially over those who are already vulnerable, one can easily see why insecurity in itself constitutes an ideal breeding ground for sexual harassment at work.

Various factors have combined to step up the rate and increase the extent of economic insecurity since the beginning of the 90s, during which time new types of employment - with "atypical", "integration" or "reintegration" jobs coming on top of fixed-term contracts - have thrown many workers into uncertain and insecure employment. Although this is something which affects the entire production system, all enterprises - small, medium-sized and large - and all groups of employees, the main victims and the first to suffer - though not the only ones - are women who are, on the whole, hit harder by job insecurity than men. An illustration of the segregation process in increasingly diversified and insecure forms of employment is part-time work, an insecure form of employment reserved mainly for women, who account for some 85% of the jobs available.

Working conditions and practices in general and those with a bearing on sexual harassment in particular are not going to remain unaffected by increasing job insecurity for women. Given that the victims generally come from disadvantaged and dependent groups of the labour force which often have problems in exercising their rights (women, young people and immigrants), the insecurity which exacerbates women's vulnerability is seen as a real danger because it may foreshadow what will be the norm tomorrow for women at work and once individuals are in this vulnerable situation where their problems mount up, they may be caught in a downward spiral, since their weak bargaining position compels them to adjust not only to economic restructuring but also to the abuses which it causes, severely destabilising employment contracts and often forcing them into the role of victims.

Every effort has to made to ensure that women, who are worst affected by job insecurity as a result of their greater vulnerability in the labour market, are not also hit hardest by these upheavals which put them at the mercy of chance, increased subordination vis-à-vis their employers and a deterioration in their bargaining position due to their greater vulnerability.

The interviewees thus thought that an effort should be made to combat job insecurity so that a vulnerable labour force with uncertain and unstable employment does not play into the employers' hands and provide another opportunity to mount an attack on women's dignity and so that a breeding ground for sexual harassment is not created in a situation where the conditions set out below are ripe for it:

* increased inequality and discrimination against women
* reduction in the room for manoeuvre
* individual pay bargaining
* weakening of collective links at work
* increased dependency
* pressure to keep quiet about abuses.

Job insecurity for women thus impedes progress towards equality for the two sexes, because deregulation of employment inevitably leads to more oppression as the labour law protection systems and laws issued to protect workers from abuses are dismantled and job insecurity ensures that female workers are more reluctant to lodge complaints and enforce their rights. And for women, the main concern is to cover up and keep quiet about the various humiliations, abuses and harassment they have endured, fearing the consequences of exposure, which is often dismissal and is a risk which they are unwilling to take in case it starts them off on the downward spiral towards exclusion.

In the new social context of insecure employment, management uses job insecurity as a lever to exert pressure and exercise control which is compounded by the economic, sociological and psychological dependence in which more and more female workers are being plunged due to the crisis in employment and the general climate of insecurity. In such situations, which employers use and abuse, the omnipresent threat of dismissal is a permanent barrier to individual and collective strategies for resistance. Indeed, faced with an employer who holds all the cards in his hand, there is more and more of a tendency for women to become resigned to their fate, since labour market constraints deprive them of any scope for individual action.

Job insecurity for women is seen as a spawning ground for sexual harassment because it offers employers more opportunities to blackmail women in order to obtain sexual favours. Women find it all the more difficult to avoid this because the decisions affecting their jobs - regarding recruitment, promotion, renewal of the employment contract and dismissal - and their working conditions are all in the hands of male managers and supervisors who are liable to be all too easily tempted to abuse their authority and to use their prerogatives to maximum possible effect.

In this situation the European Commission should not confine itself to taking measures against sexual harassment at work but should also seek to reinforce measures against insecurity in order to put a stop to sexual harassment in our times and rid society of its hidden agenda.

7.   PROPOSALS FOR THE EUROPEAN COMMISSION

This study shows that, although the EC Recommendation and the Code of Practice have had the merit of raising awareness of the problem and prompting women to stand up for their dignity in the five countries examined, the effect on the social players in industrial relations has been more muted, and the preventive and information measures the EU recommends have not been applied in any of them.

The research also shows that none of the five countries has a law covering the entire spectrum of sexual harassment. However, the persistence and scale of the problem are not, strictly speaking, a product of the legislative vacuum but of other social factors such as:

a)   many women's misapprehensions about and lack of understanding of what sexual harassment entails;
b)   obstacles to lodging complaints;
c)   the impact of the stereotypes associated with sexual harassment and problems in changing attitudes;
d)   trade union organisations' failure to tackle issues concerning personal dignity or to tackle them vigorously enough;
e)   enterprises' reluctance to do anything about it;
f)   male complicity of the various players in industrial relations.

As a result, sexual harassment remains an unseen phenomenon, as pointed out above, and there are very few women who dare to complain about it. Measures therefore need to be envisaged which are designed to **raise the profile** of sexual harassment and make complaints about it **legitimate**. There seems no alternative to a new European directive to counter the individual and collective secrecy which surrounds sexual harassment at work.

Since the repercussions of sexual harassment are so severe for the victims, as the national studies show, policy must, above all, be geared to **prevention** rather than punishment. Rather than seeking to take punitive action – after the fact when the damage has already been done – the aim should rather be to prevent it becoming necessary. Recourse to the law can, of course, only dress the victims' wounds but not heal them, not only because of the sexual harassment they have suffered but also because judicial procedures are so cumbersome and so time-consuming. It is therefore necessary to promote a policy which takes effect at an earlier point in time because, as we have seen, there is still a lack of preventive measures.

The new directive should therefore mainly be designed to promote:
a)   a policy of **prevention**1 and not only of penalties and,
b)   a policy which genuinely encourages prevention and not one which merely purports to do so.

Such a policy would comprise:

a)   **legislative action**

Implementing an effective prevention policy in enterprises requires:

* penalties to be reinforced, since the coercive aspect of prevention should not be neglected as a deterrent;
* the onus to be placed on the employer to take preventive action.

b)   **empirical preventive measures**

Everybody – both within and outside the enterprise – who may play a key part in putting a stop to sexual harassment or preventing it from starting has to be mobilised. Apart from management, which is supposed to play its part, workers, occupational physicians, workers' representatives or trade union delegates, labour inspectors, the police, the State department for women's rights, associations and also judicial instances must be given the wherewithal to be agents of prevention.

c)   **action against victimisation**

A ban has to be placed on harassed women being dismissed when they refuse to accept harassment or lodge a complaint. In the same way, it should be the harasser who is redeployed or transferred to another post unless the victim decides otherwise.

A pre-emptive policy therefore needs to be implemented which entails:

* obligations to provide information to raise individual and collective awareness, as interviews show that sexual harassment has yet to be brought out into the open and information campaigns are needed to:
  - inform public opinion on the severity of the problem;
  - inform women of their rights, explain to them what sexual harassment entails and what underlies such practises, so that they realise what is happening to them and are given the means to complain about it;
  - tell managers and people responsible for human resources what their duties are, to overcome inertia with regard to prevention and to encourage a more pre-emptive approach;
* an obligation to train social players to alert them to the problem and make them do something about it;
* an obligation to introduce a confidential counsellor at enterprise or regional level to help victims to cope with the situation and exercise their rights;
* a policy against victimisation of harassed women which stops the measures taken by enterprises to deal with conflicts affecting women rather than the guilty parties;
* a policy for equality for men and women, since it is obvious that until the balance of power changes and there is still a sexual division of work and power, women will remain potential victims;
* a policy to combat unemployment and increased social insecurity which provide ideal conditions for abuses of power.

1.   The obligation to inform women

This need is justified all the more by the fact that, although more and more women are making complaints, the defensive strategy women still deploy most is to wait and keep quiet about harassment.

Information campaigns are indispensable to counter:
* women's lack of knowledge about their rights and the means of protection available to them in each country;
* their misunderstanding of what harassment involves, to prevent problems of interpretation, ambiguities and misunderstandings. A precise definition should be adopted in the new European Commission directive.

Women also need to be told what harassment really involves because they generally define it in restrictive terms and from the victim's point of view. They see themselves both as victims and as being to blame, because they do not understand the mechanics of power and the division of work and power between the sexes which create the climate for harassment .

Information for women - which is indispensable if they are to understand what is happening to them - thus needs to be promoted on a massive scale in order to raise awareness of the theoretical and practical implications of the problem, to open their eyes to the reality of sexual harassment and to enable them to dare to think about and exercise their rights.

Such campaigns will also enable women to take an active part in prevention in that, once they know their rights and are aware of the problem, they can do much to discourage any type of sexual harassment by making it quite clear that they regard it as unacceptable as soon as they encounter it.

However, information should not be reserved exclusively for women but must also be addressed to men to make them aware of the fact that anybody can be a victim of harassment either directly (women) or indirectly (wives or daughters). Sexual harassment is no joke and people who still think it is should realise that they or those closest to them may be exposed to such humiliating behaviour.

In enterprises, information campaigns should not address only a specific group of women but women in general and not only the staff present at a given moment in time but also all new recruits.

Media campaigns are also needed to encourage people to speak out about and increase awareness of the problem as long as:
* they are handled properly in order to avoid any adverse effects or extremist behaviour resulting from matters being taken too far or false conclusions being drawn.
* sexism through language and images is combated in awareness-raising campaigns. Although the media should obviously be playing a major part in preventing sexist behaviour, the images of women which they portray should be treated with caution.

2.   *An obligation to inform human resources departments*

In the absence of any system of prevention in enterprises, something needs to be done about the "head in the sand" policy of employers who refuse to budge on prevention and managers who wait until their backs are against the wall before doing anything. The directive needs to beef up the penalties for harassment to make deterrents one of the facets of prevention. A genuine obligation to take preventive measures which is binding on employers needs to be introduced and to this end the directive should:

* emphasise the part management has to play by placing a legal obligation on employers to introduce a preventive policy, failing which they will be held responsible;
* force employers to adopt preventive measures which must produce results, failing which penalties will be incurred, based on the principle that the mere fact that sexual harassment could have occurred demonstrates that the employer has failed to fulfil his obligations to prevent it;
* failure to take preventive action must have consequences for the enterprise and must make it liable as a legal person, incurring the penalties provided for by the law.

Heads of enterprises and of human resources departments could also be made to understand that sexual harassment not only has a human cost but also, like any deleterious working condition, has a considerable economic cost for the enterprise (in terms of sick leave, etc.) and that an instance of sexual harassment may adversely affect both the climate at work and the company's external image.

3. An obligation to train social players

All the social players both in and outside an enterprise can be encouraged to play a key role in tackling this problem, not only in terms of dealing with it and repairing the damage but also in terms of prevention – elected workers' representatives, occupational physicians, CHSCT, labour inspectors, associations, the police, civil or criminal courts, the Public Prosecutor's Office, conciliation boards, etc.

Such training activities must provide them with an approach to the problem and a working methodology so that they can act as agents of prevention.

4. An obligation to introduce a confidential counsellor

Harassed women definitely need guidance and information on the procedure to be followed. It is therefore a sound preventive measure to introduce a confidential counsellor at enterprise or regional level (in the case of small enterprises). The confidential counsellor's role could also be to ensure that situations conducive to sexual harassment do not arise and also to encourage and organise training on the issue within enterprises. Within medium-sized and large enterprises, the confidential counsellor could be chosen from the workers' elected representatives.

5. Equality for men and women to create a working atmosphere which is free from sexual harassment

To prevent a pre-emptive policy remaining superficial, it would have to seek to intervene directly to combat the **causes** of sexual harassment. The problem of sexual harassment must therefore not be seen in isolation from the conditions which spawn it, because legislation will otherwise remain a dead letter. The European Commission's proposals to combat sexual harassment at work will be relevant and will enable women to escape the role of potential victims only if they incorporate measures to foster equality for men and women. The best policies for solving the problem of sexual harassment are those linked with a general policy of promoting equal opportunities and improving the position of women, since sexual harassment goes hand in hand with inequality at work and unfair distribution of power between men and women. The European Commission should therefore reinforce existing measures to promote equal opportunities.

6.   *A policy to combat unemployment and the increase of social insecurity*

A pointed out above, the employment crisis and the trend towards insecurity are a breeding ground for abuses of power. Indeed, the increasing job insecurity which is becoming a permanent feature in the five countries in southern Europe is detrimental to equal rights for men and women insofar as it constitutes an obstacle to equal opportunities in the labour market.

Women have been found to be the main victims of insecurity and fixed-term contracts, part-time work and a whole series of employment-related measures severely undermine their financial independence and increase their vulnerability and the probability of their being a potential victim of harassment.

Here it is not only economic considerations but also all policy considerations – particularly regarding the thrust of employment policy – which must be examined. In practice, this means that any policy against sexual harassment must factor in the shortage and insecurity of employment and therefore opportunities for harassment, which are now rife. In this context it is vital for the European Commission to seek to introduce and strengthen measures against insecurity at the same time as it introduces measures against sexual harassment.

REFERENCES

Spain

Calle, M.; González, C. and Núñez, J.A., Discriminación y acoso sexual a la mujer en el trabajo, Editorial Largo Caballero, 1988.

CC.OO. Secretaría Confederal de la Mujer, Acción sindical frente al acoso sexual, Madrid, Secretaría Confederal de la Mujer de CC.OO., 1990.

European Commission, How to combat sexual harassment at work. Guide to implementing the European Commission's Code of Practice, DG V A3, Brussels, 1993.

Commission of the European Communities, Sexual Harassment, Consultation of the social partners on the prevention pf sexual harassment at work.

De La Vega, José Augusto, El acoso sexual como delito autónomo, Madrid, Colex, 1991.

Del Rey, S., Acoso sexual y relación laboral, a "Relaciones Laborales", Vol. I, Madrid, 1993, pp. 228-268.

Escudero, Ricardo, El acoso sexual en el trabajo, a "Asesoras/es para la igualdad de oportunidades", Madrid, Secretaría Confederal de la Mujer de CC.OO., 1993.

Gruber, J.E., Sexual Harassment Experiences of Women in Europe, The United States and Canada, University of Michigan-Dearborn.

Jacobsohn, F.; Cromer, S. and Hildebrandt, S., Innovatory action in Europe to combat sexual harassment, Commission of the European Communities, 1994.

Mackinnon, C., Sexual harassment of working women: A case of sex discrimination, New Haven, Yale University Press, 1979.

Maquira, V. y Sánchez, C., Violencia y sociedad patriarcal, Madrid, Pablo Iglesias, 1990.

Pérez Del Rio, Teresa, El acoso sexual en el trabajo: su sanción en el orden social, a "Relaciones Laborales", vol. II, Madrid, 1990, pp. 181-199.

Pérez Del Rio, T.; Fernández López, F. and Del Rey, S., Discriminación e igualdad en la negociación colectiva, Madrid, Instituto de la Mujer, 1993.

Sáez Lara, Carmen, Mujeres y mercado de trabajo. Las discriminaciones directas e indidrectas, Madrid, Consejo Económico y Social, 1994.

Serna Calvo, Mª del Mar, La inspección del trabajo ante la situación laboral de la mujer, Informe de la Jefatura Adjunta de Inspección de Trabajo y Seguridad Social, MTSS, Madrid, 1992.

Serrano, Ignacio, El acoso sexual, a "TAPIA", núm. 80, Madrid, 1995, pp. 19-23.

Torns, T. *et. al.*, L'assetjament sexual en el món del treball a Catalunya, Universitat Autònoma de Barcelona, Departament de Sociologia, Bellaterra, 1996.

UGT, Secretaría de Acción Social, Departamento de la Mujer, Guía sindical sobre acoso sexual en el trabajo, Madrid, 1994.

France

Action Vaucluse A.V.F.T./Inspection du travail, des Transports et de l'Agriculture, Rôle de l'inspection du travail en matière de harcèlement sexuel. Essai de méthodologie d'intervention, November 1993 (12 pages).

A.V.F.T., De l'abus de pouvoir sexuel. Le harcèlement sexuel au travail, Paris, Editions La Découverte, 1990 (259 pages/bibliography), France.

A.V.F.T., Bulletin, Cette violence dont nous ne voulons plus, Paris. 10 numéros publiés. N° spéciaux: "Syndicalisme et sexisme", N° 7, "Harcèlement sexuel et patronat", N° 8.

A.V.F.T., La Lettre de l'AVFT, Bulletin on sexual harassment at work (12 pages). 9 issues published since 1992.

Beneytout, Mireille, A.V.F.T., "Projets Féministes", proposal for a reform of labour law, N° 1, March 1992 (10 pages/Bibliography), Paris, France.

Beneytout, Mireille; Cromer, Sylvie; Jacob, Thérèse and Louis, Marie-Victoire, A.V.F.T., "Semaine Sociale Lamy", Harcèlement sexuel au travail, N° 557, July 1991 (2 pages).

Beneytout, Mireille; Cromer, Sylvie; Jacob, Thérèse and Louis, Marie-Victoire, A.V.F.T., "Semaine Sociale Lamy", Harcèlement sexuel: une réforme restrictive qui n'est pas sans danger, N° 599, May 1991 (2 pages).

ILO, Cromer, Sylvie (AVFT), Le harcèlement sexuel au travail, La Situation en France, Janvier 1992. (84 pages/bibliography, report.

Cahiers du Féminisme, Harcèlement sexuel. Une loi pour quoi faire?, N° 62, autumn 1992.

Chénard, L.; Cadrin, H. and Loiselle, J., État de santé des femmes et des enfants victimes de violences conjugales. Research report. Municipal health department. Rimouski regional hospital, October 1990.

Cromer, Sylvie (AVFT), Le harcèlement sexuel. La levée du tabou, 1985-1990. Paris, La Documentation française, 1995 (Bibliography) France.

Cromer, Sylvie (AVFT), "Projets Féministes", Histoire d'une loi, la pénalisation du harcèlement sexuel dans le nouveau code pénal, N° 1, March 1992 (10 pages).

Cromer, Sylvie and Louis, Marie-Victoire, A.V.F.T., "French Politics and Society", Existe-t-il un harcèlement sexuel "à la française'?", Cambridge, Massachusetts, Minda de Gunzburg Center for European Studies Harvard University, 1992. Volume 10, N° 3 (7 pages).

Dekeuwer-Defossez, Françoise, "La Semaine juridique", Le Harcèlement sexuel en droit français: Discrimination ou atteinte à la liberté, E.D.G.D., N° 13.

Delphy, Christine, "Nouvelles Questions Féministes", L'affaire Hill-Thomas et l'identité nationale française, 1993. Volume 14, N° 4 (10 pages).

Doray, Bernard, Réflexions sur les effets destructeurs du harcèlement sexuel, "La Lettre de l'AVFT", N° 8-9, April 1996 (3 pages).

D.R.T.E. (Direction Régionale Du Travail Et De L'emploi - Ile de France), Le rôle de l'inspection du travail, Michel Mine, Horizons - Ile de France, special issue "Femmes, 2ème partie: travail", Mars 1994.

D.R.T.E. (Direction Régionale Du Travail Et De L'emploi - Ile de France), Dossier harcèlement sexuel, "La Gazette sociale d'Ile de France", internal review of the Ile de France decentralised labour, employment and vocational training services, N° 31, June 1996.

Guerder, Pierre, "Droit Social", La Poursuite et la répression pénales des discrimination en droit du travail, N° 5, May 1995 (7 pages). Éditions Techniques et Économiques, Paris, France.

Harris, Louis, Rapport d'étude, Le harcèlement sexuel: Enquête des Français: perception, opinions et évaluation du phénomène, December 1991. (63 pages), Paris.

International Labour Office: Geneva, "Conditions of work digest", Combatting sexual harassment at work, volume 11, 1992 (299 pages/bibliography/resssources).Switzerland.

Jacob, Thérèse, A.V.F.T., "Vie Sociale", Revue de Musée Social, Le harcèlement sexuel sur les lieux de travail en France, Centre d'études, de documentation, d'information et d'actions sociales, Paris, 1990. May-June, N° 5/6 (13 pages/bibliography).

Lepastier, Samuel, Le harcèlement sexuel: une psychopathologie au quotidien?, "Psychiatrie française", N° 2, June 1992, pages 25-31.

Leymann, Heinz, Mobbing. La persécution au travail. Seuil, January 1996.

Louis, Marie-Victoire, Le Droit de cuissage. France, 1860-1930, Paris, Les Editions Ouvrières, 1994 (319 pages/bibliography).

Louis, Marie-Victoire, A.V.F.T., "Chronique Féministe", Le Harcèlement sexuel: Quels enjeux pour les féministes?, N° 44, June-July 1992 (9 pages), Belgium.

Mazeaud, Antoine, "Droit Social", Changement d'affectation et harcèlement sexuel, April 1993, N° 4.

Miné, Michel and Saramito, Francis (Confédération Générale du Travail), "Le Droit ouvrier", Le harcèlement sexuel, February, 1997 (pp. 48-73).

Moreau, Marie-Ange, "Droit Social", A propos de l'abus d'autorité en matière sexuelle, February 1993, N° 2 (7 pages).

Rubinstein, Michael, La Dignité de la femme dans le monde du travail, Rapport sur le problème du harcèlement sexuel dans les Etats membres des Communautés européennes, 2 volumes (English and French); October 1987. Europe.

Roy-Loustaunau, Claude, Study: Le Harcèlement sexuel à la "française", Commentary of Law N° 92/1179 du 2 November 1992, "La Semaine Juridique", 67th year of issue, 15 April 1993, N° 15.

Roy_Loustaunau, Claude, Le droit du harcèlement sexuel: un puzzle législatif et des choix novateur, "Droit Social", N° 6, June 1995 (5 pages/bibliography).

Rutter, Peter, Le sexe abusif. Lorsque des hommes en situation de pouvoir abusent des femmes, MA éditions, 1990.

Savoie, Dominique, Le harcèlement sexuel au travail et les femmes québécoises, Thesis - Montréal University, 1984.

Université d'Avignon et des Pays de Vaucluse, Harcèlement sexuel: réflexion juridique, Seminar held on 28 January 1995.

Italy

Arnaud, Edy, 1990 Molestie sessuali e Contratti' Coordinamento nazionale donne Cgil, Notiziario, Rassegna Sindacale, N. 28, Rome.

Asso Lei, Sportello Donna, 1996, 'Monitorando Pechino. Molestie sessuali'. Rome.

Conference proceedings, Studio sulle molestie sessuali nei luoghi di lavoro, da una ricerca Cgil in provincia di Modena, Così fan (quasi) tutti..., 11 April 1991.

Conference proceedings, Fiom-Regione Emilia Romegna, 9 September 1991, Tu mi turbi, lavoro e non solo, Bologna.

Seminar proceedings, Gruppo donne della Fiom-Cgil di Bologna, 29 September 1989, Per una sessualità non violenta nella società e nei luoghi di lavoro.

Basso, L. 1995 "Un' esperienza di approccio nei casi di molestie sessuali nei luoghi di lavoro" Il cittadino Ritrovato, dossier n° 1, Rome.

Beccalli, Bianca, 1991, in Coordinamento donne Uil, Comune di Milano - Centro azione Milano donne, 1991 'Tu mi turbi', Conference proceedings, 10 December 1991, Chamber of Commerce.

Beltrami, Orsola, 1988, "Il paradosso Beltrami", Noi donne, N. 12, (p. 12-14).

Bertarelli, Paola and Pellegrino, Andrea, 1997, "Relazione sulla diffusione delle molestie sessuali nel luogo di lavoro" , rapporto cicl.

Bisi, Roberta and Faccioli, Patrizia, 1996, Con gli occhi della vittima, Franco Angeli, Milan.

Boggi, Ornella, Cacioppo Maria (a cura di), 1994, "Chi tace acconsente?" Initial results of a survey on harassment in some sectors of the municipality of Milan, Cgil-Cisl-Uil, cicl.

Catalano, T. 1991 'Molestie sessuali nei luoghi di lavoro: può bastare la normativa? ' in Quì Fisac Lombardia.

CGIL, 1990 'Molestie sessuali e Contratti' Coordinamento nazionale donne Cgil, Notiziario, Rassegna Sindacale, N. 28, Rome.

Chiavassa, Alba and Hoesch, Laura, 1992, 'Lavoro femminile: normativa antidiscriminatoria e molestie sessuali', D&L, Rivista critica di diritto del lavoro, N.3.

Ciuti, Ilaria, 1994, "Enzina e il padroncino", Noi donne, N. 7/8, (p. 32-33).

Codrignani, Giancarla, 1996, Molestie sessuali e "In"certezza del diritto, Franco Angeli, Milan.

Municipality of Milan, 1996, 'Codice di condotta per la tutela della dignità delle lavoratrici e dei lavoratori', Civica stamperia.

Coordinamento donne Uil, Comune di Milano - Centro azione Milano donne, 1991 'Tu mi turbi', Conference proceedings, 10 December 1991, Chamber of Commerce.

Cotti, Carla, 1990, "Meccaniche molestie", Noi donne, N.7-8, (p. 28-29).

Crispino, Anna Maria, 1986, "Undicesimo non molestare", Noi donne, N. 12, (p. 60-63).

Dall'Aglio, Marzia, 1994, "Rivendichiamo il diritto a non essere molestate", Notiziario Anpi, N. 3, (p. 14).

Di Genova, Arianna, 1993, "Vuoi provarci ancora Sam?", Noi donne, N. 4, (p. 24-25).

Dominijanni, Ida, 1992, ' Violenza sessuale: un progetto di legge si aggira da 13 anni', Via Dogana, N.5e 6, Libreria delle Donne, Milan.

Ecchia, Wilma, 1991, "I primi passi delle azioni positive", Il diritto delle donne, N. 11 (P. 10).

Faccioli, Patrizia and Simoni, Simonetta, 1991, Le molestie nella percezione soggettiva. (Dattiloscritto).

Galli, Ughetta, 1990, "Molestie sessuali, gerarchie e organizzazione del lavoro", Informazioni e orientamenti, N. 3-4, (p. 29-30).

Grisendi, Adele, 1992, Giù le mani, Mondadori, Milan.

Guerzoni, Mayda, 1989, "In ospedale è peggio", Il diritto delle donne, N. 5, (p.7).

Guerzoni, Mayda, 1989, "Sulle ginocchia del capo", Il diritto delle donne, N. 5 (p. 6).

Guerzoni, Mayda, 1990, "Molestie in piattaforma", Il diritto della donna, N. 8, (p. 2).

Guerzoni, Mayda, 1991, "Ma se è solo un complimento", Il diritto delle donne, N. 11, (p. 10).

Ianniello, Rosanna, 1994, "Alle soglie del 2.000", Il Foglio de Il Paese delle donne, N. 7.

Jannelo,, Rosalba, 1995 'Relazione al conferenza: XI° Non Molestare. Azioni e progetti contro le molestie sessuali nei luoghi di lavoro pubblici', Il cittadino Ritrovato, dossier n° 1, Roma Lombardo, Leda Alice, 1995 'Le molestie sessuali nella formazione: il caso delle scuole per infermieri professionali di Padova, Abano ed Este', Il Cittadino Ritrovato dossier n° 3, Rome.

Mackinnon, Catharine, 1993, "Nei tribunali statunitensi una legge delle donne per le donne", Democrazia e diritto, N. 2, (p. 203-224).

Mauti, Paola, 1991, "Luoghi ad alto rischio", Nuova Rassegna Sindacale, N. 46, (p. 19).

Molestie sessuali, il reato che non c'è ,"Foglio (Il) de Il Paese delle donne" 1994 (supplement) Nos. 3, 7, 13, 18, 25, 26, 29.

Neonato, Silvia, 1993, "Peggio le molestie che la prima linea", Noi donne, N. 1, (p. 24-25).

Neonato, Silvia, 1994,"Dubbi tra le parlamentari", Noi donne, N. 6, (p. 25).

Neonato, Silvia, 1994, "Denuncia con tragedia", Noi donne, N. 5, (p. 38-39).

Passalacqua, Carla, 1990 'Molestie sessuali e Contratti ' Coordinamento nazionale donne Cgil, Notiziario, Rassegna Sindacale, N. 28, Rome.

Pitch, Tamar, 1993, "Per rispettarsi davvero non basta denunciare", Noi donne, N. 5, (p. 10).

Pitch, Tamar, 1994, "Quando la legge è pesante", Noi donne, N. 6, (p. 22-25).

Piva , Paola, 1986, "Reagire, sottrarsi, o 'fare fronte'?," Noi donne, N. 12, (p. 62).

Magistrates Court of the Italian Republic, Mantova, 1995 'Judgement n° 257/94'.

Magistrates Court of the Italian Republic, Milano, 1991 'Judgement n° 7430/90'.

Magistrates Court of the Italian Republic, Torino, 1990 'Judgement n° 9555/90'.

Magistrates Court of the Italian Republic, Trento, 1994 'Judgement n° 76/93'.

Provincc of Milano, Equal Opportunities Committee, 1994 'Molestie sessuali sul posto di lavoro: un ostacolo per la realizzazione della pari dignità e libertà delle persone che lavorano', Conference proceedings.

Province of Siena, 1995 'Maltrattamenti e molestie in Provincia di Siena' Rapporto di ricerca, Il cittadino ritrovato, dossier, Rome.

Ricci-Sargentini, Monica, 1988, "l bollettino delle avance", Noi donne, N. 12 (p. 15).

Santaniello, M. 1995 'Ricerca sulla diffusione delle molestie sessuali sul lavoro: il caso dell' Imps del Friuli Venezia Giulia' in Il cittadino ritrovato, dossier, Rome.

Sarasini, Bia, 1988, "Sussurri e grida, anonimi però", Noi donne, N. 12 (p. 9-15).

Sarasini, Bia, 1994, "Posta in gioco: la libertà femminile", Noi donne, N. 9, (p. 16-18).

Scarponi, Stefania, Le molestie sessuli sul luogo di lavoro: verso nuove tecniche di tutela della dignità della lavoratrice, in Cadoppi Alberto (acura di), 1996, Commentario delle "Norme contro la violenza sessuale", Cedam, Padova, (p. 465-472).

Senato della Repubblica Italiana, 1994, Disegno di legge: 'Norme per la tutela della dignità e libertà della persona che lavora contro le molestie sessuali nei luoghi di lavoro'.

Targetti,, M. 1995 'Molestie sessuali fra rifiuto e desiderio, il confronto dei lavoratori nelle assemblee sindacali' in Il cittadino ritrovato, dossier, Rome.

Tatafiore, Roberta, 1986, "Il sindacato tutelerà le molestate?", Noi donne", N. 12, (p. 63).

Tatafiore, Roberta, 1988, "Il potere è doppio", Noi donne, N. 12, (p.16-22).

Turnaturi, Gabriella, 1991, "La molestia sessuale come ideologia", Micromega, N. 5 (p. 17-24).

UIL - Unione Italiana Bancari, Castiglioni Flavia (a cura di) 'Fatti non foste a viver come bruti. Dignità della persona e superamento delle molestie sessuali nel lavoro', Coordinamento nazionale donne UIB, Rome.

Urbano, Alessandra, 1991, "Arriva il codice di buona condotta", Nuova rassegna sindacale, N. 30, (p. 40).

Ventimiglia, Carmine, 1991, Donna delle mie brame, Franco Angeli Milan.

Vettor, Tiziana, 1996, 'La nozione di molestia sessuale nei luoghi di lavoro. I rimedi processuali e gli orientamenti della giurisprudenza', Note Informative, n.6, Cgil coordinamento servizi vertenziali e legali Milan e Lombardia.

Virgilio, Maria, 1996, Una vicenda dentro e fuori dal Parlamento. Dalla VII all XII Legislatura, in Cadoppi Alberto (a cura di), Commentario delle Norme contro la violenza sessuale, Cedam, Padova, (p. 480-492).

Zuffa, Grazia, 1993, "L'insidia della moralità sessuale per legge", Democrazia e diritto, N. 2 (p. 225-230).

ANNEXES

Annex 1 - Methodological details on the survey carried out in Greece

Information on the composition of the discussion groups

The groups were made out as follows:

> 8 groups made up of employees from various enterprises located in Athens.
> 1 group made up of women from various sectors in Thessaloniki (the second largest city in Greece in the north).
> 1 group made up of temporary employees in the tourism and hotel (private) sector in the Island of Crete.

The enterprises and institutions which participated were as follows:

- State Electricity Enterprise (34 470 employees, 17% of whom are women)
- Greek Telecommunications Enterprise (24 563 employees, 16% of whom are women)
- National Bank (14 000 employees, 40% of whom are women)
- Athens Town Hall – Social and health affairs department (12 female employees)
- Petroleum Refinery Enterprise (1 200 employees, 8% of whom are women)
- AEEGA (Agricultural Insurance)
- RILKEN (Cosmetic products) (300 employees, 53% of whom are women)
- MINERVA (commercial enterprise)
-

The number of women in each group is as follows:

> Group 1 (Electricity) – 8
> Group 2 (Telecommunications – 12
> Group 3 (Banking) – 9
> Group 4 (Town Hall) – 12
> Group 5 (Refinery) – 6
> Group 6 (Insurances) – 10
> Group 7 (Cosmetics) – 15
> Group 8 (Trade) – 5
> Group 9 Thessaloniki) – 16
> Group 10 (Tourism) – 12

The employees in enterprises were in administration posts.

The women in group 6 are the ones with the highest level of education (7 university graduates) whilst the women in group 6 have the lowest level.

Annex 2 - Prevention of sexual harassment in French enterprises

What are the enterprises' strategies to cope with sexual harassment at work?

Until they are confronted directly with it, enterprises appear to dissociate themselves from the problem not only in practice - which translates into the absence of an active prevention policy - but also during any discussion of it, where silence appears to be the norm, with human resources departments refusing to comment. There is nothing new about this attitude and it is showing no signs of abating – despite the progress that should have been made in tackling this problem – since, as early as 1985 the AVFT tried unsuccessfully to conduct a dialogue with the largest French enterprises.

The fifty or so enterprises we contacted refused to be interviewed. Only one enterprise where a prevention plan had been on the drawing board for a year agreed to talk to us. They described themselves as being "the first in France to introduce plans on such a scale for prevention of sexual harassment".

Our experience seems to suggest that a certain number of conditions have to be met for a prevention plan to be introduced in an enterprise. In the enterprise in question, the problem of sexual harassment had existed for several years, but no prevention plan had emerged. What were the reasons which led the enterprise to change its sexual harassment policy and to stop covering it up:

- There was one case of sexual harassment witnessed by a trade union delegate – i.e. someone who could provide a direct testimony and not hearsay – who indignantly decided to alert management and to put the problem on the agenda for the following CHSCT:

– There was a victim who wished to lodge a complaint;
– There was a person who was sympathetic to this sort of problem, a managing director described by people interviewed as a "managing director quite unlike others and an exceptional person" ready to discuss the problem and listen, who had decided to make his enterprise a human enterprise and not just a productive one. One trade union member who was interviewed affirmed that "in the 25 years which he had been a militant trade unionist he was the first managing director he had ever met who was so open and ready to listen;
– There was an enterprise whose prime concern was its social dimension where people were motivated give priority to the social aspects of work and to protecting human dignity. As we were told in an interview "the company is a social organisation which is supposed to effectively prevent this type of practice from occurring because the establishment subscribes to values such as solidarity, emancipation and social justice";
– and, moreover, there was an enterprise which had the considerable financial resources needed to promote training.

In practice this prevention plan comprises:

– a tool – a prevention file – created by a working party (made up of representatives of the various trades). This file has to be given to all workers at the enterprise and all persons recruited subsequently (staff on fixed-term and unlimited contracts and contracted and permanent staff, etc.). It is designed:

– to alert staff to the problem, as an effective reminder that sexual harassment exists and that measures have now been taken in the enterprise to stop it from happening;

– as an instrument to give workers help and protection, i.e. to provide support to women who are not aware of the existence of specific legislation on the subject and to give the telephone numbers of people whom the victim can contact.

However, this file is not enough, being designed solely as a curative instrument to help the person who has been harassed. It is not a preventive instrument which enables sexual harassment to be stopped, except in cases where its existence might possibly discourage a potential harasser who, after reading it, realises that he will be penalised.
- introduction of training for all superiors, starting with management teams and interdepartmental, middle and junior management – a total of one hundred persons. All the members of the CHSCT, trade union representatives, occupational physicians, and social assistance will also receive training. The idea is for all supervisory staff to do the training (a three-day training course) so that each of them will be an agent of prevention and as we were told: "prevention as well as management skills and knowledge will form part of their responsibilities because they will have the information, the knowledge and the training;

- introduction of a methodology for solving the problem;
- training for workers if there is any demand; a survey will be carried out to assess whether they need training to understand the problem;
- an article on the subject in the in-house journal.

The conclusion given to us by one of the people is that the sheer scale of the scheme ensures that the prevention plan covers the entire workforce "after all that has been done here, anybody who doesn't know really doesn't want to know".

This example seems somewhat utopian and is probably not a model for all enterprises since the limits to the possibilities of transferring it to other enterprises can be seen immediately:

– it is an enterprise where everything appears to be exceptional – the managing director, the financial resources, the exhaustive training programme and the importance attached to the social aspects of work;
– the problem at the moment is that the enterprises' policies put economic considerations come before social ones and there is little priority given to the human dimension;
– overall the preventive approach – prevention of risks, occupational accidents, industrial diseases etc. – is still in its infancy in France, the law on the prevention of accidents and diseases in France only dating back to 1976. The tactic adopted is rather to decide to do something after the fact, an approach which seems to be anchored in society as a whole. With regard to the concept of prevention – how can one think about a problem before it happens? – there is a lot to be done in French enterprises where the prevention culture is only gradually taking root. Today's strategies still give pride of place to consideration of how to react to a problem. French enterprises must be persuaded to think more about what problem might arise and how it could be prevented, which also means that managers must spend some time considering a problem which may or may nor arise in the enterprise.

Comments on the Spanish study

1. Preliminary comments

The countries covered by this study are Greece, Spain, France, Italy and Portugal.
The first point to note is the different approach adopted by the Spanish researchers. Unlike their counterparts in the Netherlands, the Spanish researchers are not trying to draw general conclusions for all the countries concerned (types of sexual harassment, profile of a harasser, cost and consequences of harassment, etc.). On the other hand, the country-by-country review is fairly comprehensive.

It is noted firstly that the majority of surveys which have been carried out date from the end of the 1980s and the beginning of the 1990s, and perhaps do not provide a wholly accurate picture of the current situation, in that sexual harassment is more prominent than it used to be.

The study finds also that the term "sexual harassment" itself gives rise to confusion; when women are asked if they have been harassed, those replying in the affirmative mention only the most serious instances of behaviour, whereas if they are shown a list of types of unsolicited male behaviour to which they have been subjected, the percentage increases significantly.

The study brings out the fact that the question of sexual harassment at workplaces was taken seriously only towards the end of the 1980s, mainly in France and Italy. In the other southern countries, little importance is attached to the issue of sexual harassment, and the level of awareness is not very high. A further point to note is that the matter is addressed quite differently in France and Italy. While the debate focuses mainly on the need for legislation in France, the emphasis in Italy is on researching the subject and discussing the concept from a political point of view.

Where France is concerned, parliamentary debates have concluded that the definition of sexual harassment as sex discrimination is inadequate. The point here is that a proposed Directive at Community level is likely to be based mainly on the concept of discrimination.

As for Italy, it appears that the definition of sexual harassment adopted at Community level in the 1991 Recommendation is widely disputed as being not precise enough and not encompassing enough forms of undesirable behaviour. Here again, the point needs to be made in connection with the fact that a proposed Directive would probably rely on the definition in the 1991 Recommendation.

2. Comments on surveys and statistics

Research at national level has been carried out only in France and Portugal.The study indicates that an international comparison is scarcely possible, given that the methodology employed to gauge the extent of the problem is not consistent and that, for several countries, there are no surveys at national level.

The researchers nevertheless consider that the results provided by the different studies show that the percentage of women claiming to have received unwanted sexual proposals may be situated between 30% and 84%. However, they also show that this percentage falls sharply to between 25% and 45% when the women are asked if they have been harassed or if they have been subjected to advances or solicitations of a sexual nature. However,the distinguishing criterion does not seem to be very clear.

The researchers conclude from these surveys that, in the southern countries, sexual harassment at workplaces is not an occasional occurrence but, on the contrary, is something which happens all the time, and which the women themselves accept as something they have to put up with because it is part and parcel of being a woman.

Besides the absence of national surveys in Spain, Greece and Italy, it has to be said that very few surveys or opinion polls on the subject of sexual harassment have been conducted in the southern countries. It should, however, be noted also that the surveys conducted more recently have gone into greater depth and have focused on analysing the roots of sexual harassment and its impact on the working and private lives of victims. This positive aspect is nevertheless viewed with caution by the researchers, who note that there are no surveys charting the development of the situation and attitudes towards harassment, nor are there any recent data for evaluating the results of measures taken to combat sexual harassment at workplaces, particularly in France, where the legislation in force since 1992 has not been evaluated in any way.

From the surveys carried out, some conclusions can be drawn for each country.In *Spain*, it seems that sexual harassment is very frequent and that the women who suffer it generally see it as inevitable. Similarly, the male harassers tend to regard their behaviour as natural. The women who suffer most from sexual harassment are those who work in socially and economically low-status sectors, as well as single women.

In *France*, sexual harassment takes many forms, although the non-verbal variety is less frequent. On the other hand, verbal expressions of harassment in the form of sexual requests are experienced by more than one woman in two. Physical harassment (bodily contact, fondling) is mentioned by more than one woman in three. One woman in ten claims to have been the victim of rape or attempted rape.

The employment-related implications for a person suffering harassment are clear. According to one study, 71% of those claiming to have suffered sexual harassment lose their job, through resignation (as a result of difficulties in performing their work) or dismissal. Those who keep their jobs are for the most part employed in the public sector. The repercussions career-wise are also a source of complaint. Related effects on health give rise to frequent absence from work as a result of sickness (sleeping disorders, weight fluctuations, anxiety, sexual problems). The most frequently cited effects on a personal level are loss of self-esteem and a feeling of being a sex object.

Unlike the situation in Spain, in France it does not appear that the majority of women suffering harassment are from the most disadvantaged groups socially or economically. The range is much wider. Many of the women are well educated and have professional experience. They are neither very young nor very old.

The handful of surveys carried out in *Greece* are based on very low samples. What can be gleaned, however, is that sexual harassment affects more than 70% of women, is generally perpetrated by superiors in the hierarchy, is not perceived as such by the harassers and is rarely denounced for fear of dismissal.

In *Italy*, the surveys show that sexual harassment occurs a lot, with the verbal form being the most widespread; the most serious cases involve superiors in the hierarchy. Responses to sexual harassment appear to vary, depending on whether it has to do with a hierarchical superior or a colleague. In the former case it is denounced, whereas in the second case the women's attitude tends to be more passive. Sexual harassment mainly affects very young women or single or separated women. The employers' reaction seems to be to "cover up" sexual harassment, especially in the case of small businesses; in large companies, it is increasingly common for the dispute to end with the dismissal of the person suffering harassment, i.e. the person who is perceived as potentially being most troublesome for the company.

In *Portugal*, the surveys which have been carried out are too specific and are based on samples which are too small to provide a comparison. It appears, though, that a perpetrator of sexual harassment is never penalised, on the grounds that there is no reference in labour law to this type of behaviour, nor is there a definition of sexual harassment at the workplace. It is interesting to note that a survey has also been conducted in conjunction with the study carried out for the Commission. One of the main points emerging is that persons suffering harassment are, for the most part, to be found in insecure employment (fixed-duration contracts, dependence on the harasser for promotion or contract renewal).

3. Comments on the national legislative framework

Only France has a specific law on sexual harassment; the other countries merely have certain articles of different laws which may be applied to sexual harassment.

In *Spain*, the various laws covering sexual harassment deal with it only in a hierarchical context. However, case law covers the eventuality of the harasser being a colleague. Moreover, the different articles are drawn up in such a way as to give the courts wide room for manoeuvre.

In *France*, a 1992 law created the offence of sexual harassment, defined as sexual aggression (unwanted behaviour of a sexual nature affecting the working environment is not therefore targeted). Moreover, the only scenario covered entails abuse of authority linked to the job performed in order to obtain sexual favours (sexual blackmail carried out by a person of equivalent hierarchical standing or of a lower rank does not therefore constitute sexual harassment). The effects of sexual harassment on the employment of the person being harassed are considered as discrimination. Law enforcement goes beyond the working environment and applies also, for example, to doctor/patient or teacher/pupil relations.

Under the penal code, the offence of sexual harassment is punishable with up to one year's imprisonment and a fine of FF 100 000, while labour law provides for the possibility of disciplinary action against the harasser. The question of the employer's civil liability may arise, especially if no action is taken when a case of sexual harassment is brought to his or her knowledge.

There is also a law whereby the employer is required to take preventive measures, particularly as regards information.

Legislation in *Greece* does not contain a legal definition of sexual harassment. Various articles of diferent laws could nevertheless be applied to sexual harassment, although only two decisions have so far emanated from the Greek courts, allowing the claims of victims.

Italy does not have any specific law on sexual harassment either, and the bills currently being discussed by Parliament are highly problematic.

In *Portugal*, the legislative vacuum means in particular that it is impossible for the labour administration and the courts to tackle this problem adequately.

4. Comments on the position of companies with regard to sexual harassment

The Spanish researchers carried out a "mini survey" on the position of companies with regard to sexual harassment, sounding out six companies per country. One interesting point to emerge is that several companies which were approached categorically refused to be interviewed, on the grounds that the issue did not concern them. Of those which agreed to be interviewed, some did no more than state that sexual harassment is prohibited and there is therefore no point in having a preventive policy (only one company took preventive action). The others distanced themselves greatly from the problem.

From the few interviews carried out, the Spanish researchers detected certain trends: trivialisation of the problem; restrictive interpretation of sexual harassment (particularly in its verbal form); lack of knowledge on the part of human resource managers about the situation within their company as regards sexual harassment; desire to defend the image of the company. As for the methods used to settle disputes, the majority of human resource managers avoid giving the slightest publicity to the cases brought to their attention, settling them with the utmost discretion. The tendency is for disputes to be resolved by moving the person suffering harassment rather than the harasser.

In conclusion, the Spanish researchers emphasise the glaring lack of visibility of the problem in most companies, and the reluctance to construct an information policy on the issue.

5. Knowledge of the Commission Recommendation on sexual harassment

On the whole, the Spanish researchers found that people are unaware of the existence of the Recommendation and the Code of Conduct on sexual harassment. Moreover, several companies stated that they are not in favour of such a Code, believing that each country has the wherewithal to control the problem and that it is up to each company to devise the most suitable strategies for countering sexual harassment.

6. The trade unions' position on sexual harassment

The Spanish researchers also met with trade-union representatives in all the countries concerned.

Most of them acknowledge the importance of the matter and accept that it is harmful to the integration of women on the labour market and to equality between women and men, but admit that the problem is not of major concern to them. The researchers consider, however, that a trade-union organisation's awareness of the problem is determined largely by the influence exerted by females within the organisation and by the visibility of the problem within society. It seems that awareness is greatest in Italy and Spain. In France, it appears that the existence of a specific law to counter harassment has greatly curtailed trade-union intervention, although a change of strategy is now noticeable. In Greece and Portugal, it seems that this issue is discussed very little at trade-union level.

7. Proposals put forward by the spanish researchers

The researchers base their findings on the premise that sexual harassment is still a hidden reality, which very few women dare to denounce. They are in favour of measures aimed at heightening the visibility of sexual harassment and bringing the perpetrators to book. In view of the seriousness of the repercussions for victims of sexual harassment, they stress the need for a policy geared primarily to prevention.

European Commission

Sexual harassment at the workplace in the European Union

Luxembourg: Office for Official Publications of the European Communities

1999 — X, 233 pp. — 21 x 29.7 cm

ISBN 92-828-6217-8

Price (excluding VAT) in Luxembourg: EUR 15